Modern Languages

Modern Languages

Learning and Teaching in an Intercultural Field

Alison Phipps and Mike Gonzalez

Sage Publications
London • Thousand Oaks • New Delhi

First published 2004

SAGE Publications Ltd
1 Oliver's Yard
55 City Road
London EC1Y 1SP

SAGE Publications Inc.
2455 Teller Road
Thousand Oaks, California 91320

SAGE Publications India Pvt Ltd
B-42, Panchsheel Enclave
Post Box 4109
New Delhi 100 017

British Library Cataloguing in Publication data

A catalogue record for this book is available from the British Library

ISBN 0-7619-7417-2
ISBN 0-7619-7418-0 (pbk)

Library of Congress Control Number 2003115340

Typeset by Pantek Arts Ltd, Maidstone, Kent
Printed in Great Britain by T.J. International, Padstow, Cornwall

Contents

Acknowledgements

We would like to take this opportunity to thank numerous friends and colleagues. We have gained immeasurably from working with students of German and Hispanic studies and of Anthropology at the University of Glasgow. Their openness and engagement have sustained us throughout. In particular we are profoundly grateful to our respective partners Clare Maclean and Robert Swinfen for patiently tolerating our often excessive enthusiasm for this project. This book would never have been possible without our involvement in the Barcelona Group. Our thanks to Melanie Walker, Quintin Cutts, Judy Wilkinson and Chris Warhurst for creating new critical spaces in the institution. We learned much from Ron Barnett and Jan Parker who took the time to read drafts of the manuscript at various stages. Their conviction that the project was worthwhile sustained us.

We are grateful to our initial reviewers and readers for their warm endorsement and practical, critical suggestions. All errors which have escaped undetected in the final process are, however, our own responsibility.

Foreword

The study of modern languages lies at the intersection of many routes, and provides a way station on many itineraries. It is consequently diverse and ever changing. And while change and diversity are stimulating and enriching, they sit uncomfortably with the stability and sense of a settled identity that provide comfort and recognition to many students and staff. 'Language people' usually have enough personal and professional versatility to navigate the complexities and uncertainties, even if they sometimes feel a yearning for the more settled 'home' that their counterparts in some other disciplines appear to enjoy (Evans, 1988). This versatility has stood them in good stead during the lean times and the crises that have buffeted languages in higher education every ten or fifteen years. It has rarely been more needed than today, when soaring demand for language learning by students of many different subjects seems to go hand in hand with declining demand for specialist language degrees (Kelly and Jones, 2003). As a result, teachers and support staff are increasingly challenged to rethink their approaches, from the design of programmes through to the style of their personal engagement with students.

However versatile individuals might be, they need the resources of shared reflection and collective imagination to respond creatively to new and daunting demands. This is the challenge to which Alison Phipps and Mike Gonzalez have risen so magnificently. In a radical reappraisal of the theory and practice of modern languages, they draw on a wealth of insights taken from some of the most exciting thinkers of our time as well as from more venerable sources that have not lost their freshness. They confront fundamental issues of the purpose and rationale for learning languages, and subject the dominant alternatives to an unflinchingly critical gaze. On the one hand, they reject a purely instrumental approach which sees the overriding purpose as the acquisition of a skill to enhance employability. The preponderance of this rationale for learning languages has been a key feature of public policy declarations in recent years, but has tended to dehumanise languages, reducing them to a one-dimensional activity. On the other hand, they reject a purely cognitive approach which sees modern languages as a body of arcane knowledge, valued for its own sake. This rationale was the traditional justification for literary and philological degrees, but tended to reduce languages to a conspicuous marker of distinction for a cultured elite. These approaches have tended towards an artificial polarisation in which each of them feeds off its contrary. The authors argue passionately for a different way of thinking about languages, as an embodied activity whose value lies in expressing and enriching human beings in all of their dimensions. The generous and inclusive humanism that pervades their thinking also provides a degree of leverage, necessary to escape the exacerbated binary oppositions that have tended to close down dialogue and sterilise debate.

What they propose is nothing less than a shift from *avoir* to *être*, from *having* to *being* (Marcel, 1949). Rather than a set of skills or a body of knowledge to be acquired, they conceive learning other languages as something to do and something to be lived: an activity and a way of being. The key concepts they introduce, of 'languaging' and 'intercultural being', are unfamiliar and no doubt awkward to use, but the conscious defamiliarisation may also serve to jolt readers out of ingrained habits of mind and enable them to reframe their perceptions. It is an invigorating approach, which opens the space for a fundamental rethinking of languages. More sceptical readers may wonder how this approach will 'play' with quality assurance units, or whether it will 'align' with the strategic priorities of funding councils. They need not fear: the approach fulfils and hugely exceeds the limited objectives of administrative frameworks. The authors encourage us to raise our gaze and be led rather by our long-term aspirations, since they are what give life, meaning and purpose to our teaching and learning. The many concrete examples extracted from the rich pedagogical experience of the two authors are evidence of what can be achieved. They show that life can be breathed into apparently dry or daunting subjects, and that teaching and learning can and should be punctuated by epiphanies and personal transformations.

In some respects the authors propose a utopian vision, but a practical utopia, which shows that it is possible to step outside the well-worn frameworks of thought and practice. New and different ways of teaching and learning are demonstrated and argued for in chapter after chapter, addressing almost every aspect of the modern languages experience. Most teachers (and many learners) will recognise the problems to which the authors propose imaginative solutions, and most will put the book down reluctantly, feeling energised by the ideas they have found. I expect it will become a much-thumbed handbook for teachers in search of inspiration, and I am sure it will be a catalyst to further debate and exploration. But I suspect it may also become a turning point for thinking about modern languages. This book exudes life and hope. It shows a future where languages can thrive because they are an integral and indispensable part of what it means to be human. It is an exhilarating prospect to help to bring that future closer.

Michael Kelly

Director, Subject Centre for Languages, Linguistics and Area Studies
University of Southampton
August 2003

References

Evans, C. (1988) *Language People: The Experience of Teaching and Learning Modern Languages in British Universities*. Milton Keynes: Open University Press and Society for Research into Higher Education.

Kelly, M. and Jones, D. (2003) *A New Landscape for Languages*. London: Nuffield Foundation.

Marcel, G. (1949) *Being and Having*, trans K. Farrer. Westminster: Dacre Press.

Introduction

This book is written during a time of upheaval and crisis in the field of modern languages and in the context of higher education. As such it bears the marks of the experience of writing, thinking and reading in a time of uncertainty. The speed of change and sheer pace of development of the crisis in modern languages and in higher education makes any attempt to capture the nature of the status quo impossible. This book is, then, an attempt to work with the uncertainties and radical unknowability that characterise the fragmenting field of modern languages. The context is the same for learners and teachers alike. This book is not a manual. It is a critical resource for modern language teachers in higher education. Its central premises build out from cornerstone concepts of *languaging* and *intercultural being*.

THE ARGUMENT

The argument of this book is that languages are a social justice issue. Languages, skilfully embodied and enacted, are part of the richness of human being. Languages are not skills or competences. This book contends that the ways in which we teach and learn languages today are so marked by functional and technicist approaches, in the service of employability and the market, or in the service of philology, that they have become detached from human ways of being. It also argues that the concepts that have served us in the past will do no longer. Fresh thinking is required to enable us to move out of the binary impasses of languages versus culture, literature versus language, language elitism versus language populism, structural versus communicative approaches.

If our teaching is to enable the development of dispositions that can become intercultural, fully awake to the possibilities and pitfalls of global citizenship, then new concepts are required, tools to help prise open ways out of our defensive stockades and to begin shaping a space for languaging and intercultural being.

The analysis

We analyse the discourse and practice of language teaching in higher education critically. We situate ourselves within the broad tradition of cultural studies. It is, of course, possible to smooth over supercomplexity (Barnett, 2000) with simplistic explanations and technicist solutions. However, to do so, in our view, is neither interesting nor productive.

Throughout our analysis of languages in higher education we foreground our concern for questions of power, inequality, social justice, for marked patterns of difference and division between rich and poor, male and female, black and white. Cultural studies has a particular history, a characteristic style and a distinctively political way of questioning given facts. In questioning facts, cultural studies invites us to engage in a process of learning and relearning, of deconstruction and reconstruction. With Giroux (1992) and Freire (1998), we believe that teaching is a form of political and cultural action and we explore this proposition in the context of language teaching and intercultural action in higher education.

Stories matter

Alongside the cornerstone concepts of *languaging* and *intercultural being*, we work with certain principles-in-action. These apply to the process of creating this text, and to the process of being languaging teachers in higher education. These principles are those of exchange, engagement, equality, of a struggle with the difficulties of power and a continuous, reflective practice of collaboration. From the empirical ground of projects that engaged us both in action research in our institution, aspects of which are reflected elsewhere (Walker, 2001, 2002), and from the resources of our engagement as teachers, we have developed stories as resources for hope, for resistance and for realising the project of languaging.

These stories, grounded in 'data', are offered as part of the business of making meaning in an age of supercomplexity, and in an age which requires languaging. Structurally our stories have a dual purpose. Firstly, they break into the text to create a moment for a different mode of reading and reflecting, for a different form of engagement and exchange. They enable the injection of different voices, tones, colours into the thrust of the argument, bringing the discussion back to the ground and helping remind us of the work we have to do. Secondly, they aim to act as a springboard for further conversation, for the telling of more stories in such a way as to create an environment where talking of teaching is not a taboo. The current managerialist ideology in higher education is not conducive to open exchange, bringing, as it does, more fear than freedom. But we have a commitment and a hunger for intellectual debate as academics, and our current circumstances, and the inherent injustices in the patterns of language provision, demand that we use our best resources to this end. Some are stories to live by, others are stories to resist.

CREATING SPACE

To teach as a languaging, intercultural being, in higher education, is to develop a different disposition for action, it is to be in a continual process of becoming an interdisciplinary academic. To this end, we continually look inside the field of modern languages with the purpose of deconstruction and critique, examining our cultural history and the material circumstances that have grown current practices. We then look beyond ourselves in search of theories and methods for appropriating new worlds and new experiences of languages. We look to learn lessons from other fields and other ways of questioning the world, fields that have long worked with border crossings and where languages and intercultural experience form part of the territory.

Our proposition for languages is resolutely not one of a technicist compromise. We offer an alternative to the discourse of skills and competences and do so in a quest for co-creation, meaning-making, relation, exchange, fluency, being.

The politics of languages

THE CHALLENGE WE FACE WORKING TOGETHER WITH WORDS...

I gave my talk in English at this ancient Portuguese university. I did so comfortably and yet with some discomfort. The occasion is a lecture for teachers of languages. We have come to the question session and those with me on the platform have varieties of English, Portuguese, German, French. From being a monolingual presentation we begin a multilingual conversation, in languages, about languages. There is intense concentration. I have no Portuguese and am embarrassed by this, but if I concentrate hard, and let the last few days, my first days in this country, do their listening, struggling, work for meaning, then fragments cluster to give me the beginnings of sense, and I can at least mix a word, a polite phrase, in my equally multilingual responses.

Power switches back and forth in our conversation, taken up responsibly in turn by others who live and work in languages, as I do. We do not need to explain or argue for the validity of such an exchange, we are working together with words and we know ourselves to be enriched.

And yet at the same time there is a *profound crisis* in modern languages. The number of students applying for undergraduate courses is declining, and the siren voices asking what 'use' such courses are grow more shrill by the minute. Emergency conferences gather to define the origins of the coming disaster, and to justify the continuing existence of modern languages in terms of the values that prevail throughout higher education. Mergers of departments across institutions are offered up on the altar of 'viability' and 'efficiency' – the twin shibboleths of a new managerial layer trained in the ethics of consumption and profitability. An alternative response is to justify the survival of their departments by reference to a university-wide 'market' for languages; new degree courses marrying languages with management or law or engineering, for example, are enthusiastically offered as a way forward.

Languages as commodity

These, and other similar responses to the current emergency have two features in common: they are defensive, and they concede without a fight the concept of *languages as 'skills'*, technical adjuncts to the real business of managing, engineering, drawing up contracts and so on. A principled advocacy of modern languages as an *intellectual discipline* full of possibilities, a source of understandings and insights that can empower and enrich human life, is rarely if ever heard.

It is our belief that the truly powerful arguments for the study of languages cannot have their origins in any variant of the cost-benefit calculations that underpin the 'skills' argument. If students are voting with their feet, it is because they are forced to make their choices in the framework of utilitarian criteria which directly link decisions about education to the shape of the labour market. Increasingly languages are being pushed out of secondary and higher education into primary education or are sold as packaged commodities in the life-long learning market (Kelly and Jones, 2003).What kind of job you will be able to get with this or that qualification is the sole consideration in many cases. Modern languages cannot justify its existence by promising returns on an investment of time and (increasingly) of money on the students' part. At least, it cannot provide any assurance of *material* returns.

It is our view that this commodity view is disempowering and destructive of the value of education as opposed to training. We argue throughout this book that there is an alternative way of approaching the business of learning languages as skill-acquisition. We describe that alternative as *languaging*, a term to which we shall return throughout. We use it for a purpose.

Languages are more than skills; they are the medium through which communities of people `languaging` engage with, make sense of and shape the world. Through language they become active agents in creating their human environment; this process is what we call *languaging*. Languaging is a life skill. It is inextricably interwoven with social experience – living in society – and it develops and changes constantly as that experience evolves and changes. The student of a language other than their own can be given an extraordinary opportunity to enter the languaging of others, to understand the complexity of the experience of others to enrich their own. *To enter other cultures is to re-enter one's own*, understand the better the supercomplex variety of human experience (Barnett, 2000), and become more deeply human as a result.

This purpose is incontestably profound, humane and educative; its 'profit' is existential, personal, social, and the 'return' on what is given or exchanged with other cultures and languages is immense. In these terms, the consequence of the study of modern languages can be the evolution of what we term *intercultural being* – the understanding of the varied and multiple reality of which we are part.

From language learning to languaging

Table 1.1 represents the shifts between conceptual frameworks that a focus on languaging as opposed to language learning may allow.

TABLE 1.1 *Languaging and language learning*

	Language learning	Languaging
Purpose	Pragmatic skill	Ontological skill
Context	Classroom focus	Whole social world
Outcome	Assessed performance	Feel and fluency
Aim	Accuracy and measurable knowledge	Meaning-making and human connection
Disposition	Competition	Open, collective exploration and exchange
Agency	Intercultural communicative competence	Intercultural being criticality
Creativity	Prescribed by form	Freed through form
Cultures	Learning about	Living in and with
Position	Language at a distance	Language from within
Environment	Objectivity of languages	Material life of languages
Task	Complex	Supercomplex

(Adapted from Barnett, 1994: 179)

ON ORIGINS: THE DISCIPLINE OF MODERN LANGUAGES

'Modern languages', as opposed to ancient or classical languages, is a relative newcomer to universities. It could be argued that it is not a discipline at all, or at least that it did not have cohesion or a set of shared perceptions until the creation of a strategic alliance of individual language disciplines mobilising as a united body in the face of a crisis. At all levels, the debates concerning the future of modern languages, either as a newly united body or as separate autonomous disciplines, display a marked tension between 'a responsible concern for the maintenance of social order, and an irresponsible concern to pursue knowledge' that may be traced back to the eighteenth-century debates around the purposes of education between Kant, Schleiermacher and Humboldt (Nuffield Languages Inquiry, 2000: 44). So such concerns are hardly new; they are and always have been a central argument within the academy.

Crisis in the humanities

If these tensions and concerns are now making themselves felt in modern languages, it is as part of a more general crisis of direction within the humanities as a whole. For Ronald Barnett (2003), for example, the increasing dominance within higher education of models of performance signals a prevailing positivism and a potentially pernicious technocratic ideology that make it increasingly difficult to argue that the humanities should address the broader issues of human value, conduct and purpose which he describes as 'supercomplexity'. Such issues, after all, are hard to translate into the language of a marketplace that requires that each activity be described easily as a commodity and be quantified accordingly.

Supercomplexity, for Barnett, is more precise and descriptive a term than that of postmodernism. It describes the condition of contemporary western life where values and positions are brought into conflict and competition in ways which are irreconcilable. Consequently, educators in an age of supercomplexity need to be engaged in the development of new ontologies, and new dispositions that equal the challenges set.

In *The Postmodern Condition*, Lyotard (1984) devotes a whole section to the discussion of 'Education and Its Legitimation through Performativity'. He describes how education, redefined as the *transmission* of knowledge rather than its pursuit, is driven away from the speculative aims of *Bildung*, of 'knowledge for its own sake', and towards performativity, whose purposes are efficiency, skills and func-

performativity

tion. This is not a distinction between that which is ideological and that which is not, of course. Lyotard is clear that *Bildung* is neither more nor less ideologically motivated than performativity. Indeed it is a 'legitimizing myth', serving grand ideals such as the universality of philosophy and the liberation of all humanity.

> *The desired goal becomes the optimal contribution of higher education to the best performativity of the social system. Accordingly, it will have to create the skills that are indispensable to that system. These are of two kinds. The first kind are more specifically designed to tackle world competition. They vary according to which 'Specialities' the nation-states or major educational institutions can sell on the world market [...]*
>
> *[In the second case], the transmission of knowledge is no longer designed to train an elite capable of guiding the nation towards its emancipation, but to supply the system with players capable of acceptably fulfilling their roles at the pragmatic posts required by institutions.* (Lyotard, 1984: 40)

Although written nearly twenty years ago, Lyotard's work is a startlingly prophetic assessment of the shift in what may be considered to be 'legitimate' knowledge and its consequences for higher education. Yet unlike Bourdieu (2000), Barnett (1994) and other commentators on the humanities and in the literature on modern languages, Lyotard takes no position on the question.

That neutrality has earned him criticism, notably from Fredric Jameson, who emphasises the need to challenge 'the dystopian prospect of a global private monopoly of information' through political, as opposed to symbolic action (Jameson, 1984: xx). It is a need made more urgent by the proliferation, in the United Kingdom for example, of initiatives like 'lifelong learning' or 'continuing professional development' programmes, whose firmly functional or performative character is expressed in its emphasis on the acquisition of 'skills'.

The general shift is precisely echoed in modern languages in higher education, where, in Kelly's description:

> *The term 'languages degrees' has always been highly coded. For most of their century or so history (sic), language degrees have incorporated a distinction between language on the one hand, viewed as a technical means of access, and content on the other hand, viewed as a legitimate object of study.* (Kelly, 2001: 82)

The curriculum debate

There is a paradox here, however. Debate as to what should be the legitimate object of the study of modern languages continues with varying ferocity. Yet it seems that there is one answer for undergraduates, for those few students who do manage to leap the multiple hurdles placed before them and embark on postgraduate work, and quite another for those paying for courses through adult education programmes.

Undergraduate courses seem to be moving inexorably in a performative direction. It is a matter we shall address in detail in later chapters. But in general terms it would be hard to deny the shift, reflected in modularisation and the imposition across the board of standardised forms of assessment that accompanies it. Functional courses occupy an increasing space in the curriculum, and practical and applied language exercises absorb a growing proportion of student time. This is even true of Masters courses which in many cases, but not all, seek legitimacy in instrumental terms.

When it comes to postgraduate *research*,   disciplinary research
however, whether at Masters or Doctoral
levels, it seems that different values prevail. A glance at the range of modern languages research topics at these levels reveals a list of familiar traditional topics informed by universal humanism. This is the contradiction: on the one hand, the values and methods that inform such research are less and less likely to have been learned in the course of undergraduate study; yet is assumed that they will have been absorbed somewhere along the way, and that students will be ready to enter a realm whose values, orthodoxies and practices are wholly different from anything they have previously encountered.

Similar developments are occurring in the context of the United States, as Kramsch testifies:

> *The traditional lines along which power and legitimation are distributed in the general discourse of academia are being put into question through four recent developments: the intrusion into academia of nonwritten forms of knowledge, the proliferation of alternative modes of knowledge delivery, the advances made in information-processing technologies, and the rise of the social sciences. These four areas of change challenge traditional academic discourse in its four distinct characteristics: literacy, schooling, interpretation, canonicity. (Kramsch, 1998: 26)*

THERE IS MODERNISATION...AND MODERNISATION

The challenges we face are unavoidable. The greatest error, however, would be simply to turn our back and reject them as 'bad modernisation'. The situation is far more complex. The imagined 'good old days' when a disinterested humanism prevailed, to the extent that they ever existed, were double-edged. The dominant high culture, for example, gave short shrift to the broad spectrum of cultural products and activities not contained within the narrow literary canon. It was an intellectual culture that was overwhelmingly elitist, narrow-minded and discriminatory towards marginalised or minority expression. And while it made obeisance to a concept of tradition and thus to historical processes, its historicism was often mechanical or irredeemably idealist in its refusal to anchor the life of the spirit in the terrain of the material.

On the other hand, the move towards 'performativity' or skills, for all its potential limitation of the speculative spirit, has given a new legitimacy to oral forms, communicative competences and areas of non-academic knowledge (from popular culture and storytelling to ritual and performance). The growth of interest in applied linguistics and the new disciplines of foreign language education and second language acquisition, have been another, perhaps unintended, consequence. As they have gained 'legitimacy' within the academy, they have begun to contribute important research to the study of literature, for example through their concern with literacy (Kramsch 1998).

'Applied language'

As modern language departments have moved increasingly towards 'applied language', another potential conflict has become apparent. Kelly (2000) highlights the possible contradiction between the private and the social purposes of language learning, on the one hand, and on the other the specific purposes of applied language in particular fields, as language departments and centres have moved into areas like business, law and medicine as well as anthropology and sociology.

Projecting the logic of the process into a probably not very distant future, Kelly points ahead to a situation in which there would be no language degrees as such, but only language study associated directly with each separate discipline (Kelly, 2000: 91). While he refrains from suggesting how this might be resisted or addressed politically, he makes clear what the long-term consequences are likely to be. Language departments would be transformed into service units, providing skills additional to the core capacities required by other areas of professional activity. In other words, languages will be uncoupled from what we see as the central activities of *languaging, being intercultural* and living with supercomplexity.

For the modern languages teacher or scholar in higher education, the effect would be a massive deskilling, a devaluing of all those areas of human knowledge and understanding which, as we argue throughout this book, can and should be the necessary and liberating outcomes of the study of modern languages and their cultures. The irony, of course, as we suggested earlier, is that the impact of that process of deskilling will fall on those who, having learned the discourse of humanist criticism and literary analysis, will return to an increasingly performative higher education environment as teachers – almost certainly at low rates of pay and on short-term contracts which offer no opportunities at all to contest the shape and direction of higher education.

A deeper crisis?

It is these actual or threatened paradigmatic shifts in the status and transmission of knowledges that have produced a sense of crisis and the sense of angst and uncertainty that accompanies any liminal phase (Turner, 1995). This sense may be felt not just in modern languages, but across the humanities and in some areas of social science (particularly those which are most remote from the requirements of social engineering and closest to the exploration of social experience). Nonetheless, it does seem that the crisis is deeper and more pressing in modern languages than in, say, history or English. There are several reasons for this.

Because modern languages can be seen as an applied discipline, for example, the performativity argument seems both more immediate and more compelling. It could be argued that modern languages are by definition a performative skill. At the other end of the spectrum, the traditional study of literature seems to belong to a species of speculative scholarship lying at the furthest remove from functionality.

The space between – the terrain of intercultural understanding where social being, exchange and languaging interconnect – often seems deserted.

And the divide between these different   intercultural studies
and opposed (or mutually contemptuous)
perceptions has meant that in modern languages there has been very
little sign of the rigorous intellectual defence of the study of culture
within a framework of social knowledge and multicultural diversity that
has been mounted in other disciplines. The reluctance to absorb the
ideas of cultural studies, and of intercultural studies, into modern
languages departments has left an embattled traditionalist redoubt
increasingly isolated. Whatever the long-term dangers for the discipline, on the other hand, market-oriented studies have grown more
influential in so far as they reflect and reinforce the utilitarian perceptions of education that are increasingly dominant across the university
sector as a whole.

Conference papers and publications in modern languages in recent
years have often expressed fears of an imminent loss of identity and a
privation of professional status and income, yet with little willingness to
offer any intellectual defence of the discipline. There is very little sense of
how we came to be where we are, or what we have lost or gained along
the way.

What practical solutions are offered seem to clutch at straws. Coleman
(2001), for example, places the emphasis on practical pedagogy and language awareness. Others suggest defensive, rather legalistic responses
like languages charters (Brumfit, 2000, 2001) in the face of increasing
pressure from English as the dominant language. Some call for a
retrenching of positions against upstart elements in the individual disciplines (Haug, 1999), while still others argue for more interdisciplinary,
intercultural approaches to modern languages (von Graevenitz, 1999).

Underpinning all these approaches   the unacknowledged question
is an unacknowledged question: what
is the theoretical and methodological basis of modern languages? If the
question is not made explicit it may be because it has simply never been
articulated as anything more than common sense. Until it is articulated,
modern languages is unlikely to be able to go beyond a defensive posture. This may have something to do with the fact that as a discipline,
categorised academically as such, modern languages, as opposed to
French, Spanish or German, is a new kid on the block and has barely
had the time to elaborate the reasons for its existence before it finds
itself under threat. We shall return to these various initiatives in more
detail later.

GLOBAL SPEECH?

Who cares if 70 percent of those who graduate from America's colleges are not required to learn a foreign language? Isn't the rest of the world speaking English now? And if they aren't, hadn't all those damn foreigners better GET WITH THE PROGRAM? (Moore, 2002: 92)

It is now the case that the learning of English comes first among other pluricentric 'world' languages such as German, French, Spanish, Russian and Chinese. It is not a simple case, however, of anglophone linguistic hegemony. On the one hand, other languages do enjoy an increasingly prominent role – Spanish is the obvious example – while the star of others, like Russian, appears to be on the wane. But it is impossible to approach questions concerning the teaching and learning of languages other than English without taking into account the dominant position of English on a world scale.

In the United Kingdom any coherent policy for foreign languages must start with the central fact of the British situation – that English is the main language and that, because of the dominance of the United States, it is the language of world economic power. (Brumfit, 2000: 97)

It is often argued by university administrators and some monolingual politicians that English has already become the global language, following on the heels of the dominant actors in the world economy and the international financial institutions whose common language is almost invariably English. And it is true that in the realm of computer technology and software, English and Microsoft appear to be the principal points of reference. That certainly underpins the aggressive search for fee-paying overseas students by British, Antipodean and American institutions of higher education. The presumption is that the attraction is not just the specific knowledge-base of any given department or university, but particularly the possibility of learning English in a university environment. On that basis, it would seem to follow that learning a second language (other than English) is unnecessary, a waste of valuable time and resources.

The power of 'world' language learning

On the other hand, however, increasing numbers of business and management, law and industrial design, medicine and engineering courses, are offering the possibility of learning a language as a value added, and even in some cases as an inducement to intending entrants. For the most part, of course, the languages offered are the other 'world' languages that share, albeit in an inferior position, the space of a world market. Thus the value-added is functional, and the language courses offered very rarely contain any critical, cultural or historical component. This serves to reinforce the perception of modern languages as essentially, and purely, performative.

These developments present traditional cognate degree subjects with a dilemma. On the one hand, more students will be drawn into foreign language learning – an important consideration when departmental budgets and allocations are largely determined on a per capita basis. On the other hand, their involvement will be on a far more restricted and almost entirely instrumental basis. That is not to say that students in non-humanities subjects cannot be drawn into the journey of cultural awareness and the complex understandings for whose acquisition we are passionate advocates. But to the extent that it does occur, it will be in conflict with the general direction of their studies, in which languages are a peripheral or at best a secondary component.

Without wishing to sound cynical, it is highly   social experience
unlikely that non-language departments offering
such courses have anything but quite short-term, opportunistic purposes in mind. They will wish to add 'colour', a gloss of multiculturalism which is not reflected in any other element of the course, offer the acquisition of a new social skill, or open the door to the increasingly available opportunities to undertake part of one's degree course in law, management, medicine or engineering abroad. On the other hand, the specificity of abroad will rarely be a consideration of much weight – beyond a very general and ill-defined benefit of accumulated social experience. Does medicine with languages, for example, embrace an exploration of the meaning of health, the language of bodies and so on in other cultures? Do engineering courses with languages address the impact and significance of technology in other societies? At the moment, that does not seem to be the case.

The problem and the contradiction is that just as internal budgetary pressures will drive university departments towards service provision for these students, the same cost-benefit calculations make it increasingly difficult to defend the non-language components of the course. This is not to say that there will necessarily be a large-scale disappearance of language departments – but it is already the case that they are increasingly populated by service providers and overwhelmed by short-term demands for a kind of provision which will not enrich their other activities.

'Communicative skill' for 'brief encounters'

The Nuffield Languages Inquiry, whose conclusions were published in 2000, addressed the low level of language competence in other languages in the UK context. The stimulus to the inquiry, however, was the pressing need for the training of 'personnel with technical or professional skills plus another language' (p. 4). The international competitiveness of British business, it argued, is adversely affected by a generalised lack of competence in languages. As so often before, the argument for education provision arose out of economic need. And it was clear that the inquiry's perception of 'communicative skill' derived from success in doing business in the global market, albeit with non-English speakers. The solution offered is *'bolt-on'* language courses to serve business. Now this presumes that complex intercultural and existential insights have no significance in the world of business. In a human, languaging world this is simply not the case.

What passes for cultural instruction rarely goes beyond the *niceties of social ritual*, invariably illustrated by reference to the formalities involved in doing business with Japanese corporations – the exemplary Others who are nevertheless so like Our Global Selves (Wink, 1992). Thus what is at first sight an argument for more language provision effectively reinforces a narrow, market-based definition and allows the requirements of capital to ascribe the functional limits to what may be learned. It is rather like taking a nut to crack a sledge hammer. In the final analysis, this is an argument *against* intercultural education in favour of training for brief, instrumental encounters with other dominant actors in the world economy.

More significantly, however, the inquiry does point to the social exclusions that accompany monolingualism:

'monolingualism implies inflexibility...'

> *English alone is not enough. In a world where bilingualism and plurilingualism are commonplace, monolingualism implies inflexibility, insensitivity and arrogance. Much that is essential to our society, its health and its interests – including effective choice in policy, realisation of citizenship, effective overseas links and openness to the inventions of other cultures – will not be achieved in one language alone. (Nuffield Languages Inquiry, 2000: 14)*

During public debate in 2003 around immigration 'tests' for 'Britishness', UK Home Secretary David Blunkett suggested that bilingualism is somehow a social disadvantage. Against that the position taken by Nuffield is salutary. In fact, although bilingualism has often been stigmatised in monolingual countries, research has now shown that children are not disadvantaged by a bilingual upbringing – quite the contrary, it is a major addition to their intellectual horizons in the long run, even if it creates some short-term interference (Kimbrough Oller and Eilers, 2002).

Nuffield's view, however, needs to be appro-   developing critique
ached with caution. The Commission's stance on
monolingualism does not stem from a different set of premises from the rest of its report. It encourages the learning of global languages (the greatest of which, of course, is English), but it does not for a moment suggest that learning Gujarati, Turkish or Arabic can fulfil their recommended functions. And yet, in terms of a critical and confident intercultural being, the learning of minority languages can often be a form of resistance, of critique of the prevailing cultural values. Within Nuffield's terms of reference, language learning for that purpose can in no sense correspond to its criteria.

And yet under the prevailing global economic condition, where wealth accumulation is associated with certain languages, we see patterns of language learning which distinguish languages in interesting and complex ways, in a struggle for life's expression, for resistance, for domination, for beauty and well-being (Bartlett, 2001).

At the 2003 World Social Forum in Porto Alegre, Brazil, there seem to be as many languages as there are people. Walking past the telephone booths is like threading the elements of this multilayered movement into a single language. In the huge conference halls, there are headphones and professional interpreters. But in the smaller rooms, where 150 or so of us will meet to explore the future, there are no such facilities. Instead I speak between and in and out of Spanish, Portuguese, French and English in a discussion so animated and passionate that very soon we finish each other's sentences.

Different languages will provide different bases for different kinds of experience. Some (particularly the major languages of national and international communication, including English) will provide a basis for action in the world, as well as for learning and conceptualizing. (Brumfit, 2000: 99)

In our view, Brumfit's point is a vital, if not the vital one in favour of the encouragement of languaging as a key element in that process of human growth which rests on relationships of exchange and mutual enrichment as well as a critical engagement with social reality. It is not the only way to reach that point of self- and social consciousness, but it is one route to a kind of understanding that makes sense not only of the Other but also of the Self. However, we take issue with his notion that only some languages will provide a basis for action in the world. Languages are being preserved, learned, revitalised around the world as a direct expression of resistance.

We could not for a moment claim, of course, that such a perspective is widely shared, let alone dominant within the discipline. On the contrary, many of those with whom we have discussed issues of teaching and learning have expressed concern that, in the traditional cognate disciplines, there is an erosion of literacy in the language, a growing dependency on translated texts and a privileging of English as the language of pedagogy (although that has probably always been the case). As we shall see later, there is considerable debate surrounding the issue of so called 'teaching in the target language'. But there is a wider cultural issue here, beyond questions of method.

Cultural capital

The decision to learn another language is in the first instance a recognition of the cultural capital, the accumulated knowledge and social experience enshrined in cultural practices. It is a recognition, at some level, of plurality. As recent discussions about the importance of 'education in Britishness' as a prerequisite for acceptance into British society have made clear, citizenship for many people in British society is an experience of loss and abandonment.

Pierre Bourdieu is, typically, astute on the subject of threatened languages in France. His arguments apply equally to the status of modern languages in Anglophone and other monolingual systems:

One cannot save the value of a competence [such as classical languages] unless one saves the market, in other words, the whole set of political and social conditions of production of the producers/consumers. The defenders of Latin or, in other contexts, of French or Arabic, often talk as if the language they favour could have some value outside the market, by intrinsic virtues such as its 'logical' qualities; but, in practice, they are defending the market. The position which the educational system gives to the different languages (or the different cultural contexts) is such an important issue only because this institution has the monopoly in the large-scale production of producers/consumers, and therefore in the reproduction of the market without which the social value of the linguistic competence, its capacity to function as linguistic capital, would cease to exist. (Bourdieu, 2000: 57)

The cultural hegemony of English as the source of what is increasingly represented as the universal culture of postmodernity means that, in some sense or another, learning any other language, as well as teaching it, can become *a counter-cultural activity*, at least in monolingual regimes. It may often therefore demand some courage to argue for it, as well as practise it, in any way that goes beyond the acquisition of foreign languages either as a social embellishment or as a restricted functional skill. Indeed we would argue that a case for foreign language that is couched in terms of those justifications is an argument already lost whatever happens. For if modern languages survive only within that narrow frame, then the cultural expansion that such study should imply will, in any case, have been already abandoned.

NATIONAL LANGUAGES – GLOBAL MARKETS

Creating 'imagined communities'

In the construction of nation-states, the defining moment is the drawing of territorial boundaries; that is a necessary, but not a sufficient condition. As Benedict Anderson (1991) discussed, national projects are concerned with the creation of 'imagined communities' whose shared identity may be coterminous with the spaces contained within boundaries, but is principally formed around a shared identity expressed first and foremost in a common language. In every case, the adoption of a shared language of community is also an act of exclusion and denial, the creation of self and other, of civilisations within the city walls and barbarisms at the gate. We are now witnessing this process re-enacted on a global not just a national level as we build new Towers of Babel. We need to learn to live with Babel, and without its Tower.

The centralisation of power in the Iberian peninsula under the Catholic kings and Charles V began with the dominion of Castilian; the creation of contemporary France began with the suppression of Occitan. The subsequent creation of identity rests on the formulation of national myths, epic narratives of order drawn from chaos, which are set in pre-history. Thus nationhood is inseparable from identity, as the eighteenth-century philosopher Herder argued. His notion of a 'national Soul' may later have been transformed into the more ostensibly scientific concept of 'national character', but the historical depth of the nation-state is mirrored in its language.

> *In the history of the nineteenth and twentieth centuries as populations have come to see themselves as nations, so they have sought to present their language varieties not only as languages distinct from all others, but also as single, unified languages. (Barbour, 1996: 33)*

The link between the nation-state and particular languages is an important one as it has allowed nations to construct a sense of what Barbour (1996: 33) terms a 'shared public culture' for the functioning of the state and the economy. Adopted as the currency of politics, economic life and as culture itself, other languages are relegated to the status of a kind of pre-language, to an orality insufficiently refined to bear the weight of communal representation.

Language too was an instrument of the expansion

language as an instrument of expansion

of the nation-state; imperialism expressed itself as linguistic dominion. For the subaltern to find a voice (to paraphrase Spivak) it must be in the language of the conqueror; indigenous Americans spoke Nahua or Quiche only in secret, the slaves musicalised and languaged their Yoruba or Lucumí so that the plantation owners would not recognise it.

Dominance and resistance

With imperialism and global expansion, the linguistic boundaries are extended beyond the frontiers of the nation-state; there comes to be a differentiation within the cultural space, since the culture may cross many frontiers, yet power – economic, political and cultural – continues to reside in nation-states. English is the common currency of the British Empire in India, Spanish the language of most of the countries of the South and Central Americas, Russian the lingua franca of twentieth-century Central Asia not only in the communication between centre and periphery, but also within the periphery itself. The colonial subjects communicate in the language of the imperial power, now transformed into the bearer of a universal culture that can only be expressed in the dominant medium.

However, some care is needed here. English and other 'world' and 'colonial' languages can be languages of resistance, of practicality, of celebration, anger, joy as well as domination, erosion, loss (Brutt-Griffler, 2002). Within the political conflicts and supercomplexity of languaging choices we see the development of intercultural dispositions. Without an awareness of the histories that inform social and individual attitudes to language learning, and without the action-in-the-world that languaging represents, the project of forming critical citizens for an intercultural world will founder (Guilherme, 2002). Consequently the historical origin of the rise and dominance of 'modern languages' is embraced within our definition.

And yet, in the very course of the building of cultural and linguistic hegemony, a deep **critical reappropriation** and enduring contradiction has occurred. For although resistance to the hegemonic power has been expressed in many cases in the recuperation of 'invisible', suppressed languages, the imperial languages have themselves undergone challenge, splintering and counter-hegemonic recasting from within. Thus Caribbean 'nation-language' is not mere dialect but a reconstruction of English as critique; Spanish has long since ceased to be the language of the vice-regal bureaucracy and is now a world language adopted as their own by excluded groups in the name of their own cultural counterthrusts. Thus up to 30 million Spanish speakers in the United States have discovered a sense of power through the language of the historic conqueror (Hidalgo, 2001). French is no longer the language exclusive to the Quai D'Orsay and the *corps diplomatique* – it is spoken, remade, in Haiti, Martinique and Guadeloupe and in the French colonies of Africa and in a Québécois emphatic in its difference from European French.

The implication of all this is that the powerful languages of the world may express national identities, or they may be the medium for the expression of other collective identities distinct from or even in conflict with the nation.

Human beings often have complex, multiple identities – local, regional, familial, religious, ethnic; the dominant nationalist ideology dictates that one kind of identity, national identity (often closely linked to language) be paramount. [...] Just as an escape from the primacy of national identity can allow other identities to flourish, so an escape from the tyranny of the uniform national standard language can strengthen threatened dialects in small languages. (Barbour, 1996: 42)

Global diversity?

We are not idealising local languages as forms of resistance. The emphasis for us is on being intercultural, languaging, mutual exchange for mutual enrichment. In such a context 'Babel is more like the name of a life force' (McWhorter, 2002).

The 'other' is no longer 'out there' in the colonies and in 'exotic' far-flung places. The other is no longer, if indeed she was ever, contained within the boundaries of a nation and its one language. It is now not surprising to hear a plethora of languages in the western metropolis. Indeed it is no longer necessary to leave home to encounter members of other cultural groups and native speakers of other languages.

Language has been taken as a key 'sign of belonging', yet that belonging has itself become problematic.

At the end of one of my lectures on German tourism a couple of students came up and began to engage with some of the questions I'd been raising about hospitality and languages. I'd mentioned the way that languages work to welcome or to exclude, I'd mentioned that I'd been struck in recent months how often references to asylum seekers are accompanied by references to their major 'problem' – their 'poor' English. Perhaps, in our endeavours to offer hospitality, we might reach for the tools of dialogue ourselves, trying out words that make someone genuinely feel 'at home'. 'Just watch a hesitant word of welcome made in a language that is not ours bring back memories of place, and taste,' I said.

The students tell me their own stories. One has vivid memories of being brought up in a guest house in the North of Scotland and looking forward to the annual visits from a family from Bavaria, how his family began to learn German to speak to their guests, how he was given clothes their son had grown out of. The other student, rather shyly, confesses to volunteering in an asylum centre in the city. 'I've started learning Arabic to help with this,' she says, 'and you are so right. I take my homework to the centre and the women are just delighted to help me with my grammar and conversation. I'd never thought about this making them feel at home, but it does, and it makes them smile too.'

The old notions of 'home' and 'abroad' have broken down, if they were ever really fully tenable. Indeed, as Crowley argues (1996) 'European History is the deployment of the vision of the monolingual, monocultural nation for reactionary purposes.' Coulmas (1992), by contrast, investigates the correlation between the number of languages spoken and GDP. His interpretation is similar to Anderson's, though with less focus on the growth of the nation-state, in that he sees mass literacy (*Schrift*) as a key reason for the western tendency towards monolingualism in languages which are adapted to the needs of a literate culture. In some ways, however, this is a circular argument – and while there may be fewer languages used in contemporary literature, there is nevertheless a clear ideological shift towards the recuperation of language as a challenge to cultural hegemony.

What are the implications for modern languages, then, given the propensity towards universalisation of the languages of the materially dominant powers on the one hand and the multilingual reality arising out of the growing movements of populations on the other (Bauman, 2000)? Absorption and incorporation may be the preferred option for the powerful; for others – the majority, we suspect – the plurality and diversity of human expression, even within the world's most powerful languages, is what the intercultural approach, moving from language learning to languaging, can both celebrate and encourage. The point is that it cannot any longer be sufficient simply to reproduce the cultural models of the dominant classes within the nation-state as if they were the components of a global culture. It is more diverse and more profound by far than that.

Languages in higher education are suffering multiple challenges, not least of all those of an all **a way forward** pervasive functionalism and of the global dominance of English. Academic departments of modern languages are fighting for survival and struggling to articulate justifications for their existence. In the midst of the gloom and the supercomplexity comes the discovery of a central weakness in modern languages as a relatively new discipline in its own right. It has no clear theory or method of appropriation or knowledge of the world. It is therefore our task in the next chapter to begin to discover a way forward, to find theory and method sufficient to the task of creating critical dispositions for languaging and being intercultural.

Key references

Barnett, R. (2000) *Realizing the University in an Age of Supercomplexity*. Buckingham: Open University Press.

Di Napoli, R., Polezzi, L. and King, A. (2001) *Fuzzy Boundaries? Reflections on Modern Languages and the Humanities*. London: CILT.

Kelly, M. and Jones, D. (2003) *A New Landscape for Languages*. London: Nuffield Foundation.

Lyotard, J.-F. (1984) *The Postmodern Condition: A Report on Knowledge*. Manchester: Manchester University Press.

The Nuffield Languages Inquiry (2000) *The Nuffield Languages Inquiry (2000): Languages: The Next Generation*. London: Nuffield Foundation.

Websites

http://web.inter.nl.net/users/Paul.Treanor/lang.issues.html
http://www.lang.ltsn.ac.uk/resources/guidecontents.aspx

Encyclopedia

Byram, M. (2000) *Routledge Encylopedia of Language Teaching and Learning*. London and New York: Routledge.

2

Signs of belonging

In the previous chapter we demonstrated that, under siege from functionalism and from the global market, languages begin to lose their right to exist in higher education. Under such crisis conditions we discover the central weakness of modern languages, that it has, as a discipline, neither the theory nor the method for engaging with the material world. In this chapter we explore the fact that these crises lead us into such a defensive position and set of practices that there is no room left to manoeuvre, no space or time for serious reflection or creative thinking. There are a number of panic measures (often externally imposed by other academics thinking as administrators) which enclose us in an even narrower space.

Our response is (a) to critique the foundational assumptions of modern languages, using the perspectives of cultural studies, in terms of race, gender and class, and then (b) to argue that modern languages is in possession of a theory and method for being in the world.

Maeve's story: My Year in Cuba

The aim of my year abroad was to develop my Spanish language skills and my passion for the subject, and it certainly fulfilled it.

Highlights of my year: Getting mistaken for a Spanish person by Cubans! Being able to understand everything people are saying and loving the language more than ever before.

It was fascinating, bewildering and uplifting to live in such a different society, in terms of political system, ideals and practical reality. Although many aspects were frustrating and difficult, it was invaluable to be there at this time and has taught me a lot about the strengths and weaknesses of our own society. For example, during the Hurricane, people really pulled together, worked as a team, always put the greater good above their own immediate needs, and I felt unity.

INSIDE THE STOCKADE

At times of crisis, it is natural enough that people will seek refuge in common-sense assumptions and unquestioned values, or turn nostalgically towards the intellectual habits of the past. There is safety, after all, in pulling up the drawbridge and resisting change, rejecting the strangers at the gates. There is also a very different response to crisis – a kind of immersion in the immediate, as if the shape of things were beyond our grasp and control and events were subject to arbitrary and unknowable laws of motion. In both cases, the consequence is that we cease to be thinking subjects, agents in our own world. In this way we submit to our own sense of powerlessness – and the dominant values triumph without a fight.

There is, however, a third response to crisis, a response we find in Maeve's story. This is the response that teaches us about the strengths and weaknesses of our own ways of being. It is a way that is fascinating, bewildering and uplifting, at times frustrating and difficult. It is a way that allows pause for thought and for finding ways of being above the immediate needs, that enables the development of love and passion for other languages and other peoples. Most importantly, it is an encounter which transforms both parties and which enables both, through languaging, to embark upon new journeys of self and social discovery. It is a journey into intercultural being. Without Maeve's openness, in languaging, we are condemned to endless, sterile repetition of habits and practices; founding ideas are left undiscovered, visionary purposes never articulated.

It is the difficult task of this book to explore potential forms of intercultural being in and through the politics of pedagogy.

> There is no identity without a struggle against the constrictions of the forms inherited from 'tradition'. [...] The aim is not to identify oneself with a tradition, but to construct a nucleus of values, a personal identity, both rebellious and loyal, towards one's own roots. (Barba, 1994: 197–8)

Language encounters

The traditions of languages are histories of encounters with speakers of other languages. The contexts in which these encounters occur are contexts of multiple power relations. The encounter between English and any other language is not an open exchange but a struggle for domination. This is perhaps nowhere more evident than in the hegemonic struggles between Spanish and American English along the Mexican–US border:

Obliterating cultural barriers as though they were trade barriers will become the most onerous task of partners that have worked for 150 years under basic principles of inequality. In anticipation of the millions of Spanish speakers that are going to live, work, and receive education in the United States in the course of the twenty-first century, the English speaking superpower and major leader of globalisation will have to put to a test an unprecedented exercise in cultural democracy by opening public spaces to the Spanish language. (Hidalgo, 2001: 71)

The dominance of French in UK schools and universities is an accident of history and geographical proximity. In fact this dominance is presently challenged by the European Union's policy of language diversity, and by the growth of air travel, which makes Cancún as accessible as Carcassonne. To repeat an earlier point, in Britain it is predominantly European languages which are available for learning within higher education, although there is a growing interest in Chinese and Japanese among politicians with an eye on globalisation. There is of course no guarantee that this will last. During the Cold War there was a strategic interest in Russian and Slavic languages. Today departments of Slavic languages are disappearing from higher education at a rapid pace. Languages and their learning become important pointers to shifting strategic alliances in business and political terms, in a technocratic world.

The ability to speak another language fluently, with ease, can also be a marker of personal distinction. The learning of other languages, particularly for 'individual' rather than 'social' purposes (to use Kelly's (2001) distinctions) may be seen, at least in the UK, as a class pursuit.

Until comparatively recently, indeed probably until the immediate post-war period, modern languages were seldom learnt as a means to communicate – to transact business, or to interact with others. Learning languages was seen instead as an individual pursuit, a mark of refined culture, the ultimate expression of a disciplined intellect. (Grenfell, 2000: 2)

The ability to use another language with some degree of fluency is a skill valued largely by the middle classes, who have the means to spend structured learning time abroad. 'Ease is so universally approved only because it represents the most visible assertion of freedom from the constraints which dominate ordinary people' (Bourdieu, 1984: 255).

This does not of course mean that languages lack social meaning. In Ivy League universities in the US and at Oxbridge, graduate seminars in the humanities will assume a working knowledge of key languages and their literatures, and an ability to work with dictionaries and grammars in order to read a text in the original. It is presumed that this rigour with languages will produce a disciplined intellect, a marker of class and a marker of professionalism. The performative turn, however, means that the linking of languages to medicine, law, business, engineering is an example of the professionalising and functionalising of language learning which is also linked to the professional classes. It highlights the relatively new assumption that, far from being a plaything for the leisured and for the gentleman-scholar, another language may be useful in the workplace.

In 1968, the production line at the Renault-Flins Factory outside Paris was staffed by workers from a wide variety of linguistic backgrounds. Members of the same linguistic group were systematically separated from each other and their movements were controlled by the notorious 1,500-strong security squad. From the management perspective it was an effective way of preventing any kind of joint action by the workers. In May of that famous year, strike action brought the factory to a halt. The workers had found ways of speaking to one another with the enthusiastic help of students from the modern languages faculty at the Sorbonne. They had produced strike posters and propaganda in all of the languages represented among the workforce on the production line.

This was a prophetic example of the application of language learning to life – it is a further demonstration of the point made by Maeve, in her story, of the way that languages enable us to transcend immediate concerns and find ways of mutual being and mutual comprehension for practical action.

It does not follow that distinction will go to all those who are fluent in another language. Consider the ambiguities that surround attitudes to bilingualism. It would seem that the value placed on bilingualism relates to the ability of the language learner to write the language as well as to speak it (Coulmas, 1992). But that in its turn is calculated in very specific ways – by assessing its weight of what Bourdieu terms symbolic capital. The bilingual speaker will usually employ both the dominant language and what are usually characterised as 'community languages'. This is a term whose racist overtones are obvious and ignore the historical depth and symbolic power of languages like Urdu, Hindi or Arabic, with their centuries-long accumulation of formal expressions, and addressing them as if they were only oral codes.

World and heritage languages

In any event which language we end up learning will largely be accidental and could easily cease to be an accepted social achievement if political circumstances change. What would be the reaction today if you chose Swahili over French? By and large it is Western European languages together with their American variants which are learned and taught. It is surprising, perhaps, how narrow that range is. French, Spanish, German and to a lesser extent Italian have maintained their status as world languages thus far; modern Greek, Russian, even Portuguese are marginal. It is doubly curious, given the patterns of travel, tourism and migration, that Turkish, for instance, is not a widely learned language in Germany, or that Greek or Arabic is not part of a curriculum that prepares people for holidays in Crete or Tunisia. Some minority languages like Irish and Scots Gaelic are enjoying protection as 'heritage' languages for those with ethnic links to the languages but who have not learned them bilingually. But it is a very few only that enjoy this languaging privilege.

> I'm on my way home, waiting for the train at the station. A family stand next to me is chatting English. A young woman walks onto the platform and is recognised by the man in the family. He speaks to her in Gaelic and they laugh and enjoy an exchange. He then introduces his family and his partner in particular. She is learning to teach and is learning Gaelic as part of her training. The family live on the Isle of Islay, the children attend a Gaelic medium school and are being raised bilingually. The political status of their language is a living concern, what they speak is the object of their attention. How it should be pursued and made to live on is as natural an opener to these languagers as talking about the weather.

A further cultural aspect of language learning that arises in the context of this discussion is gender. The notion of mother tongue (*langue maternelle*, *Muttersprache*, *lengua materna*, etc.) associates languages with gender, at a symbolic level. It is true, for example, that the majority of language learners and hourly paid teachers at university level are women. Gender issues are thus clearly at play in this situation. The question is, what are the issues and how have they come to be so constructed in this particular field?

In the same sense, there is an increasing tendency to allocate modern languages to a region of 'leisure' or 'tourism' or of 'liberal arts'. Modern languages in the past were seen as 'Classics for middle-class women'. Research in cultural studies (Chodorow, 1989) has pointed to the way that certain aspects of social and cultural life come to assume gendered characteristics, often along binary lines of work and leisure. Sherry Simon's (1996) view is that they correspond to the 'soft' (feminised) area of social accomplishment rather than 'hard' (and presumably masculine) functionality. 'Work' categories are accorded masculinised status, leisure is feminised. In this reading languages become feminised activities and consequently of lesser economic significance. This in turn legitimises cutbacks in the face of a shrinking base of interest. In this sense, issues of power in gendered form enter the academy by yet another name.

The characteristic current response, which is to justify modern languages in the discourse of hard-nosed, business-led education, does not address or contest this issue of inequality; on the contrary, it reinforces the divisions and assigns languages and women to pre-existing categories that remain undisputed intellectually in the field of modern languages in higher education. Again it is our task in this book to question the underlying assumptions that led to such an impasse and to the perpetuation of such inequalities.

Let us take translation as an example, to which we shall return in Chapter 9, of how these gendered aspects are made manifest. Translation, according to Sherry Simon, is an activity that has long been stigmatised:

> *Because they are necessarily 'defective', all translations are 'reputed females'. In this neat equation, John Florio (1603) summarises a heritage of double inferiority. Translators and women have historically been weaker figures in their respective hierarchies.* (Simon, 1996: 1)

Languages, then, are markers of identity, they have the potential to fetishise the speaker, to signal race, gender and class. They have had social and cultural uses historically which persist to varying degrees, but predominantly the thrust of language learning today is functional, with some notable exceptions such as heritage language learning.

CLEARING THE WAY

Languages are signs of belonging. Learning another language is an exploration of the multiple experiences and cultural resonances that are embedded in and accrue to other languages and their cultures. Picking up a new language is not picking up a pristine, untainted, ahistorical object. Nor is it, to employ a different metaphor, an empty desert – any more than any culture is an empty space, or any learner is an empty vessel. It is an already peopled territory of social being in which, like the territory we ourselves have come from, there are pre-existing constraints, stories, struggles, tastes and smells. These must shape what can be said as well as how it is said. They are part of the mutual process of discovery of relationships and provide space for the intercultural process of negotiation, encounter and exchange. In order to understand another world, to be intercultural, to language, it is not sufficient to know your own world only. That world must be changed and challenged and enriched by others. Nor is it the case that all we need is a few grammar tools, a vocabulary list and the ability to apply performative tools in order to resolve practical problems.

This complex negotiation is what we understand by languaging. The starting point is to recognise that the divisions within society will find their expression in language just as they do in other places, and the organisation of language learning and teaching will also reflect these divisions. We can seek out variety and diversity in another language if we seek them out in our own lives. The disposition for such negotiation, such exchange, such mutual recognition and transformation is, for us, what is at the heart of the notion of the intercultural being. It is made manifest in the reflexive work of translation, of languaging.

Languages and intercultural communication

Our alternative in this book is a new variety of modern language studies – in a phrase: a field of languages and intercultural communication that has embraced the interpretation of culture, the lessons of second language acquisition and applied linguistics, the deconstruction of texts, and the development of cultural studies approaches to questions of race, gender, class, nationhood. We need first to identify and set aside the obstacles which stand in the way of this development.

Will's story

[This extract from a published learning journal introduces us to Will's reflections on his year abroad, part way through his time and the changes it has wrought on his life.]

During the conversation, it occurred to me the distances between my various worlds. That's to say my life here, my life in Spain, at home in C. and finally at L. The strangest thing is how I'll go to each one and people there will be glad to see me asking questions about the other places in my life, but only to a point. They'll never be anywhere as near into each place as I am and a lot of time will only ask them out of politeness. There's that, compared with me feeling deeply about each world and having spent significant moments of my life there. Like I said: distance.

These worlds are very distant, in that they are separated from each other both by geography and the type of life there. The only link between each one is me, and that's not always an easy thing for me; that I can never fully share these feelings and experiences with others.

(Crawshaw, Callen and Tusting, 2001: 107)

Being intercultural, being the languaging link, is – as Will says – about distance, but distance experienced from within. It is about finding ways to answer the questions – never really asked in modern languages – intellectually: What difference does it make that this is not my language or my culture? What difference does it make that I dwell in between, or that I 'dwell-in-travel'? What difference does it make, to use Clifford's (1997) words, that it is no longer a question of 'where I am from but of where I am between'? Questions of gender since the 1970s have forced a complete rethinking of many issues of society and culture along the lines of the difference it makes to be a woman at a certain time and place. The postcolonial debate has opened whole worlds of inquiry and experience, again questioning the difference it makes to be either a postcolonial or a colonial subject. This debate has often involved the acknowledgement of profound differences even within the same language. Consequently, under this line of inquiry, the question of being intercultural is a question of understanding the difference it makes to be the languaging link between multiple worlds.

Table 2.1 represents the shifts between conceptual frameworks that focus on being intercultural as opposed to intercultural competence.

Broadly speaking the growing interest in an intercultural focus on language learning has principally informed debates in relation to primary and secondary education. In the UK, pioneering work in the field of cultural studies, intercultural communicative competence and language

TABLE 2.1 *From intercultural competence to intercultural being*

	Intercultural competence	Intercultural being
Epistemology	Prescribed by disciplinary paradigms, e.g. literary, geographic, linguistic	Engaged with the whole social world, embodied disposition for action
	Engagement *of* self and other	Reflective engagement *with* self and other
Situations	Learned from and in a discipline Defined by academic fields	Discovered in action, reflection and recursion
		Transdisciplinary
Focus	Skills of interpreting, discovery and interaction	Skilful
	Skills as outcome	Skilling as process
Education	Political education	Languagers-in-action
	Critical cultural awareness	Critical intercultural being
	Sojourning	Reflective sojourning
Learning context	Classroom conditions predominate	Whole social world
Communication	Language learning	Languaging
	Intercultural speaker	Intercultural speaking and listening
Value orientation	Competence, communication and awareness	Border crossings
Boundary conditions	Knowledge of borders, translation, languages	Being border crossers, translators, languaging links

(Adapted from Barnett, 1994 and Byram, 1997)

learning has come from a variety of research projects led or inspired by the work of Michael Byram and aimed at secondary schools, curriculum development and teacher training. The students who have benefited from some of this work are now reaching the universities and the innovative thinking embedded in much of Byram's work is only beginning to be embraced in new fields such as languages and intercultural communication. The difficulty is that this new and potentially invigorating debate is taking place against a background of crisis and is under extreme pressure to develop along pragmatic, performative lines. The urgent task for us, for the future health and growth of modern languages, lies in recognising clearly the threats that these instrumental pressures pose and enabling the alternative vision of intercultural being and languaging to be articulated:

> *In this perspective, the learner and the teacher as co-learner question and elicit from the native an account of his* (sic) *culture which, together with other accounts, native and learner interpret jointly. (Byram, Estarte-Sarries and Taylor, 1991: 11)*

Transformation of the learning subject

If the question of intercultural being becomes the central concern and foundational position in our discussion of teaching and learning modern languages in higher education, then language learners may yet become what Byram calls 'intercultural speakers'. The focus is not the acquisition of a sham otherness or of cultural awareness (Cryle, 2002), but instead the transformation of the learning subject not just through learning a different language but through languaging and intercultural being.

It is important not to suggest that we are involved in the business of creating perfect performers, some kind of ideal along the same lines as the idealised and impossible notion of the 'native speaker' (Kramsch, 1993). As Will's story reminds us, what matters is the dynamic, often broken yet engaged process of intercultural encounters and the transformation of being. But this does not for a moment minimise the importance, nor the radical potential, of attempts to shift the focus away from the mechanics of the language and its 'mastery' and on to the cultural subject. Some of these attempts may be, of necessity in a crisis, utopian in character (Bauman, 2002).

Our concern, then, is how to 'maintain the coherence and integrity of (personal) development in the cultural chaos [and supercomplexity] of modern living' (Byram, Zarate and Neuner, 1997: 5).

In its 1997 report on language learning the **Council of Europe report on language learning** Council of Europe emp-hasised that language learners are not mere vessels to be filled; learning itself has begun to be seen as rather a more porous activity than the technocrats would have us believe. The aims and objectives for language learning and intercultural competence outlined in this report and also developed by Byram (Byram, Zarate and Neuner, 1997) stress the capacity of the language learner to effect social change. The report concludes with a range of objectives that include the demonstrable ability to be open to other cultures, to act as an intermediary, to be critically reflexive about cultural distance (Byram, Zarate and Neuner, 1997: 14–15). In short, to be like Will and Maeve.

> *The learner's ultimate goal is to achieve a capacity for cognitive analysis of a foreign culture, people and its artefacts – whether intellectual or other – and for affective response to the experience of another culture which neither hinders his (sic) perception of self or others nor prevents his adaptation to new environments. (Byram, Estarte-Sarries and Taylor, 1991: xiii)*

In subsequent chapters, we shall explore the implications of this view for both learning and teaching in modern languages. We shall argue that, from this starting point, we may yet articulate and develop a theoretical and methodological framework. There are still many debates concerning the 'best' way to teach language. In the field of second language acquisition the point has been made that the focus on speech in linguistics and in communicative language teaching has been to the detriment of literacy (Coulmas, 1992; Kramsch, 1998; Kress, 2003). Indeed Brown (2000: 185) suggests that through a narrow focus on communication language learning experiences have been greatly diminished: 'opportunities for learning about cultural issues, for extended reading, for talking about the ways in which language works are all being lost.' For our purposes it is important to take stock of the implications for higher education of this fundamental shift away from the language learning and towards languaging, away from living abroad to living in languages and being intercultural.

Academic staff complain constantly that students arrive at university 'illiterate' in their second language (or indeed in their own), unable to manipulate text, to read or to write. This is then taken to explain and justify a 'necessary dumbing down' of the early curriculum for languages in universities. Ironically, the truth is that the new cohorts of language learners often have well developed communicative skills. They are also largely members of more elite social groups:

> *[...] Figures suggest that there has been a growing elitism in languages. It is likely to be in part an academic elitism, which encourages the more able students to tackle A level languages, and provides them with better and more focused teaching. It may well be compounded by an element of educational elitism in which languages are more concentrated in academically more successful schools. The greater emphasis on languages in the independent sector is well known. (Kelly and Jones, 2003)*

New courses...vs languages as philology

In some institutions the new courses have been constructed with a genuine concern for the communicative competences that the students do already possess. In others there is a continuing assumption that the schools have prepared their most capable students for a university specialism in languages by ensuring they are entirely competent to read and translate large quantities of literature in the original language, i.e. for languages as philology not for languages as studies for intercultural being.

If existing social experience and communicative ability are deployed in a relationship of critical exchange between teacher and learner of the kind that Byram advocates, then other capacities can be built on that foundation. That foundation is, importantly, one of openness and mutual respect for each other and for the subject, not of domination by the teacher. That this is often not done may arise from a conservatism exacerbated by the sense of crisis. It may just be that changing how we do things is difficult, that giving away power in mutual exchange requires a certain openness and vulnerability.

It may also be the consequence of an increasing trend in universities to allocate much of the early undergraduate teaching to hourly-paid or part-time graduate teachers or native language assistants. For such staff, on highly vulnerable contracts, the giving away of power becomes well nigh impossible.

Departments [in the USA] face serious faculty resource mismatches when senior and experienced faculty members, who typically are educated in the literary field, teach few students, while novice graduate TAs teach the bulk of students in language classes. (Byrnes, 1998: 10–11)

This casualisation simply serves to separate the basic language learning from the range of cultural activities, and in many cases to reserve access to advanced intercultural literacy encounters to those at the higher (or honours) levels of undergraduate involvement.

Modern languages is at a crossroads. As the Nuffield Inquiry put it:

Nuffield languages inquiry

Languages are in crisis. Most university language departments are regarded as operating in deficit, and an increasing number are under threat of closure or reduction. Some have already closed. This is in part a product of funding formulae that do not adequately recognise the cost of language teaching, and reflects a national context where individual universities are not actively encouraged to enhance their provision of languages. Higher education is a diverse and fragmented sector, which lacks both the will and the means to address UK-wide strategic issues in languages in a sustained way. There is no government-led strategic agenda for languages to which higher education could respond. (Nuffield Languages Inquiry, 2000: 54)

The comment begs a number of questions, of course. The 'national need' referred to is left undefined, as are the 'strategic issues' – and there can be little doubt that the profession has become so absorbed in matters of administration and response that the much-vaunted 'blue skies' thinking that was supposed to accompany innovation has been conducted by a small and embattled group of colleagues with vision. It must be clear to everyone by now, however, that a cost-benefit analysis will only hasten the transformation of languages into commodities bought and sold for their usefulness. Performativity will become the norm of assessment and the result can only be the ultimate abandonment of that human process of developing understanding, of enrichment of the self and of that other, expansive, kind of globalisation that emerges out of collaboration and exchange, rather than competition and the destruction of values.

The report *A New Landscape for Languages* (Kelly and Jones, 2003) identifies a number of potential scenarios that may face modern languages in the future. It also outlines the courses of action already taken managerially to deal with the deficits in departments of modern languages, including: the merging of departments into schools of modern languages or single-language departments; the incorporation of languages into business schools or humanities departments; the disbanding of languages units and the relocation of 'valued' staff into other cognate departments; the pursuit of synergies between local universities in language programmes and the creation of specialist language-only units which deliver 'key skills and language services' but not 'academic' content.

In this chapter we have engaged with and critiqued the foundational assumptions of modern languages, in so far as they exist. We have cleared the pathways out of the stockade towards a terrain in which language learning reconnects with the worlds in which we speak and act in multiple ways that are intimated, connected and mutually enriching. Having the courage to leave the stockade will also require risk and vulnerability, possibly failure. It is always difficult to resource a siege mentality when the future is yet to be built. But it is the necessary precondition for embarking on the languaging project.

In the chapters that follow, we have set out to pursue the logic of our general critique of a field trapped between the narrow elitism of a latter-day public school refinement on the one hand, and a functional perception in which languages are at best a mode of minimal communication on the other. Our argument is that an aggressive search for new markets for service teaching or functionality is no answer to the crisis in modern languages. It can only lead to its submergence into a general area of detached services.

The alternative is to reconstruct the new discipline of modern language studies using its greatest strength – as a means to become critically engaged through an awareness of others, to become a languaging actor in the world. Thus we contest the narrow, the functionalist and the hegemonic by exploring diversity and plurality. To 'develop the learners' capacity for independent thought and critical reflection' entails 'a readiness on the part of teachers and teacher trainers (and learners themselves) to explore what it is to be human and to rebuild pedagogy from first principles' (Little, 2000: 25).

Key references

Byram, M. (1997) *Teaching and Assessing Intercultural Communicative Competence*. Clevedon: Multilingual Matters.

Byram, M., Zarate, G. and Neuner, G. (1997) *Sociocultural Competence in Language Learning and Teaching*. Strasbourg: Council of Europe Publishing.

Byrnes, H. (ed.) (1998) *Learning Foreign and Second languages: Perspectives in Research and Scholarship*. New York: Modern Language Association of America.

Crawshaw, R., Callen, B. and Tusting, K. (2001) 'Attesting the Self: Narration and Identity Change', *Language and Intercultural Communication*, vol. 1, no. 2, pp. 101–19.

Hidalgo, M. (2001) 'Spanish Language Shift Reversal on the US–Mexico Border and the Extended Third Space', *Language and Intercultural Communication*, vol. 1, no. 1, pp. 57–75.

Kelly, M. (2001) '"Serrez ma haire avec ma discipline": Reconfiguring the Structures and Concepts', in R. Di Napoli, L. Polezzi, and A. King (eds), *Fuzzy Boundaries? Reflections on Modern Languages and the Humanities*. London: CILT, pp. 43–56.

Websites

http://www.lancs.ac.uk/users/interculture/
http://www.lang.ltsn.ac.uk/resources/guidecontents.aspx

Encyclopedia

Byram, M. (2000), *Routledge Encyclopedia of Language Teaching and Learning*. London and New York: Routledge.

Culture in pieces

It is not simply enough to just break out of the stockade. We need to develop a disposition that will enable us to enter the broader field of intercultural experience and material life that we commonly call 'culture'. This is a terrain without walls, a world which is not divided up into the convenient corridors of the academy but which spills out and overflows in unpredictable and messy ways. Engaging with this is where the future of modern languages can lie.

We begin, in this chapter, to demonstrate the implications of the continued atomising of culture and the relegating of material life to a backdrop to literature, to so-called 'content' courses. We argue for a rediscovery of the integrity of cultural practice as part of the embodiment of languaging and the bedrock of intercultural being.

Canon versus culture

It's 9 o'clock on an October morning. The lecture hall is not packed. In these days of attrition in modern languages those choosing to take German are counter-cultural souls – often sole survivors of what were once strong departments in schools. Or, even more likely, they have been to public school, where the fees support the few to gain access to languages and cultures, fund foreign trips, exchange programmes and buy the time and resources required for such tuition. Modern languages are now both as marginal and as privileged as classical languages.

I look out at the sea of faces. Some know each other already, having met by chance in the week of revelling and trepidation that preceded this. Mostly there is an unknowing stillness in the lecture theatre, no great anticipation, just a waiting for the show to begin.

They are probably expecting a lecture on contemporary German culture. That's the title of the introductory course. I pause, smile, take my own nervous breath – this is always a hard time of year, the stage fright never diminishes – and we begin.

First of all I invite them to move closer together and closer to me. Then I invite them to speak to each other and to brainstorm the simple question: 'What comes in to your mind when I say the word "culture"?' There is initial surprise, bodily reluctance to engage in some, an embarrassed shuffling in others. And then the gentle murmur that I love so much, of learners learning and laughing. The noise level builds. These days I know how to gauge the right moment and to draw them back together. I invite their responses and words pour from the chalk on the broken blackboard: architecture, music, literature, art, dance. I pause for a moment and visibly shudder as my fingernails catch the board. There is more laughter. I feel them to know me to be human. The next task is eagerly engaged. 'What comes in to your mind when you think of "German culture"?' There is no need to issue the instruction, they are already back in their clusters, laughter is immediate, life is full. The noise is rich. Is this learning, I wonder for a moment? Is this knowledge? I join in the laughter this time. I assert an authority from experience. 'Hands up if you wrote down "beer".' A forest of arms wave. More laughter. 'What about Lederhosen?' More waving hands. 'BMW?' I love this moment, this feeling of us all seeing the connections together. It's in this laughter, bodily engagement, dialogue, levelling and in this particular contradiction – between 'culture' and German culture – that I know we have a genuine beginning, an introduction to culture and beyond.

'Culture' in the curriculum

There can be very few single words that provoke such fierce debate as 'culture'. It is bitterly disputed territory. The far right describes culture as an embattled fortress threatened by the barbarians at the gate; it is a synonym of purity, caste and historical continuity. And it is a fiction. This static and unchanging thing that is French or German, Mexican or Russian culture, set in a conserving material of some mysterious kind that neither changes nor deteriorates with the passage of time, does not, of course, exist. The reductive description of collective characteristics associated with one or another nation-state is pure reification. That is to say, it is an abstract idea that has come to be seen as if it were a real, tangible thing. Since the nation-state itself emerges from conflict, struggle, and the impulse to territorial cohesion, then its culture too is historically specific.

We need to explore the reasons why the historical and temporal sources of ideas of fixed cultural stereotypes are buried, made invisible, mythified. But if we do not place the definition itself back within the flux of history we will inescapably become recruits to the defence of immobilising and reactionary fixities. And these are invariably exclusions. Yet we argue throughout this book for a dynamic and inclusive conception of culture which both echoes the continual compromises, encounters, fusions and intersections of the history of culture, and articulates a conviction that the projection of that process into the future is the only real guarantee of the development of human understanding in the realm of freedom.

And yet, paradoxically, the concept of culture 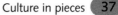 has become central to the marketing and recruiting of students to modern languages degree programmes in recent years. Many departments have rebranded themselves as areas within Schools of Modern Languages, Literatures and Cultures (Kelly and Jones, 2003). On the surface, this would seem to represent a significant change from the days when culture was limited to courses providing what was called 'background' to the discussion of literary history, where it was seen as a support to the 'real' work of literary studies. In this framework, culture, at two removes from the real business of literary study and accorded no more importance than a condiment to the main dish, could never be a subject included in modern languages curricula in its own right.

The philosophical and ideological underpinings of modern languages were rarely exposed to view – though not far beneath the surface lay the 'Spirit of the Age' (*Geist, Esprit*), and this general idea of culture defined the soil in which these blooms would grow and flourish. But the combination of growing agents was too accidental and too arbitrary to be of any interest. The optimistic universalism of this view found its continuation and affirmation in F.R. Leavis's conception of a 'great tradition'. The realities of the postwar world, however, made it difficult to posit the existence of a single and uncontested path to human liberation. In the context of the Cold War and the proliferation of movements of national liberation, the prevailing cultural categories were necessarily also contested – and art and literature became one of the sites of contestation. But only one.

Cultural studies

The emergence of a stance that has been termed 'post-disciplinary', that of cultural studies, attested the multiplicity of such sites. Cultural studies, in seeing itself as post-disciplinary, offers a mode of engagement in a wide variety of fields that is primarily political. Its commentary on literature, film, art and architecture, music and daily life focuses on questions of power and inequality, of social justice and questions of identity and difference. In a world of supercomplexity, where the frameworks of knowledge and understanding are in hopeless conflict, new ways of engaging culturally with the world and our understanding of it require new political and intellectual forms of expression. Modern languages, by embracing culture, it seemed, could be enlivened in its own endeavour to work through the contradictions of culture and language.

Looking at the curricula of modern languages degree programmes today, it becomes clear that `curriculum change` a major shift has taken place. The days of the dominance of the canon of literary, predominantly male, cultural giants is over. Most courses now include ample reference to women writers, to gay expression and, in almost all European languages, to a postcolonial phenomenon which poses explicitly and implicitly a direct challenge to the universalisms of the spirits of the age. At first sight, then, it would seem that cultural studies has come in from the cold and taken its place beside the other components of the modern languages degree. In reality, however, the extent to which the so-called cultural studies elements of modern languages programmes are actually derived from 'cultural studies' is debatable (von Graevenitz, 1999). What seems to be a major shift is, in fact, often little more than window dressing. The key question, articulated in Chapter 2, of what it means, in terms of theory and of method, that this language or that culture is not my own remains unasked.

It is true that 'culture' courses in many contemporary curricula do not start from 'high art' concepts; indeed they are often critical of them (Eagleton, 2000). They have also opened a permitted space for a discussion of other areas of cultural production – in particular cinema as well as other, usually genre-based, bodies of work. Equally, the 'great canon' is and has been amply shown to be amenable to such critical, cultural studies readings. This will often create the feeling of a patchwork of elements, contiguous but not combined; this impression is only emphasised by the modular structure of many and increasing numbers of degree courses. The situation is more confusing still when postmodernism is invoked to legitimate a kind of fragmentation of view, so that the proliferation of courses is accompanied by a notion of the autonomy of each area of cultural practice. In this way a detailed analysis of each vitiates any holistic analysis of the totality of culture as practice and process. How helpful 'postmodernism' may be as a conceptual tool to deal with such a situation is, in our view and that of others, highly debatable (Barnett, 2000; Callinicos, 1989).

Yet neither of these approaches, in our view, represents a continuity of the framework of cultural studies, an overtly political and essentially Marxist interpretation of culture, which emerged largely from the work of the Frankfurt School and the Birmingham Centre for Contemporary Cultural Studies which built on and developed its legacy. Cultural studies is not and never was conceived as a catch-all. It is situated within a historical, coherent, intellectual tradition. Latterly the fusion of cultural studies with poststructuralism, feminism and postcolonial studies among others has produced an understanding of the complex processes of the consumption and production of everyday life, including literature.

In most modern languages curricula in higher education, however, the influ- 'cultural studies' approaches

ence of cultural studies has been interpreted in a quite different way. As we have already noted, issues of race, gender and class are now frequently raised in the context of literary study, and there will often be courses on postcolonial writing or on women's writing. But in most languages departments, these are largely token affairs. On the other hand, courses that break with the idea of an aesthetic hierarchy are few and far between, and the more radical understandings of culture find little acknowledgement in practice.

Models of culture

The models of culture embedded implicitly or explicitly in typical 'cultural background' courses assume that reality is 'constructed' ideologically, and thus deny material life any agency in the formation of human behaviour (Archer, 2000). They find echo in poststructuralist models of cultural studies, particularly those prevailing in the humanities. Yet understanding gender, race and class in selected texts is not necessarily the only useful framework for the interpretation of culture, nor yet the most complete.

Perspectives developed within anthropology can open up the concept of culture in directions unavailable to modern languages under siege, but necessary for the development of theoretical and methodological frameworks for languaging and intercultural being. The anthropological perspective on culture is both general and specific, acknowledging that it is *both* a phenomenon common to all human experience *and*, as is the case with the cultures associated with individual languages, associated with specific cultures. Culture therefore has important, universalising and particular links to material life. Bourdieu makes this point succinctly:

> One cannot fully understand cultural practices unless 'culture' in the restricted, normative sense of ordinary usage, is brought back into 'culture' in the anthropological sense, and the elaborated taste for the most refined objects is reconnected with the elementary taste for the flavours of food. (Bourdieu, 1984: 1)

This view allows us to understand specific cultures, not so much as black boxes to be described or solely as constructs of the mind, but as fluid, contested and shaped by a variety of agents. The consequence is that the discussion of culture requires reflection on material practices. This view of culture as both general and specific, coupled with the political and critical perspectives of cultural studies, opens up an as yet untapped potential for rethinking modern languages in higher education. Without it we condemn modern languages to the kind of bland diet and slow starvation that characterises any siege.

BENCHMARKING CULTURE

It is worth us engaging in the exercise Bourdieu suggests here by bringing the sense of culture in modern languages benchmark statements together with that of anthropology. Other statements, such as geography, economics, history, linguistics, classics, would suffice here, suited as they are to the supply of theory and method for the purposes of languaging and intercultural being. The anthropology benchmarks enable the contours of 'culture debates' to be most clearly articulated, given that culture is, in effect, anthropology's work. (Table 3.1 contains extracts from the UK Benchmark Statements for subject knowledge in Anthropology and Table 3.2 contains extracts from the UK Benchmark Statements for subject knowledge in Languages and Related Subjects.)

It is revealing to juxtapose these two benchmark statements. We do not do this in order to demonstrate the superiority of anthropology over modern languages but in order to underline how differently the two speak about and understand culture. Culture has been described as anthropology's gift to the world. It has a long, reasoned and often critically fraught tradition of studying culture through its changes and developments. This is reflected in the integrated way in which processes

TABLE 3.1 *Anthropology: subject knowledge, skills and understanding: social anthropology*

Benchmark

- An understanding of the nature and extent of human diversity and commonality as seen from a variety of perspectives (e.g. social, cultural, ecological, biological).
- An awareness of the repertoire of concepts, theories and key research methods used in anthropological analysis.
- An appreciation of the relationship between local social and cultural forms in relation to global processes and broader temporal developments.
- An awareness of how anthropology articulates with cognate subjects.
- Alertness to the potential applications of anthropological knowledge in a variety of contexts.
- An understanding of how human beings shape and are shaped by social, cultural and environmental contexts.
- An ability to question cultural assumptions
- An understanding of the social and historical processes that influence the objects of anthropological study.
- An ability to interpret and analyse a variety of textual, oral and visual forms.

Source: http://www.qaa.ac.uk/crntwork/benchmark/phase2/anthropology.pdf (2002).

TABLE 3.2 *Languages and related subjects*

Knowledge of related studies

As determined in the individual programme specification, graduates in the discipline of LRS at honours level will be expected to:

● demonstrate an ability critically to evaluate through appropriate methodologies one or more aspects of the literatures, cultures, linguistic contexts, history, politics, geography, social and economic structures of the societies of the country or countries of the target language(s);

● demonstrate a broad knowledge and, using appropriate methodologies, a critical understanding of the cultures and societies of the country or countries of the target language(s) gained through the study of the literatures and/or other cultural products of the target language(s).

Intercultural awareness and understanding

As determined in the individual programme specification, graduates in the discipline of LRS at honours level will be expected to:

● demonstrate a reasoned awareness and critical understanding of one or more cultures and societies, other than their own, that will normally have been significantly enhanced by a period of residence in the country, or countries, of the target language(s);

● demonstrate an ability to describe, analyse and evaluate the similarities and dissimilarities of those cultures or societies in comparison with their own.

Source: http://www.qaa.ac.uk/crntwork/benchmark/phase2/languages.pdf (2002).

evolving in time and space, together with thinking about those processes, are brought together in the benchmark statement. It is worth noting the stress in this confident anthropological discourse on interdisciplinarity, on the relationship between different social and cultural, global and local, temporal and spatial experiences.

'Culture' = 'background'?

Culture in modern languages has long been understood as literature with some elements of 'background'. The languages benchmark statement offers no criticism of this narrow view. On the contrary, it is reinforced by the insistence on distinct *methodologies* [*sic*] 'appropriate' to each distinct field. This parcels up culture into bits, tidies them up and wraps them in brown paper. The point is that this approach to culture is a million miles away from the integrated vision and comparative understanding that has grown in anthropology and can embrace all forms of cultural experience in their relationship to one another. And, indeed, it seems legitimate to ask here whether issues of methodology in modern languages are ever overtly addressed in most modern languages curricula, whereas in the case of anthropology it is constantly addressed as an integral way of being and becoming an anthropologist.

No cultural activity is simply a product – as the modern languages benchmark suggests. As we have repeatedly emphasised *culture is process* – is verb and adjective. By the same token a crude and ill-defined search for assumed 'similarities and dissimilarities' is hardly an appropriate prelude for an exploration of intercultural being.

It is worth reflecting here on how it is that these two entirely different approaches and expressions of teaching and learning 'culture' have come about. The material fact of the matter is that modern languages are indeed divided and parcelled up and each fragment is wholly separate from the other, with no sense of it being part of a coherent, integrated, disciplined whole. If, as we have argued, the 'discipline' of modern languages is indeed a new phenomenon in its current guise, then little more could be expected. Anthropology, on the other hand, for all its different areas of concern, does have a sense of its own methodology – that of ethnography – and of its history (with its roots in colonialism). It also has a sense of the political issues inherent in cultural description and cultural comparison, and of the need for languages to be what is lived in. In anthropology, importantly, culture is integrated into the social, biological, material, languaging processes of human life.

Teaching methods

In modern languages we have borrowed theories of literature, culture, history, social change, economics and geography, and there are multiple, hotly disputed methods for teaching and learning languages. To repeat: modern languages does not have its own theory, nor does it have its own method. The very fertile ground of difference, of cultural and linguistic difference and otherness, has not yet been developed into a coherent curriculum or project. Hence the evasive discourse of 'appropriate methodologies' in the benchmark statements.

Critiquing 'text'

When faced with its own crises around questions of representation, truth and history, anthropology took a long hard look at its own theory and method and some radical and reflexive developments occurred. Culture, for instance, came to be understood as 'text' (Geertz, 1973). The texts that were the staple product of ethnography and anthropological training were consequently subjected to rigorous critique (Clifford and Marcus, 1986). In addition, anthropologists began to look more critically at the roots of their discipline in colonial travel and to acknowledge their place in imperialist projects. These, and other crises, have led to a radical rethinking of subject, theory and method in anthropology and have resulted in a vigorous reshaping of the discipline. There is, in our view, much that modern languages could learn from the lessons taken in other disciplines from their own ethical dilemmas and epistemological and ontological crises.

This is not to suggest for a moment that modern languages find themselves *crisis in modern languages* in a situation of crisis simply because of a lack of vision and creative thinking in the subjects. Wider social, cultural and political forces are clearly at play in the current situation. 'A demoralised nation tells demoralised stories to itself [...]. A people are as healthy and con-fident as the stories they tell themselves. Sick storytellers can make their nations sick. And sick nations make for sick storytellers' (Okri, 1997: 109–10). Engaged in a war of attrition, fighting falling numbers, faced with the inexorable rise of global English, with languages depart-ments round about being closed down, then the stories in the staff rooms – if these still exist as such – are of rearguard actions, last ditch defences or defeat.

Where student numbers are steady or rising, where the medium is English, where the subject is culturally sexy, then there are pressures, but the stories have more room to breathe. Vision, innovation and creative energy do not come from nowhere. They come, yes, from adversity as well as strength, but they require time and space to be tried out, for suc-cesses and failures to produce humour and hope, for lessons to be truly learned. Vision requires material resources. When retreating or defeated these are in short supply. For us to truly reinvigorate the field we need supplies, aid from richer neighbours. In short, modern languages need collegiality, need the real vision of a university, not balance sheets and declarations of debt.

It is of paramount importance, not just for modern languages, but for the wider project of mutual prosperity, hospitality and diversity, that languages live and are lived. It is important for intellectual work in all subjects that languages grow, that public intellectuals are languagers. We need more than one vision and ideology for the broken world of human relations and human communication. Let us make no mistake here. The argument of this book is about finding and creating new stories, new ways of being out of the current defeat. But it is about more than this. Much more.

Fundamental changes

In some places, where energy has been found and released modern languages have experienced and provoked fundamental changes in the way they are taught. Area studies, communicative language teaching, the incorporation of the occasional study of popular culture, film and media studies and linguistics have changed the shape of the discipline. Some students do have good stories to tell. The exclusive study of literature has at least sometimes given way to more varied and multiple programmes, and the consequence has been a redefinition – by custom and practice at least – of the concept of culture deployed in modern languages departments. Culture *is* now understood in a more complex manner as material practice and social interaction, in other words as a verb or an adjective, as process and description rather than a noun which reifies.

The problem is that several of the publications and courses which market themselves as cultural studies actually still take an approach based on a concept of culture as artistic and intellectual activity (Burns, 1995).They are thus essentially an extension of the literary cultural paradigm which has dominated the study of modern languages until the last decade. Despite all the shifts and the acknowledgement of some of the potential of cultural studies, so-called culture courses continue to examine intellectual life, the media, institutions, political figures and events and even geography, but do so using the same methods and theoretical framework as literary studies, often even mistakenly employing concepts like 'discourse' to validate textual analysis rather than as a variegated mode of cultural commentary. In and of itself there is nothing wrong with this type of analysis – but it is still a restrictive method, and one that presumes that to teach culture means little more than teaching literature, so that the material life of culture is reduced to a slightly expanded notion of text:

This is the 'philologism' which, [...] tends to treat all languages like dead languages, fit only for deciphering; it is the intellectualism of the structural semiologists who treat language as an object of interpretation or contemplation rather than an instrument of action or power. (Bourdieu, 2000: 53)

To expand the notion of text to include all of social and cultural life ultimately means that the questions asked of other languages and cultures, in the dominant learning activity of interpretation, are questions pertaining to meaning, or deciphering. To follow one line of questioning excludes others which may be equally productive. For instance: What does this text (object, music, dance, food, poem) *do*? How might I understand my distance or difference in language and in culture as it changes over time? Where do I stand, in time and place, as I seek to understand? How am I practically engaged and changed by the bodily action of languaging? How might I, by my own effort, share in a different social and cultural life? What does it feel like, taste like, smell like, to live in this language, to language in this way?

From the perspective of our general argument, these alternative questions of culture and of the self have a far-reaching consequence. For as long as the implicit or explicit reference point is a canon of excellence, that is interpreted with the tool of unchanging ahistorical reason with a view-from-nowhere, then the business of 'learning culture' is little more than the absorption of pre-existing, pre-packaged rules and criteria which are then tested against given works. This can be true even where the texts addressed are not 'great works' but genres and works produced within other cultural fields and frames – popular culture for example. There is still no place within this context for an exchange of cultural experience with the text, which we have argued is the core of an active, intercultural learning process.

Interviewer: And what surprised you about the course?

Student 4: *I like the way it doesn't limit itself to just German language or culture, you know, and it deals with so many different aspects of society. I find it really interesting because you could use it, you could take the course as a starting point and then use it for different things and that is how you start getting your courses to relate to each other. I find that much more interesting than just, you know, doing one course and that is it.*

Student 1: [...]*the fact that it's not just about German. It's not, you know, like sitting down and you read Kleist or whatever and then it's sort of over. It goes on and you can apply it to different things that you are doing in different subjects.*

Student 2: *I think that everybody at university should do a course like this because you talk about issues that are important in today's culture because it is about popular culture and I know a lot of people who are doing other subjects like geography who study the same things as we're studying in this course just now, so you know, we're having really interesting flat conversations too, so I really think that you can apply it to today and your culture.*

Student 3: *I've been quite cynical up to now about university in general, I've just been disappointed by it all and I think this course has really, not changed my mind, because they're all still out there, [laughter] but there seems to be a bit of light...*

Student 1: *I've very much done a literature degree because all the subjects I've done have had that component...you know, to do a novel ... I learn it, I learn quotes, I learn themes, I do this, that and the other with it, but then after the exam I've not really kept much from it.*

The concept of culture as material practice presumes that the cultural encounter is dynamic, 're-actualising' in the sense that meaning is discovered in an encounter between text and learner in a specific time and space – that is the material practice to which we are referring here. It is not the presumed quality or otherwise of any given cultural process or product that makes it more or less valuable, but rather its ability to elicit languaging.

CULTURE WARS

As we have seen, in the context of the modern languages curriculum, its is not always clear what is meant by 'culture' – though it is subject to redefinition in the context of a discipline under siege and under pressure to broaden its market appeal. The inescapable consequence is a blurring or even a serious dilution of the concept.

In translating the ideas of cultural studies into modern languages, much of the teaching on gender, society and ethnicity has become atomised, and the radical potential of cultural theory has been locked into a structure of identity politics and literary study, perpetuating old paradigms that serve particular interests. This must be at odds with a mass higher education system which sets out to develop individuals with a disposition for critical thought and autonomous learning. In the words of South African novelist André Brink:

> Culture is that territory or dimension of experience in which meaning emerges; more precisely, that experience of meaning in which the individual is creatively related to the collective. (Brink, 1983: 224)

Again, we may learn from anthropology where its vision is integrative. The task that we face, therefore, is to reconnect and reintegrate each of these areas into modern languages, in such a way that culture is the framework of learning and not merely one in a series of warring topics.

This is in no way a simple task. Academic life and its ways of working and being atomise experience and set apart social and practical life:

> Imputing to its object what belongs in fact to the way of looking at it, it projects into practice an unexamined social relation which is none other than the scholastic relation to the world [...] they [academics] tend to conceive every understanding, even practical understanding, as an interpretation, a self-aware act of deciphering. (Bourdieu, 2000: 53)

Given this intellectual milieu such a state of being raises fundamental and radical questions about what it might mean 'to teach culture', not as background or as text, not for distanced appreciative interpretation but as part of the social and material fabric of life.

SO WHAT DOES IT MEAN TO TEACH CULTURE?

Studying women's writing or postcolonial literature expands and undoubtedly challenges the hegemony of a white, male canon, but it does so using the discourse of culture when in reality it has little interest in anything but the literary category of culture and a few tools it has bricolaged from cultural theory.

What appears to take on board the developments and refinements of social thought that have evolved through the women's movement, in debates around modernism, out of the acknowledgment of popular culture can easily become simple transpositions of the atomised visions of cultural history. These are then simply imposed onto other areas of artistic and cultural practice. Terms and tools which can be extraordinarily useful – 'discourse' or 'ideology' spring readily to mind – are used to isolate particular realms of experience, to tell their histories without reference to others and, perhaps most damaging, to isolate thought and expression from material life. So we may have a history of women's writing, or of the romantic novel, whose presumptions and reference points are much the same as their earlier more limited predecessors.

The confrontations between these versions of cultural study and the conception of cultural studies as a dynamic and integrated totality have been described as 'culture wars'. They find their practical expression in curricula in modern languages departments.

It's mid way through the academic year and a new lecture course on Popular German Theatre is about to start. So far, throughout their course, students have studied the rise of fascism and the failures of democracy in twentieth-century Germany. They have seen films of Auschwitz and Hitler and the building and tearing down of the Berlin Wall. Recently they followed a course on Nietzsche. Many are taking options on National Socialism, Freud and Jung, Realism, Thomas Mann and Kafka. The poetry they read in their first year was bleak, as were the plays. Their second year focused on Faust and literary pacts with the devil.

There has been some relief, for those seeking it. Some occasional romantic poetry, some stories and fairy tales, comedies and other aspects of 'popular culture'. The value of studying popular culture has to be constantly defended as a serious scholarly enterprise. This is never the case for the diet outlined above. The departmental lines are drawn ideologically and passionately. We fight our culture wars vigorously, embodying our values and passions in our teaching – for good and ill. But I wonder what it is like for my students, sitting somewhat sullenly as I move to begin my course. What picture do they have of German culture? What does this say about our own warped relations to our culture of choice? What we've given them is a long and unrelenting set of sick stories. This is the canon we have chosen out of all the vibrancy and complexity of German cultural life.

Let there be laughter and life, I think, and begin.

Indeed the culture wars identified by Eagleton (Eagleton, 2000) are fought with great energy and more than a little fear in the pages of the stock journals of the respective modern language disciplines (Haug, 1999; von Graevenitz, 1999):

The phrase 'culture wars' suggests pitched battles between populists and elitists, custodians of the canon and devotees of difference, *dead white males and the unjustly marginalized. The clash between Culture and culture, however, is no longer simply a battle of definitions, but a global conflict. It is a matter of actual politics, not just academic ones. It is not just a tussle between Stendhal and Seinfeld, or between those churls on the English department corridor who study line-endings in Milton and the bright young things who write books on masturbation. It is part of the shape of the world politics of the new millennium. [...] It is just that the culture wars which matter concern such questions as ethnic cleansing, not the relative merits of Racine and soap operas. (Eagleton, 2000: 51)*

Eagleton's point is fundamental. The debate about the teaching of culture

humanism or deconstruction

can so easily be caricatured as a confrontation between nostalgia for the elitist humanisms of the nineteenth century and a fashionable discourse-based deconstruction that eschews all general statements about the human experience. The result is a supposed 'wholeness' born of arrogance or it is an endless fragmentation:

Difference does not have to result in the pathology of closure. [...] However, understanding the other may be enhanced less by a radical fetishisation of difference than by deepening a sense of our shared humanity. (Cronin, 2000: 91)

Our argument here is founded on a profoundly different conception that pursues cultural life not as a revealed truth but as a dynamic process and practice, and where the search is not for hidden mystical essences but for the relationships, encounters and changes that are the foundation of the engagement with the social that we understand by culture.

Most importantly, however, as Eagleton so passionately underscores, cultural understand- **critical universalism**
ing is an appropriation of the world as it is. That is not to say, of course, that we should address in our teaching only the immediate and ignore the past. Nor does it mean we should ignore either difference or the universal. It means that we should engage in what Cronin terms *critical universalism* as opposed to *pathological universalism*:

> *Critical universalism is a celebration of difference that leads to an embrace of other differences, the universalism lying not in the eradication of the other but in sharing a common condition of being a human other. (Cronin, 2000: 91)*

The process we are describing is one that is profoundly aware of the past, of tradition, of the weight and presence of complex histories, of the sense in which the concept of culture is dense with accumulated experience, is humming with life. What we are saying is that that concept is encountered in a historical present – made new, so to speak, for each languaging learner. That, essentially, is the task of teaching culture – to facilitate that encounter. With an awareness of the past and our own history as modern linguists in place, bedded into new curricula, we may begin, collectively, to articulate methods for languaging and theories of intercultural being.

Key references

Bourdieu, P. (1984) *Distinction: A Social Critique of the Judgement of Taste*. London: Routledge.

Bourdieu, P. (2000) *Pascalian Meditations*. Cambridge: Polity.

Clifford, J. and Marcus, G. E. (1986) *Writing Culture: The Poetics and Politics of Ethnography*. Berkley and Los Angeles: University of California Press.

Cronin, M. (2000) *Across the Lines: Travel, Language and Translation*. Cork: Cork University Press.

Eagleton, T. (2000) *The Idea of Culture*. Oxford: Blackwell.

Websites
http://www.qaa.ac.uk/crntwork/benchmark/phase2/anthropology.pdf
http://www.qaa.ac.uk/crntwork/benchmark/phase2/languages.pdf

Encyclopedia
Byram, M. (2000) *Routledge Encyclopedia of Language Teaching and Learning*. London and New York: Routledge.

4

Culture and beyond

A TRAVELLER'S TOOL KIT

In a time when the dominant conceptions of educational value return to ideas of functionality and see languages only in terms of simple 'skills', the question of why it is important to teach culture and teach through culture has to be addressed. In part, we have already offered in our opening chapters what we hope is a rounded critique of functionalism and elitism in modern languages. In the previous chapter we examined the atomising and fragmentation of culture, proposing instead an integrating encounter. Nevertheless, since our argument is that, once out of the stockade, the teaching of modern languages must develop an intercultural theory and method, then it is the task of this chapter to describe what this may mean conceptually and in practice.

In order to move beyond atomised approaches to culture we need, firstly, to engage with the history of modern language learning and to incorporate this history into our teaching, just as anthropologists or sociologists or historians teach the history of their own disciplines as a matter of course, precisely in order to demonstrate the historical foundations of their theory and method.

FUNCTIONALISM AND IDEOLOGY

In one sense, the learning of modern languages has always been functional, if we embrace within that concept an *ideological* function – the possession of the values and legitimating myths of domination. Languages were learned primarily by the elite, by the kings and queens, courtiers and monks, in the service of politics, religion and state building. The Grand Tour gave the bourgeoisie reasons for learning languages such as French, German, Italian, etc., for the cosmopolitan purpose of communicating with those encountered on their tour. Indeed accomplishment in the upper middle classes, particularly for women, included the ability to speak a different language. The teaching of modern languages in private schools or by private governesses thus provided an essential accoutrement of a certain bourgeois lifestyle. Modern languages were taught alongside embroidery. Miss Bingley and Mr Darcy solemnly proclaim their definition of an accomplished woman to Elizabeth Bennet in *Pride and Prejudice*:

> 'Then' observed Elizabeth, 'you must comprehend a great deal in your idea of an accomplished woman.'
>
> 'Yes, I do comprehend a great deal in it.'
>
> 'Oh, certainly,' cried his faithful assistant, 'no one can be really esteemed accomplished, who does not greatly surpass what is usually met with. A woman must have a thorough knowledge of music, singing, drawing, dancing and the modern languages, to deserve the word.' (Austen, 1813: 85)

Languages were not taught in a disinterested manner because of some overwhelming belief in their ability to serve an Entente Cordiale. They brought status and potential for wealth, travel and leisure; they brought cultural capital. This aspect of language learning, conducted in the same way as the learning of ancient languages – that is through translation and through key texts – subordinated certain aspects of culture and elevated others, which were seen to best mirror the classical model. A canon of classical texts for each language developed whose reading became synonymous with 'being cultured'.

`cultural capital`

In this sense, therefore, language learning has long been 'functional' in the sense of accumulating cultural capital. In the early twentieth century, that function extended to certain areas of employment one of whose principal requirements was precisely the possession of cultural capital – the diplomatic corps, the civil service, the army, for example. It remained fundamental to possess knowledge of the key 'texts' and conducts of the dominant culture – tested daily by the crossword in *The Times*, the pastime of slightly eccentric gentlemen with knowledge of cricket, the classics, Romantic poetry and nineteenth-century politics as well as a penchant for obscure Latinisms. It was also desirable, in this sense, to possess some understanding of the material reality of the wider world – hence latterly the development of courses in area studies.

Thus it is that the different historical manifestations of cultural elements in the modern languages curriculum may, of course, be seen to mirror shifts that have also taken place in the use and meaning of the term culture itself and their association with different modes of travel. Raymond Williams documents this clearly in *Keywords* (Williams, 1983) showing especially the way negative connotations of the idea of 'being cultured', in the sense of 'civilised', were to the fore in the mid-twentieth century.

This historical, epistemological frame- **teaching disciplinary history** work goes largely unacknowledged in the modern languages curriculum in higher education. In anthropology, to return to our benchmark example from the previous chapter, however, teaching the shifting cultural changes that form the discipline is very important (Kuper, 1996). A perception of disciplinary history is at the heart of some disciplines and helps deconstruct the ideological and cultural frameworks otherwise taken for granted. The aim of such teaching is to enable students to discover and understand the biases and assumptions inherent in academic work and in disciplinary frameworks. We would argue that teaching the cultural history of modern languages, as an intercultural discipline, is of crucial import to a reinvigorated, critical modern languages. In other words, modern languages, as a disciplinary field, is as amenable to critical reading as Racine.

I've been set the task of preparing a five-week course of lectures on 'Why learn a modern language?' for our first year students. I've also been given various starter packs and sets of materials. There are different books on my desk sent to me by publishers which I could adopt. The subject centre has sent me a marketing kit for languages. The 'usefulness' of languages for careers seems to be the point all these publications are making. I look at the circulars and memos on my desk from the university principal inviting staff to consider early voluntary severance, telling us of the management group decisions on modern languages, showing me how I can help the funding crisis and smile at the irony: pressing in on me from one side the 'usefulness' story, on the other the reality of the contempt in which our culture has learned to hold language learning. I begin preparing my lecture, jotting down headings and questions as part *of the slides. I begin with this story and with this particular conundrum. Who is right here? And how did we get here in the first place? How can we know if languages are useful and make clear decisions about their role in a place such as this without understanding how this came about? And so the structure begins to emerge, meandering into history, Grand Tours, Italian journeys, the Entente Cordiale, threats of war and hopes of peace, and always languages living out the hope.*

TO TRAVEL AND TO TRANSLATE

History is a living thing and finds its imprint in present cultural practices, including language learning. It seems likely that most learners would argue that learning modern languages is useful in order to travel and to translate (Cronin, 2000). We argue that this assumption needs to be grounded in a cultural understanding of the history of language learning. The association with leisure on the one hand, and with privileged entry to the fullest range of expressions of a universal culture on the other, remains the dominant one. Learning a language does require significant investments of time and energy, or the financial resources to move freely between countries. In the past, languages gave the Grand Tourists and their successors right of access to the sites of cosmopolitan culture – Florence, Rome, Greece, the Valley of the Kings and so on.

There is very good evidence in the shifting patterns of contemporary tourism, furthermore, that [packaged culture] that impulse is resurgent – for a number of complex reasons. We see the rise of packaged culture, in tourism as in modern languages education, in the growing proportion of travellers electing city breaks, ecological packages and 'cultural' holidays to historic sites (Kirshenblatt-Gimblett, 1998). This is, for the most part, 'culture lite' – without languages. But if travel has been in that sense democratised, the other element of the binary – namely translation – has been compromised. The combination of the two remains a privilege dependent on leisure time and money.

This then is the paradox that the question of teaching and learning culture dramatically poses. As with the integration of the history of modern language learning into a new curriculum, so it is with the cultural, social and material practices which have languages at their heart, namely translation and travel. On the one hand, the availability of travel and the facilitation of access to historic sites would appear to make it possible for a much wider layer of people to accumulate cultural capital. Yet on the other hand, the leisure to explore other cultures through languaging within the education system is less and less available in the anglophone world. In Britain, for example, the national secondary school curriculum is systematically marginalising modern languages, while in higher education, as stated previously, languages are now often attached to other areas of study which provide the content – the 'language and or with…'.

The curious thing is that growing numbers of people are devoting some part of their leisure time to language learning in evening classes and the like. And in many senses that is an extremely positive expression of a general and growing interest both in culture as tradition and in culture as modes of living. But eventually the language is being sold as a commodity on a virtual shelf. It is a completely different thing to engage critically with intercultural complexity as a long-term commitment to intercultural being and to languaging. These are dispositions which cannot be bought in off-the-shelf packages.

On the other hand, for a modern languages discipline gazing wide-eyed into the abyss ___packaged otherness___ there is little of comfort in such packaging of cultures and languages. For these activities – of travel on the one hand and the accumulation of cultural capital on the other – are becoming detached from language. Travel, for example, increasingly involves journeying into environments domesticated and prepared for a monolingual tourist or business traveller, whose experience of intercultural communication is minimal – even though he or she may indeed enrol in a language class prior to leaving. The desire to communicate in the language, however, is most often frustrated by the lack of leisure time and resources. Thus cultural capital remains firmly with those who control society's material resources, and 'otherness' remains a pre-packaged commodity sold as a brand.

Travel in this context is evidence of that 'cosmopolitanism' which allows the traveller to carry her literal and symbolic baggage wherever she goes, and to live out of that one suitcase. It is perfectly possible for the twenty-first century traveller to go thousands of miles to a resort owned and administered by a corporation based in her home country, to eat food prepared and freeze-dried not far from her place of residence, or at the very least prepared from ingredients grown or refined near there. The sun tan oils, entertainment, reading materials, TV programmes and even the music derived from local traditions will almost certainly be supplied from the same source. As John Berger put it, 'The twentieth century (now the twenty first century) consumer economy has produced the first culture for which a beggar is a reminder of nothing'.

> The Observer newspaper advertises its new 'Point It: Traveller's Language Kit' on television in the following way. A thief approaches an elderly British couple in a Spanish street, pulls out a gun and demands their money and jewellery in Spanish. The couple, smiling with a kind of naive charm (both have northern English accents), purport not to understand until they pull out their 'Traveller's Language Kit' which enables the thief to point to the objects he requires – wallet, money, watch and so on. In this encounter between stereotypes, there is no verbal communication at all. Thief and victims collude in their own cultural imprisonment, and foreignness is preserved as an impenetrable otherness. And somehow, in a distorted and grotesque way, travel is represented as both full of risk and manageable with the instruments of home. This is the logical outcome of decades of teaching languages as bolt-on kits for travellers.

Where is the place of modern languages when travel and translation are disengaged from one another, and the encounter with the 'Other' is commodified, contained and mediated? There is no space for reflection on the teaching of such fundamental issues in the traditional modern languages curriculum. Yet it is precisely in this kind of cultural encounter that the issue of languaging, or indeed its absence, is highlighted to most effect.

To turn this argument on its head, however, enables us to challenge the idea that 'culture' is only encountered through travel, i.e. through people travelling and translating. Materials migrate; languages migrate; cultural texts, images, artefacts all migrate. Languaging and intercultural being develop as dispositions in the often highly contested spaces and places of encounter and exchange. 'Abroad' is as much in the classroom or corner of the street as it is across some national border. So languaging and intercultural being are about dwelling-in-travel and translation, they are *not*, functionally, *for* travel and translation. They are here and now and not solely for the acquisition of some prospective economic and cultural capital.

PROSPECTING FOR CULTURE

So where do we find culture in the field of modern languages and in what guises? In an attempt to address the crisis that currently pervades modern languages in the UK (and the situation is not very different in the US), languages champions have tried to attach language learning to prospective economic or cultural capital. To study for a higher degree in divinity or medieval studies now sees tacit and at times official acknowledgement that learning German, Medieval French, Italian will make for better researchers. More significantly, perhaps, languages have become significant modular add-ons to degrees in engineering, business and law among others. It is assumed that, actually or virtually, this will enable the student to travel across the world albeit within their own field; so in a curious way the travel will always be virtual, since it can only involve an exact exchange of like for like, an encounter that presumes that no change will result from it – or at least no qualitative change.

The Nuffield Report (Nuffield Languages Inquiry, 2000) not only assumed a link between language learning and wealth creation, but took it for granted that this link was unproblematic:

> *Cross cultural communication: a key skill...*
>
> *The UK has no automatic monopoly on political or economic success. In a world of alliances and partnerships we need to understand where others are coming from. In a competitive world we cannot afford to be without strong and complete skills: no skills – no jobs. The need to strengthen our children's literacy, numeracy and technology skills is clear and we support it. Side by side with these should go the ability to communicate across cultures. It too is a key skill. (4)*

This quotation reveals, albeit inadvertently, some of the tensions at work in the culture wars that have become modern languages teaching. On the one hand the concessionary final sentences acknowledge, as does the recent Benchmark Statement referred to in Chapter 3, the centrality of intercultural communication; the sting, however, is in the tail. 'It, *too*, is a key skill.' The rest of the paragraph makes very clear that employability in a mobile world is the key criterion. The same is true of many mission statements in modern languages, where the gesture in the direction of interculturalism is counterposed to a notion of functionality or performativity embedded in the slippery idea of 'skills' and 'employability'.

For those of us in ailing modern languages contexts, Nuffield's supportive rhetoric is obvi-

> **saving the discipline?**

ously music to our ears; we all have a vested interest in maintaining the jobs and careers of modern languages professionals. It has to be acknowledged, however, that the teaching of modern languages nationwide – of languages, *not* of cultures – is carried out predominantly by part-time or hourly paid workers, the majority of whom are women, with minimal employment rights. And unfortunately for us a considerable body of research demonstrates both empirically and theoretically that learning languages brings no significant individual or even national economic reward (Grin, 1996b).

But the possibility that languages may not actually bring economic rewards, or that functional arguments may not actually serve to save the discipline, is never really questioned. Indeed it remains generally true that the arts and humanities as a whole continue to buy and sell the myth of a direct link between their brand of education and national wealth creation. It may or may not be the case that critical engagement with the arts and humanities brings economic reward. What is clear is that as this argument unravels, and the discourse of denial intensifies, the collective panic in the higher education languages sector becomes increasingly focused on ideological divides, the division between those who believe that teaching languages – not literature or culture or film or area studies – will be our salvation, and those who believe that we should cut our losses and uncouple from the 'menial' task of teaching languages. Some argue that we should accept that 'no capital' of any kind accrues to the activity of language teaching and stop the pretence before 'we are all down-graded into service language teaching', 'stuck in dead end jobs', for which only 'unthinking senior, non-linguist academic administrators and university finance managers' actually believe we are qualified. In this prolonged squabble, the critical, intellectual issue of what it means to teach languages and C/culture, gets lost.

MESSY CULTURES

In an age of 'liquid modernity' (Bauman, 2000) it is useful to detach languages and the learning of languages from cultures and from Culture – 'useful', that is, where the main considerations at work in higher education are instrumental and quantitative, and where uniform and transferable programmes are the objective, and standardisation the instrument, Cultures are messy, heavy, people-ridden; Culture – or culture packaged – is light and universal. As Eagleton puts it: 'The point about Culture is that it is cultureless; its values are not those of any particular form of life, simply of human life as such' (Eagleton, 2000).

Cultures, not culture, in this way of thinking, get in the way, they need managing and understanding and dealing with, through a variety of 'intercultural training programmes'. They are a problem.

Where the rhetoric of siege and defence dominates every area of cultural and political life, people from other linguistic and cultural backgrounds are increasingly represented as threats. Of course, the deeply problematic implication is that the danger comes from black, non-European cultures rather than our (largely white and Christian) neighbours. In fact, at a time of massive transnational migration – economic and otherwise – and in a postcolonial world – the other is no longer safely 'abroad' in the colonies but is very close to home, is ourselves and is our fellow citizen (Guilherme, 2002).

Marija's story

It's mid way through term and we've been examining Brecht's poetry over several weeks now. The tutorial group is small and responsive. The class works well, there is always easy discussion. Ideas and reflections are generated, texts are read and prepared in advance. I enjoy working with these students. I look forward to this class. Today they have prepared reflections on the different sections of Brecht's amazing poem An die Nachgeborene. Its not easy for them, or for me, to feel our way into the time and fears and guilt of Nazi Germany. We've talked a lot so far about the specifics of history and writing but I am keen for them to know that poetry also has other messages for other peoples and other times in history. I *want them to understand something of my love and passion for this writing, why it speaks to my life. And this is part of the sharing in the class.*

Some students make connections to the concern with environmental destruction or world poverty as issues in our own times that are provoked in them when they read such lines.

We come to the third part of the poem and I read out the lines calling for leniency, understanding, forgiveness 'Gedenkt unsrer mit Nachsicht'. One student begins to weep. Marija is Bosnian. This poem speaks to her heart, she says, these are her feelings, her experiences, this is her story too. We are appalled that the conflict, still raging, has suddenly, powerfully, shockingly entered our corner of the world. We hold on to her weeping in the gentle, shocking silence. We are all entirely lost for words but we have found a new meaning to these lines.

CULTURE AND POLITICS

We have shown that studying and teaching 'culture' is often based on static understandings linked to vague notions of future prospects, imbued with potential for cultural capital. In fact cultures are fluid and mobile. English, the new lingua franca, passes with the same decultured, deracinated ease through the world as the Latin of the equally deracinated Catholic church passed through the Holy Roman Empire. It flows uninhibited through those who have had the leisure to learn but gets stuck and fails for those who have not.

So the question of what it means to teach 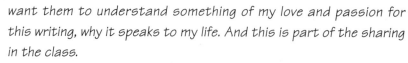 *teaching C/culture*
C/culture, becomes highly politicised and problematic. For some, teaching C/culture may ultimately mean clinging on to literature as symbolic of an idea of the nation-state as strong and solid and secure; for others, it may mean problematising dominant aspects of a nation's culture through a focus on women's writing or minority representations in film or fiction. Only in exceptional cases, however, is it actually seen to be about engaging with the practices of everyday life and of new cultural, post-national constellations, such as Atlantic Studies or Intercultural Studies.

These aspects of teaching culture are taught primarily from research strengths and trainings, unlike the vast majority of language teaching – which, although on balance is probably done well, is executed, to the relief of the research professors and lecturers, by desperate and exploited young graduate teaching assistants who are told and believe it will be good experience for their academic CVs (though in practice most modern languages post-doctoral students struggle over the crumbs of careers in modern languages departments too).

Do departments of modern languages actually want hordes of students who have nothing but a functional, economic belief in the long slog of language learning? Modern languages professionals in higher education all know, implicitly, that such an understanding of languages is not sufficient motivation. What does motivate is relationships, understanding, integration with others, growth and exchange; becoming critical, intercultural beings who laugh and cry and read and sing and love and learn in other languages.

The problem is that the material circumstances and the institutional frames in which we teach are dominated explicitly or not by functional imperatives of the sort embedded in the language of 'skills' and 'employability'. To insist on the centrality of the teaching of culture thus becomes something of an act of defiance or resistance to the inexorable march of global capitalism – at least in the sense of challenging hegemonic ideas about culture as civilisation, travel as mere *flânerie* and translation as exclusively concerned with making sense of otherness *for us*. This often means that for those involved in teaching modern languages, in anglophone contexts, the experience of pedagogy is more like a war of attrition against a background of managerial pressure, shrinking budgets and the constraints of targets and productivity.

And it is increasingly untenable. So what can breathe life into the dry cultural and canonical   revisiting 'function'
equations? Perhaps the answer lies in returning to the question of function and rediscovering its meaning outside the history of social engineering and marketisation.

Of course the concept of function that we would wish to deploy, bound up as it is with a concept of culture as lived experience and material practice, concerns our functioning as conscious, critical individuals in a social context. It presumes that higher education is not a training ground for functionaries or higher-order technicians but a space in which it is possible for learners to encounter history, the social reality and the complexity of human expression as materials of personal growth. In short, to encounter cultures at the core of that experience is the fruitful exchange of values and knowledges. That, to repeat, is how we understand the meaning of 'being intercultural'.

The key issue at this stage of our argument, of course, is the place of modern languages in that process. Would psychology, or social science, or the new humanist geography, or the history and philosophy of science, or philosophy, not fulfil similar functions? The answer to that, in each case, would be a provisional yes – since all of these areas of human understanding lend themselves to this notion of learning – but not necessarily so. It depends how they are taught, and in a broad sense on the extent to which independent learning in a social context and on the basis of an ethics of learning can take place. It depends on the capacity for critical engagement with the questions thrown up in each field.

We would not be so foolish as to try and erect a hierarchy of values, a league table from the most to the least desirable of academic disciplines. That would render everything we have argued so far quite meaningless. The point is that modern languages is one route to that critical engagement with the dominant civilisational ideology which is the core of any meaningful process of educational development. Indeed, because it asks the learner to be multiple in expression, to move between universes of thought and value, between historical visions, it may be particularly well-suited to that process. The kind of functionality that we are seeking for modern languages, therefore, rests on a radically different vision of the learning process in higher education in which the learning of languages would play a core and central role.

In the past university departments taught Culture as part of the project of building the nation-state; culture was national, exclusive and defined by its univocal qualities. For over a hundred years, the departments of modern languages existed side by side with departments of anthropology and of folklore studies, all of them translating disciplines which identified nation-building with the construction of civilised society and a rational order. Their use of the term 'culture' was exotic; it was 'what other people have' (Thurlow, 2002). As Aaltonen points out:

The aim of a translated theatre text is very seldom, or never entirely, to provide an introduction to the Other or to mediate the Foreign. Instead foreign work is given the task of speaking for the target system and society. The aim is not that the audience be brought closer to, or made familiar with the foreign tradition, but rather that the foreign tradition is, to a greater or lesser extent, transformed according to the different conditions of specific fields of reception. (Aaltonen, 2000: 48)

The nation-building projects of Germany and Finland, to name but two examples, both actively sought and translated 'high' culture texts from other strong nation-states, such as France and Britain. Anthropology has taken a long hard look at itself as a discipline over the last thirty years. The complicity of anthropologists in the colonial projects, the need for the Western Empires to understand and manage and inferiorise those they colonised – all of these aims were served by anthropologists' eroticising myths. Equally, as Said has demonstrated, C/culture worked hard, in producing its various representations of otherness, to demonstrate, unquestioningly, the *cultural superiority* of the occident over the orient. We do not need to rehearse these arguments here. Some of their critical rigour would not go amiss in the field of languages, however, when to teach languages is in the service of Culture and when Culture has been, though is really no longer, in the service of a privileged elite. After all, as Eagleton points out:

> *Those radicals for whom high culture is* ipso facto *reactionary forget that much of it is well to the left of the World Bank [...] What matters is not the works themselves but the way they are collectively construed, ways which the works could hardly have anticipated [...] It is not Shakespeare who is worthless, just some of the social uses to which his work has been put. (Eagleton, 2000: 52)*

In the past, we have needed languages for various social, collective and ideological purposes, as part of the project of nation-building (Anderson, 1991). At other times they were a mark of accomplishment for the nation-builders and their wives (*sic*), and more recently we have needed languages as part of the Entente Cordiale and the project of political reconstruction following the Second World War. Now we would appear to only need languages to make capital in various forms. What purpose, in addition to making money, can languages serve today?

CULTURE IS FOR THE ATTIC

Where does this leave us then? What might be the way forward, beyond the stockade, when there are such conflicting understandings of languages and cultures in the modern languages curriculum? We would argue that there are two very different available answers. The recent Benchmark Statement on Modern Languages offers both as if they were not discontinuous and opposing (see Figure 4.1).

FIGURE 4.1 *Extract from Benchmark Statements on Modern Languages.*

Language skills are likely to include a sub-set of related skills. These will vary from the relatively simple to the more complex, and could include such activities as email correspondence, talking on the telephone, video-conferencing, and the use of target language documents for carrying out research or writing reports.

Students of LRS [languages and related subjects] will be effective and self-aware independent language learners. Their language-learning skills might extend from strategies for learning vocabulary to awareness of learning style and the identification of appropriate learning opportunities. These skills equip them to learn other languages with relative ease; they enhance their command and awareness of English and have been shown to increase their employability.

In particular, their competence in the target language means they will have an appreciation of the internal diversity and transcultural connectedness of cultures, and an attitude of curiosity and openness towards other cultures. The skills and attributes concerned include:

- a critical understanding of a culture and practices other than one's own;
- an appreciation of the uniqueness of the other culture(s);
- an ability to articulate to others the contribution that the culture has made at a regional and global level
- an ability and willingness to engage with other cultures;
- an ability to appreciate and critically evaluate one's own culture.

Source: *http://www.qaa.ac.uk/crntwork/benchmark/phase2/languages.pdf* (2002).

It is our feeling that while both are given equal weight in the statement, the realities of higher education in a functionalist early twenty-first century leave very little doubt as to where the balance is currently tipped. On the other hand, what may be little more than gestures towards cultural understanding and communication could indeed become the spinal cord of a renewed, critical discipline of modern languages in a different university sector committed to equity, social justice and the development of free and informed individuals for whom the experience of higher education has been an emancipatory one.

Student 2: *First of all the fact that in a German sort of language and literature degree, you got something suddenly saying you can study things about Germany today and you know actually being able to do that was very different in the first place.*

Student 3: *It wasn't just about Germany as well, it was a bit more diverse. We were doing a bit of sociology and anthropology, other subjects which were quite interesting and you don't really get the opportunity to study as much.*

Student 4: *We had just had our year abroad and everything. We had all these great experiences and we came back, all bursting with what we'd done and everything then, to go back to all the usual kind of studying, all the literature and stuff that we really can't apply any of those experiences to directly, to study something that we were doing there, it was based on everyday things that happen in Germany [...] and I think it made a big difference because you could actually use your experience and bring that into it, just because it was kind of up to date.*

Student 1: *You actually have to go out and speak to German people [...], because usually in a course, you have some contact with German people but not really and this was a chance where you actually had to go out, find people and speak to them yourself and I think you learn quite a lot from doing that.*

Student 3: *And also from speaking to each other on the course [...] I think the first two hours that we had, it was right away 'Right get into groups and do this,' you're thrown together with all these people that you don't know at all. [...] You suddenly think 'This isn't what I thought I was going to do. I thought I was doing a course where you usually go in and you sit down, you write notes and you get told things [...]' and suddenly it was just 'Well, here you are – discuss' and you were like 'Ooh'.*

Modern languages have taken a cultural turn of sorts,   `cultural turn` but as we have argued throughout, this turn ducks the issues and is mired in static, functional, conflicting notions, making the cultural turn a rather 'thin' turn. What we are here proposing is a 'thick' turn, an authentic transformation of the discipline.

There is no doubt that the kind of awareness that we are arguing for can only imperfectly come in a classroom set within another language community. The opportunity to spend a period in the country of the language, and to reflect upon this experience critically and creatively, is therefore an absolutely integral and indispensable part of any modern languages course. We are all familiar with the endless cost arguments that call this component into question; its defence is, however, integral to the vision of a future and reinvigorated discipline of modern languages. That it should be structured or organised in some way is also beyond question, but the purpose of being abroad should clearly be a consequence of being there. No amount of home-based tasks carried out in a different place nor imprecise notions of assimilation can meet the purpose. Residence abroad should be seen as exploration, assimilation and an opportunity for transformation. We address this issue in detail in subsequent chapters.

Throughout the course of this chapter and the preceding critique of fragmented views of culture we have stumbled again and again over the culture *concept* as an obstacle. Culture is a problematic term. It is ideology ridden. It starts culture wars, it atomises, it creates understandings of difference that stand, ultimately, in direct opposition to the kinds of integrative, intercultural being that we are advocating throughout, for modern languages. The logical end of our argument is the same as that reached by Eagleton, that the term needs to be put firmly in its place, for it has become too overweening, too woolly, too imprecise. Culture is no longer a helpful discursive construct. It creates more problems than it solves. Tim Ingold speaks for us when he maintains that for us to truly progress, 'the culture concept [...] will have to go' (Ingold, 1993: 230).

The concept of culture

This is not to say in any way that the culture concept has not served us well in the past. The strides made by, among others, Raymond Williams or Pierre Bourdieu in attempting to get around the high/low culture debate and divide have been immensely productive. Without their insights we would not have the cultural studies and critical insights into social and cultural life that we now have. Without their work and those following in their footsteps some of the innovative moves in modern languages curricula may never have come to pass. Without their work there would be little foundation for advocating change.

It is also not to say that the terms will not be useful again. Although not currently a useful conceptual tool to think with and through, 'culture' as a term may well benefit – as say the term 'ideology' has done (Barnett, 2003) – from a stint in the attic. It may then be taken down again in years to come, dusted off, cleaned and found to have new uses for new historical moments.

What we are advocating here, then, is that we move beyond 'culture'. To continue to see culture as a bounded component of a fragmented modern languages curriculum simply does not work intellectually or even practically, as we have demonstrated in these chapters on culture. It just makes for an intellectual and practical mess, a heap of often randomly assorted items on a stall, all hastily and defensively rebranding themselves as culture.

We are working, throughout this book, with the notions of lan- languaging and intercultural being guaging and intercultural being. These two concepts are rooted in the discourses on culture of the recent past, they sit firmly within this critical holistic discourse. By using these concepts and by focusing on relational engagements, encounters and exchange, on meaning, understanding and critical being, then we believe we are able to move beyond the idea of language versus culture. We see these concepts as helping us to develop the kinds of intellectual foundations for a reinvigorated discipline that theorises distances and differences, that works with critical universalism, that values practical questions in addition to interpretation, that attends to the social, languaging world with others in everyday contexts of practical action.

Key references

Bauman, Z. (2000) *Liquid Modernity*. Oxford: Polity.

Cronin, M. (2000) *Across the Lines: Travel, Language and Translation*. Cork: Cork University Press.

Ingold, T. (1993) 'The Art of Translation in a Continuous World', in G. Pálsson (ed.), *Beyond Boundaries: Understanding, Translation and Anthropological Discourse*. Oxford: Berg, pp. 210–30.

Kirschenblatt-Gimblett, B. and Brunner, E. M. (1992) 'Tourism', in *Folklore, Cultural Performances and Popular Entertainments: A Communications Centred Handbook*. Oxford: Oxford University Press.

Williams, R. (1983) *Keywords: A Vocabulary of Culture ad Society*, 2nd edn. London: Fontana.

Websites

http://www.lang.ltsn.ac.uk/resources/guidecontents.aspx
http://www.lang.ltsn.ac.uk/languagesbox.aspx
http://www.qaa.ac.uk/crntwork/benchmark/phase2/languages.pdf

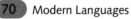

Encyclopedia

Byram, M. (2000) *Routledge Encyclopedia of Language Teaching and Learning*. London and New York: Routledge.

Languaging matters

MOVING THE FURNITURE

'Languaging' may be a slightly uncomfortable term at first, but it should only be a sign of that unease that precedes new ventures and discoveries. Language learning, after all, is more than reading and writing (though it is also that), more than the accumulation of techniques and skills. It is, as we have argued, a point of access to ways of being in the world, to new insights and understandings. In that sense, it should always be an open door.

There are assumptions about language **classroom organisation** learning embedded in the physical organisation of the classroom. The authority of the teacher, of the central bank of knowledge, are enshrined in the sight lines of communication; the arrangement of the furniture is determined by the authoritative eye, the relationship between teachers and listeners. Typically, the latter are passive, the former active; the anticipated posture is one of attentive acknowledgement.

> *The chairs and tables are set in rows; they seem to scrape especially noisily on the floor when you politely ask if you can pass behind the ones who got there early. There is some conversation – but you don't know many people. In any case, you could only really speak to the people on either side – the ones in front are looking at the empty board and the guy behind is still listening to his Walkman and tapping his feet on the back of your chair. Then, quite suddenly, the talking stops: the fellow behind takes off his phones. There's someone standing at the big table at the front – waiting.*

When chairs and table are set in rows, transverse communication, conversation among the learners and eye-contact across the room are achieved

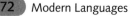

only at the cost of discomfort, a twisted neck, a sidelong glance. In any case, it is an unnatural posture in the lecture hall, a temporary distraction from the task in hand; this is a place for teaching – delivery and reception – not a place for interaction and contact, for learning.

DISCIPLINARY VIOLENCE

Michel Foucault exposed the inherent disciplinary violence of such situations.

> *Thus discipline produces subjected and practiced bodies, 'docile' bodies. [...] It is [...] a multiplicity of minor processes, of different origin and scattered location, which overlap, repeat, or imitate one another, support one another, distinguish themselves from one another according to their domain of application, converge, and gradually produce the blueprint of a general method. (Foucault, 1991: 138)*

The description of the architecture of educational institutions and the impact of arranging learners' bodies in fixed rows still resonates for some, perhaps the majority, of lecture, classroom and even language laboratory situations.

> *Two colleagues of mine responded once to the final report of a two-year committee of enquiry into teaching methods by refusing to entertain any change of method. I asked why. The response was that 'we prefer the traditional methods'. 'What are they?' I asked. They were unable to reply.*

What was the difference between us? And why were they unable to reply? It was a difference of relationship rather than methodology. Perhaps they saw the debate as *lèse-majesté*, an assault on their position in the class-room. Or perhaps they were so wedded to the common-sense, dominant and uncritically accepted modes of teaching language that had been passed on to them through their own language learning that they were unable to see the need to question or reflect.

Cultural studies and anthropology, as well as other human sciences, have taught us clearly that the more obvious something is the more ideo-logical it is. So in a way, perhaps they were right to be defensive (though the proposals were rather less radical than they feared); ideology fails when it ceases to be what Gramsci called a 'secular religion'. The arrangement of space and furniture gave a clear answer to the question – how is language learned? In their view, it was by the deployment of rules and procedures which produce an utterance which is correct (or otherwise). This is a very different outcome from an activity of languaging that embraces accuracy and appropriateness as part of the search for living expression and complex meaning. The presumed, embedded relationship was therefore hierarchical and unequal; the teacher vouchsafed the rules and procedures in pre-existing, decontextualised frames and the students demonstrated in a range of tests their absorption of the same.

The students in such learning regimes are not consciously mobilised as learners in a way that could *empty vessels?* make learner and teacher active participants in dialogue and mutual development – collaborating creators of 'ontological energy'. They are deemed to come without relevant knowledge, and are seen as 'docile bodies' or 'empty vessels', with nothing to contribute to the collective process (Vygotsky, 1978), let alone the individual project – as objects awaiting the exercise and demonstration of authority and power.

This arrangement has very little to do with the 'development of individual resources and skills, the multiple investigation of possibilities and problem-solving capacities' (Pennycook, 1994). Yet these are key aspects of a languaging activity. Neither could it assist or encourage learner autonomy – 'the struggle to become the author of one's own world, to be able to create one's own meanings, to pursue cultural alternatives amid the cultural politics of everyday life' (Benson and Voller, 1997: 39). Languaging, after all, is at its core a question of *agency*, of individuals accumulating powers and understandings to enable them to become actively critical social beings.

It may be that such active, creative processes are more easily available in the social science or even (sometimes) cultural studies milieux. A modern languages environment is regarded as a location where these concerns somehow cease to be relevant, as if that business of the making of meaning in an everyday world ceased at the classroom door. The experiences and knowledges that students bring with them are not regarded as relevant because the learners do not yet 'have' the language. The mark of that is the sudden and dramatic silence that happens as soon as students cross the classroom threshold, as if the networks of relationships through which we live in the world and even the corridor outside cease to operate once across the portal. An active learning environment, by contrast, is one that continues that process through and into a different way of being.

It is crucial to acknowledge that learners do not arrive in the language

mobilising creativity and ability

classroom bereft of instruments. Since the task is the continuity of 'meaning-making' or 'languaging' as Halliday calls it in Doughty and Thornton (1973: 59), then students come with considerable relevant creative powers, practice and ability which can be mobilised and deployed in language learning.

The condition for languaging to take place is a shared exploration of personal responses and understandings, and their exchange. It is not an unfamiliar process at all. What happens in a conservative, functional environment, however, is that that experience is marginalised, made strange; it is as if the learning space were a different place to which they did not belong. Far from 'being intercultural' the student, as often as not, is infantilised, reduced to stuttering and repeating on cue (Mann, 2001), and that is a function of a power relationship established, at least initially, by an arrangement of furniture.

Here, as elsewhere, we function best – we humans – as social beings, to the extent that we collaborate, negotiate and shape our understandings through experiment, observation, collaboration and critical appraisal. We learn by seeing ourselves in different mirrors, at different angles, by dressing ourselves in our new knowledges and by engaging with others to see what works. The external (institutional) environment in every possible way stresses and encourages disciplined individualism and a competitive attitude. Every activity, from weekly exercises, to regular testing, to final examinations and assessments, to prizes and honours, are rooted in that possessive individualism and in the exercise of control of the student learner by the policies and political agendas of the teaching institutions.

Foucault notes that 'the examination combines the techniques of an observing hierarchy and those of a normalizing judgement. It is a normalizing gaze, a surveillance that makes it possible to qualify, to classify and to punish' (Foucault, 1991: 184). Yet language is socially and cooperatively learned. Meaning is negotiated and given a context, social and cultural. This is not necessarily an easy or painless process. As often as not, it passes through misunderstanding, argument and early incomprehension. And we would not want to argue that languaging is always a happy process, in one's own or another language. Yet for all its risks, it is always part of the positive pleasure of becoming human.

A language spoken by one person alone is
devoid of meaning and has no practical use.

dialogic understanding

How, then, should we address this apparent paradox at the heart of the material, social and institutional conditions in which we labour with our ideals? Language learning is not exempt from the necessity of self-reflection. The fact that it is largely taught as though it were does not make it so – as we have argued in the previous chapter. One way to address the paradox is to attempt to understand critically its ideological underpinnings, whose effect is to distort the process whereby we come to understandings through dialogue, in the deepest sense, by seeing ourselves through others. Unless that is a guiding principle in every area of language learning, we are reduced to an obstacle race in which we leap endlessly over artificial hurdles that bear no relation at all to the complexities of everyday life.

The pedagogy that we envisage engages with those complexities in a classroom that is plural and defined by a process of exchange and mutual recognition. This classroom does not exist in a vacuum, any more than the students are empty vessels. This classroom is a real, material place, just as students are real, material beings. It is part of the process of gaining the insights and understanding that will help them to find their way in and through the world.

In *Beyond All Reason: Living with Ideology in the University* (Barnett, 2003) Ron Barnett sees the task of living with multiple ideologies – pernicious and virtuous – as one of the key challenges in contemporary higher education:

> *Ideology has gained such a grip in universities that it is no longer clear that the idea of the university – as pointing to a site of reason – can be realized. In a sense, universities may not be 'Universities'. However, there is still mileage in the idea of the university: with generosity, cool heads and determination, universities may yet be reclaimed as Universities.* (Barnett, 2003: 1–2)

Reclamation is a material act. It is not just about abstract concepts. It is about a material change in the condition of our learning and teaching endeavours in the university. The shift to a problem-based learning medical curriculum in 1995 at our own university has led to the building of an entirely new medical school, where the architecture supplies the physical conditions for a new vision of engagement with knowledge.

Those conditions demand flexible environ- | flexible environments
ments and an open engagement with the
materials of living and learning. This will inevitably involve crossing boundaries, borrowing resources and materials from other places. In some sense, the material basis of this kind of teaching and learning becomes a kind of hunting and gathering, analogous to the experience of learning in the world.

If modern languages have at their heart the ability to 'enhance the locales in which they secure themselves', if they may be reflexive *idealogies* (the neologism is Barnett's) 'deliberating picking up virtuous ideals embedded in human institutions' (Barnett, 2003: 181), then the working out of these *idealogies* will be manifestly material. Thus we should begin by moving the chairs, removing the tables and distributing student bodies around the room, so enabling talk and exchange.

THE POTLATCH PRINCIPLE

(Potlatch: the communal meal where each person brings a dish. More than eating, this is a ritual of exchange, a sharing of gifts and a socialisation of individual labour, giving everyone to everyone.)

The much criticised principle still embedded in many classroom practices is that students arrive as blank sheets, as empty vessels. This may be true as far as the particular structures and mechanisms of this or that specific language are concerned. But this does not in any way mean that the learner, whoever he or she is, is without knowledge. Even more to the point, there is no learner who comes without knowledge of languaging; there is no learner who does not already live in and through language, though the ubiquity of that process may not have been made conscious yet. Learners may not possess as yet the means to describe how language works to enable living and expressing, functioning and imagining – yet they use it to those ends in a thousand ways. Beyond that, every learner brings knowledges of one kind or another to the classroom; whether or not those knowledges are mobilised or deployed in learning language is another matter.

I've been asked to run a workshop on languages for non-language learners. It's part of the kind of outreach strategies that go alongside widening participation. It is a lot harder than I'd first imagined to think through the issues that come to be obstacles. I set out the parameters of group work, stressing that I'll be asking people to share from their experience and that they should, of course, only do so in so far as they feel comfortable or able. I make sure that I give clear timings for talking and for listening to give everyone a say and I ask them to work through a sheet of questions and activities. Every now and then I pull the small groups of five back into the bigger plenary of around forty and we share some insights.

- *What languages (if any other than your parent tongue) did you learn as a child — in school or home? What was this like as an experience of language learning and of interacting with people whose culture is associated with that language?*

- *Share stories of situations where you did not speak the language being used. What did you feel? How did it make you feel about the people speaking? Did people translate for you — and what did that feel like?*

- *Write a list of all languages other than English which people in the group can speak (even a few sentences). Find the one that the most of you can speak and try to have an exchange in that language, however halting and brief (say hello, talk about the weather, etc.). What feelings did this evoke in those of you speaking?*

This final task was a revelation. Suddenly the murmur of talk and the quiet of listening turned into laughter. Snatches of Italian, Latin, French and some German could be heard. The groups became animated — one of them was gesturing, another miming breaststroke. The medley of tongues increased and I found it increasingly hard to actually stop them all languaging. Reluctantly I brought them back to the plenary for the last time and for some final reflection. Their faces were transformed, exhilarated, as though they'd climbed a mountain and seen the view for the first time. The 'preparation' for this was not long, or arduous, in terms of being time consuming. But it was arduous emotionally, for all of us. It involved engaging feelings and vulnerabilities and being in a place which felt safe. This space wasn't created simply by my imposition of rules, it was co-created and languaged.

The point here is that, in a particular kind of teaching milieu, learners can be made to feel that they are without understanding (the infantilisation process alluded to earlier) – they can be emptied of self-belief. This makes them considerably easier to manage, of course, for if they are empty then all the teacher has to do is fill each with exactly the same material. This implies a prior and wholly positivistic perception of language on the part of the teacher – that language is essentially a collection of functions. The result is disabling – and also controlling and oppressive. It mimics not the process of languaging through culture and history, but rather the rote-learning that tests only discipline and obedience.

If, on the other hand, we as teachers evoke the learners' knowledges as the material of 'meaning-making practice', then we also mobilise the supporting networks of cultural understanding that underpin them. Those practices will find their correspondences in the target language community. The process, in other words, will be the same. Valuing and acknowledging the learner's existing knowledge, and learning from and through their life histories, transforms utterly the relationship between teacher and learner, and between learner and learner, so that it becomes an authentic exchange.

> *An individual's capacity to know himself as an individual, his ability to develop a sense of self…is a function of the capacity to language. (Doughty and Thornton, 1973: 61)*

The implication for the teacher is that power and control have to be acknowledged, shared and struggled against. We do not underestimate the difficulty that this may involve nor the disorder that might ensue. But it may well be that creative disorder is a fundamental condition for languaging.

This said, entering the classroom should never be an experience of loss of autonomy, of a history, or of a connection with culture, for either teacher or learner. Learning should be a process of enhancing not diminishing being. Engagement with language should be meaningful and purposive from the outset, an addition to and enrichment of the knowing self.

It is well-established, for example, that adults cannot learn to read using John and Jane or Dr Seuss. This is not just as a result of the humiliation of seeing themselves as foolish or childlike; it is also because it denies the value of their life experience, which may well have been complex and rich, as authentic experience, and negates language (even their own in this case). Language, however, is the very medium through which they may continue to develop by enhancing their understanding of the process, becoming autonomous subjects of their own lives. As a method of language learning, minimising what the learner brings to the process, intentionally or not, cannot but fail; 'successful learning requires negotiation by the learner of what she already knows in the face of and in the light of the new' (Candlin, in Benson and Voller, 1997: xii).

It could be argued that this is not the task of language learning; therapy, political activity and sociological research, it might be said, are the proper arenas for this kind of self-awareness. But the disengagement between the development of the social sense and the sense of self and the learning of languages is ideologically pernicious – as if the manner of saying were somehow entirely distinct from its content. This strikes straight at the heart of the ideological (and practical) separation of language and culture that we argued against in Chapter 3.

The standard form of prose translation may be seen as an example of this. A piece of text, divorced entirely from its immediate context (the whole book or article) and its wider frame (culture, history, society), is presented for translation. Such texts – and the examples are legion – might include Tolkien, Thomas Hardy, Hegel, Adorno, D.H. Lawrence, Galdós; they might equally be contemporary texts, plucked from a newspaper or magazine. The exercise is therefore random and abstract; in isolation, no discussion of language or meaning is possible. The history or location the text carries within it are not addressed. The 'how' (the mechanics) is divorced from the 'what' and the 'why'.

The result is an exercise that is deeply and essentially sterile, in the quite literal sense of the word; the block of language that is produced may be equally sterile and history-less. It can only be assessed against a similarly decontextualised linguistic model – an ideal expression without communicative intent, in that the essentially dialogic nature of language is curiously denied. Its effect is to reinforce an authoritarian version of the learning process; since there are no external, contextual or cultural referents to engage, the only possible purpose of the exercise is prediction, an elaborate exercise in telepathy without instruments. The final piece will be measured against a 'fair' or 'perfect' copy held by the teacher. It is within everyone's experience, furthermore, that these templates, these 'fair copies' may be used and reused – as if both source and target language had not changed across the years.

The professor calls each student to the front by turns, where he audibly (and to the embarrassment of those yet to come) comments on and criticises the components of the student's work. The class – now a small collection of mostly demoralised and separate individuals – ends with a reading of the 'fair' version. The written version is never shown to the students, in part because it should not be made available to them for their correction, of course, and in part because the same piece will inexorably reappear the following year and be subjected to the same ritual.

Yet the dynamics of language correspond exactly to the dynamics of social life; it is a process of emptying and filling, of investing and bankrupting communicative possibilities. It is more than irresponsible to use a dehistoricised model; it is a betrayal of languaging itself. But in the authoritarian classroom the legitimacy of the 'corrected final text' is never discussed – and why should it be, given that there is no measure of adequacy beyond the assertion of authority. Since that text too is deracinated, there is no possible further measure that can be brought to bear. The circle closes, but what has been learned beyond a lesson in power and authority?

GATHERING ROUND THE TABLE

So, how do we create a classroom where the differences in power and knowledge (not just between teacher and learner but between all those involved) can be mobilised in the service of languaging. Ideally, the furniture is moved and set in a circle or randomly around the room, the tables set against the wall perhaps. The contributions of each to the common stock of knowledge and experience are set out where they can be seen. Realistically, however, we embark on this process in far from ideal conditions.

I'm doing a few guest lectures for another department. I've become used to teaching small classes, with students I've come to know well. This department is struggling not so much with crisis but with success. With a staff team of three it is not possible for them to get to know every one of their three hundred plus first years and eighty plus second years well. There is a limit to the number of students we can hold in relation. It's a challenge for me to teach in such situations. How do I inspire? Will it just be a lecture show or can I also create conditions for the sharing of knowledge between us all? The problem is that I don't actually know. I've a few ideas up my sleeve, but it will mean trying things out. I decide to be open with the students about this. I begin by telling them of my genuine delight at having the chance to see what I teach move into fresh areas, and that teaching big classes excites me and daunts me. There is laughter. We have begun well. I remember some of the principles about 'micro-sleeps' from my early training on the new lecturers programme. 'Give them breaks, repeat points, they can't cope with sixty minutes of talking heads.' I don't give them my handout until fifteen minutes into the material. I break in at this point with a task, get them into groups, make them shuffle seats or turn round to share their immediate thoughts on a question. The room is just dire. Rows and rows of fixed benches, graffiti, ripped seats, condensation streaming down the windows, sickly fluorescent lighting and chalk dust everywhere. But they respond and then there is noise such as I've not experienced before. It's a bit scary. I begin to wonder whether this technique, which I've seen work for smaller language lectures, can work in big classroom contexts. I hesitate an 'OK, can I draw you back now' and realise that they probably can't hear me, so I use the microphone and it works. I then ask for them to shout out words and ideas from their conversations and they come thick and fast, again, the problem is stemming the flow rather than filling the silence.

One of our advantages, but also disadvantages, in our physical setting for teaching languages is that the learning does not take place in the target community (except where students are able to spend a period abroad, an issue to which we will return); how then can the classroom prepare – let alone reproduce – the experience of living and experiencing language there? We are not convinced that virtual realities can replace the actual. The immersion method is not convincing – to isolate a single hour (or less or more) in an artificial environment and attempt to convince by elaborate convention seems to us unlikely to succeed. Most fundamentally it again errs by isolating the language-learning experience from all other languaging practice, reinforcing the sense that material language learning is an activity apart and different from normal social conduct.

Benson lays out eleven possible, or perhaps ideal, tasks which may be pursued in the language class. Not all eleven tasks can be addressed simultaneously – indeed some may prove impossible to realise at all. But they do represent the range of issues that language learning must address:

1. Authentic interaction with the target language and its users.
2. Collaborative group work and collective decision making.
3. Participation in open-ended learning tasks.
4. Learning about the target language and its social contexts of use.
5. Exploration of societal and personal learning goals.
6. Criticism of learning tasks and materials.
7. Self-production of tasks and materials.
8. Control over the management of learning.
9. Control over the content of learning.
10. Control over resources.
11. Discussion and criticism of target language norms.

(Benson and Voller, 1997: 33)

What is notable about these categories is that they are all active purposes for the learner. They fall into several groups. First, the conduct of learning, which should be collective and collaborative (2, 5, 6); secondly the power to shape and direct the learning process (8–10); third, the creation of a flexible and adaptable learning environment, in which the tasks follow the direction of the learners' questions and expression (2 and 3); fourth, learning about language in use (1, 4, 6, 11).

Is it possible to learn a language alone, in isolation? The answer is almost certainly no, unless all that is learned are repeatable units – useful but extremely limited. For languaging, to repeat ourselves, is a social bodily process and a shared learning space is a necessary component of it.

To return to Benson's list, there is a missing component which touches on the reality of *learning the* 'target' language outside its community. In part, the answer is to present the work as a preparation for engagement with that community – but that preparation has to go beyond just consuming cultural objects. The procedure that can effect the aim of functioning individually and collectively in the language community must take as its starting point the nature of social interactivity and the role of language within it. In short:

> [...] a pedagogy of dialogue is therefore an open exchange of ideas that makes a difference. It is joyous, serious and challenging. It is galvanizing and reflective and it is about communication rather than persuasion, and empowerment rather than assertion. (Guilherme, 2000: 78)

We remain ourselves, for the most part, when we speak another language – or we should see that as purpose and objective. The point is that we should not find ourselves limited as beings to what we are able to say in the other language. Learning another language should never feel like a narrowing down, an impoverishment. On the contrary, the acquisition of a second language should enrich not narrow us – it should augment our stock of modes of self-expression. On the other hand, we cannot become German/Spanish/French. Indeed, that is not our purpose – but even the aim suggests that the wealth of experience and knowledge with which we come to the language learning class is not an ally but an irrelevance, an unmobilisable knowledge. What we can become, in short, are intercultural beings.

We *do* come to the second language with a   `transferable knowledge`
wealth of experience and knowledge, and that
body of understanding is immediately transferable. It is not that the language learner can immediately express the subtleties of those knowledges in the other language – but they are expressible, because experienced, in it. The struggle to express, therefore, is a struggle to express the self – rather than, in the still dominant traditional model, to express something that is either in the mind of someone else, or to function in a non-experiential, cultureless desert – where the only reason to express this or that is, ultimately, for fear of discipline.

Friday morning at 9 a.m. is never a good time for discussion or active work, particularly in an encroaching Scottish winter. In a way, I am more than sufficiently pleased that my class of 20 or so third-year language students turn up at all; that they do so smiling is a bonus.

I have one hour. By now, the students have accepted the notion of a language/translation class as an active place, where work is done in groups, the furniture is arranged in the round, and there will be talk and negotiation. I have tried to use a variety of pieces, to explicitly introduce the notion that a translatable text is any form of written (or visual) communication that can be interpreted or engaged with. We have looked at newspaper reportage, graphs and statistics, agony aunt columns, advertisements, narratives; but they have not by and large been literary 'texts'.

My anxiety was to achieve two very basic conditions: first, to disengage language work from the confines of literary translation; and second, to concentrate at this stage of their learning lives on encouraging the class to produce a meaningful and communicative written Spanish. The 'producing' was really done as home tasks; the class was an opportunity to collectively gather the resources (ideas, vocabulary, register, meanings, contexts) in preparation for that later task. The 'text' was a stimulus and an example. For the most part, I did not ask for a translation so much as a reaction.

On this particular Friday I had brought a piece from the Guardian Education which was a series of responses by Spanish students to a survey of their drinking habits. They described their own patterns of drinking and used a series of terms to describe relative states of inebriation. The students looked at different elements of the piece in groups for some of the hour and then I asked them to list for me as many terms for 'drunk' as were current in their circles. Fifteen appeared on the white board as fast as I could note them down. We discussed what distinguished them – context? gender? the age or social class of the drinker? the place or manner of consumption? The nuances were pretty sophisticated. The Spanish text gave sufficient information for students to match those features and to grade the Spanish semantically just as they had done with the English. I asked them to write a piece in Spanish about someone they knew, with special reference to their drinking patterns. The writings I was given the following week were highly individual, sophisticated in register and nuance, and almost entirely without error.

The point was that the experience that informed language was equally complex and rich in one language and the other. If translation is also a simplification, then the superior value of the source language is taken as a given. The critical interrogation of the learner's own language is a means of making sense of the languaging process in general and in particular in the other language; for expressing anything in the other language, or indeed any language, is a way of making meanings as well as simply communicating them. Of course, this process is not one that should be conducted in the realm of abstraction or theory – though it will undoubtedly be informed by it – but in relation to problems of meaning-making. The upshot is that learners will necessarily enter the realm of discussing language and how it works.

Thirdly, a notion of correspondence can then take the place of that of equivalence – a key but problematic concept particularly in the exercise of translation. Instead the learner seeks a means of expression or a way of making meaning within the structures and conventions of the host culture. As a result the learners are enriched, enlivened and enlarged by richly expanded modes of expression.

We lay great stress on collaboration and group work in the **group work and collaborative learning** learning milieu. It is important, however, to be very clear why this is so – and to differentiate here (as elsewhere) between the different uses to which similar methods and practices can be put.

There is a whole range of arguments for group work and collaborative learning which arise from the debate about self-directed learning as a more 'effective' method; it is certainly cheaper, given that there is far less need for the presence of a teacher. (An interesting issue arises here: a pedagogy of language learning arising out of critical theory almost certainly does require a teaching presence, as facilitator and mediator, rather than expert, authority embodiment of truth.) But we have to be very clear that what we have in mind has nothing to do with this 'self-policing' conception – it is not a matter of self-motivation, drilling, practice and answer books. We are in no sense suggesting a type of group work in which students take it in turns to 'correct' each other and be an alternate authority figure.

Here collaboration has two complementary purposes: one, to make explicit in discussion and joint activity the journey to understanding – making explicit both the method of questioning meaning through language and exchanging, and jointly accumulating those insights into how language works to make the world meaningful. Second, collaboration can to some extent at least reproduce the social environment in which languaging takes place, also based on the exchange of ideas, meanings and experiences.

In other words, language learnt for use in a classroom context, where it is only ever used to perform, publicly and fearfully, the task of answering a question posed by a teacher, will be of little practical or critical use in the contexts of everyday life. Languaging in a context where we believe in the possibility of communication and active meaning-making as an everyday activity, social, yet structured, responsive and respectful, is languaging with life that will cross classroom thresholds and be active in the creative work of culture.

Key references

Barnett, R. (2003) *Beyond all Reason: Living with Ideology in the University*. Buckingham: Open University Press.

Benson, P. and Voller, P. (1997) *Autonomy and Independence in Language Learning*. London: Longman.

Doughty, P. and Thornton, G. (1973) *Language Study, the Teacher and the Learner*. London: Edward Arnold.

Foucault, M. (1991) *Discipline and Punish: The Birth of the Prison*. London: Penguin.

Guilherme, M. (2002) *Critical Citizens for an Intercultural World*. Clevedon: Multilingual Matters.

Pennycook, A. (1994) *English as an International Language*. London: Longman.

Vygotsky, L. S. (1978) *Mind in Society*. Cambridge, MA: Harvard University Press.

Websites

http://www.lang.ltsn.ac.uk/resources/guidecontents.aspx

Encyclopedia

Byram, M. (2000) *Routledge Encyclopedia of Language Teaching and Learning*. London and New York: Routledge.

Languaging in time and place

She gives everybody a role and everybody feels they have a role; I don't know how she does it but I'm convinced that it's the key to the success of the course. I'm really absolutely convinced it's the community you have in that classroom. Nobody feels frightened to talk, to contribute. There really is a sense of community, yeah, the desire to exchange information, exchange experiences, sometimes quite personal experiences ...She's a listener ...and she's the encourager; that's an amazingly large part of her success, the listening and the encouragement that go on. Sometimes you think 'She can't be interested all the time, it's not possible for her to be interested in everything that everybody says', but she is genuinely interested and encouraging, though not in a totally uncritical way.

(Student interview)

VISIBLE PRACTICE

When the furniture is cleared away and the conditions for languaging have been created the task before us as teachers is to activate the space and to ensure it is a place of exchange and collaboration. There seems to be a paradox at work here, because we will be asking everyone involved to take risks, to open themselves, on the basis that the classroom is a safe place. This means that as teachers our dispositions have to be those of risk-takers and of reassurance. Our agenda must therefore be transparent; we must try to be languagers and intercultural beings as teachers and as learners. We need to be willing, in our teaching, to address these paradoxes, tensions, complexities that will arise between competing claims on language teaching.

It is hard to imagine any successful learning that does not consider the process as well as the product; but that process is not peculiar to any one language being learned, though it *is* embedded in that learning. In other words, it is crucial that learners become increasingly conscious and critical actors in their own language as a direct contribution to learning another. And that, it should be clear, is a critical, embodied process rather than a linguistic one. That is to say, it goes beyond how a thing is said to what is said and why and how the saying is forged, shaped and rendered complex and profound by the manner of its saying. The important thing here is that what is aimed at in the other language is exactly the same process of understanding as making sense of what we say and do in our own languages.

Fun, RISKY, SCAFFOLDED PRACTICE

Again and again we return to that idea of the classroom as a place 'in a state of constant, creative and useful exploratory struggle' (Carter and McRae, 1996: xiii). It is also a place where difference can be addressed, celebrated and encouraged. It is a place where 'discourses' – what Gee (1989: 6) defines as 'saying-doing-being-valuing-believing combinations' – may be practised in fun, risky, brave, scaffolded safety and, most importantly, together with someone who embodies the discourse already:

> *Discourses are ways of being in the world; they are forms of life which integrate words, acts, values, beliefs, attitudes, and social identities as well as gestures, glances, body positions, and clothes. (Gee, 1989: 6)*

Languaging is about learning discourses by enabling the enculturation of learners into social practices, using *both* their own and their other language.

> *While you can overtly teach someone* linguistics, *a body of knowledge, you can't teach them to* be a linguist, *that is, to use a Discourse. The most you can do is let them practise being a linguist with you. (Gee, 1989: 7)*

The same is true of becoming 'languagers', languagers of German or Spanish, Chinese or Urdu. The acquisition of certain instruments of language-making need not be an exercise in conformity nor a levelling; if it is, then paradoxically the instruments (grammar for example) deny the potentiality they should and can denote. In other words, the impulse to complexity of expression comes from that which is expressed rather than the limited means of expression. This is the dilemma throughout – how can we ensure that in the classroom the thought, the image, the possibility of self-expression develops at its own pace, seeking the means but not limited by them? The thought, in a word, should be in advance of the technique.

> 'The problem is I really am finding this very difficult, I feel small and I just don't think I'm making any progress.' My friend is a professional, at the top of his field, with an international profile and a schoolboy complex about his ability to speak other languages. We are talking over a drink together at the end of our respective days. I'm 'accused' again of just having a 'talent', a 'gift' for languages. I never buy this kind of accusation. My friend has recently gone back to learning languages, picking up with French, and with an admirable determination. He has one-to-one tuition, but he is frustrated by the feelings the apparent difficulty of the task exposes. 'We just work through this book' he says. 'My tutor is very good, very patient and encouraging but I worry when I haven't done my homework and I can't see that I'm getting anywhere. It makes me anxious.' 'What's the book like?' I ask. 'Pretty tedious, there are exercises,' he replies. I feel a bit helpless. Exercise books for languages are tedious, and I feel myself about to resort to my usual platitudes about language learning being a slow process, needing a bit of discipline everyday, but I know I don't quite believe this, and certainly not here. I say nothing.
>
> A few weeks later we are in conversation again. 'I had a brilliant French lesson today, it was just wonderful, I ended up jumping round my room, writing things on the board and gasping for new words. We both seemed to really enjoy it. I was talking about my work.' He smiles rather ruefully. 'You were languaging,' I think.

In presenting his model of the 'intercultural speaker' Byram (1997: 70–1), following Kramsch (1993), rejects the idea of native speaker competence as an attainable objective. He makes a distinction between Intercultural Competence – limited to interactions in the mother tongue –

intercultural communicative competence

and Intercultural Communicative Competence – which involves interactions in another language:

> *The relationship between Intercultural Competence and Intercultural Communicative Competence is one of degrees of complexity and the ability to deal with a wider range of situations of contact in the latter than in the former. (Byram, 1997: 71)*

The notion of the *Intercultural Speaker* is a useful one and Byram has made an important contribution to expanding and humanising language teaching and learning through his work. However, we do not wish our developing languaging or that of our students to be simply about speaking. The *Intercultural Listener* is as pertinent to our project. Indeed the language learning and teaching we envisage here is that of developing interculturally critical beings (Barnett, 1997).

We emphasise again the centrality of the idea of exchange. We speak in response to another's meaningful speaking as opposed to the dissociated 'thinking' utterances that masquerade as conversation in the language at artificial levels. Languagers hear what others say, mirror, absorb and re-enact, allowing the work of critical being to move life and language on. They are skilled practitioners as opposed to 'people with skills'. The idea of 'skilled practice', reclaimed beautifully by Ingold (2000), replaces traditional models of skills with a relational approach focusing on the growth of embodied skills of perception and action within social and environmental contexts of development. Languaging as a mode of being is a skilled, embodied and situated practice.

The relational and perspectival skills we are discussing do not develop solely out of loud, speaking and obvious action. Languaging is not, after all, just about speaking, but about being. So for languaging to develop as that 'full, risky, bodily, critical', skilled way of being intercultural to which we have argued we may aspire, there must also be time for quiet reflection on the process, for dreaming in the language.

> *It's the end of October. I log on to my computer first thing. There is an e-mail from one of my students who is spending a year abroad and has been away for about six weeks. 'Hello, I had the weirdest experience last night,' she writes, 'I dreamed in German.' It makes me smile and makes me remember my 'first time', on a school exchange, waking up to the knowledge that my experience of life and its expression, deep in my being, had changed and was living itself out in a different medium.*

John McRae, for example, (Carter and McRae, 1996: 180) lays great, and justified stress, on what might be described as the *fifth skill* mobilised in the course of language learning. We are all overly familiar with those 'course objectives and learning outcomes' we place now at the head of our course documents – coined according to an established and suitably meaningless formula and couched in a language of extreme and cautious safety (see Figure 6.1), not of delight and risk in the face of the great adventures that languaging in particular may enable. All the talk of outcomes remits us to performativity, to function; at a given stimulus, there will be an appropriate response.

The aims of the language element of the module are to reinforce and build on your knowledge of the structures of the language, particularly verbal constructions, to enhance your awareness of the range of register in the language by exposing you to a variety of authentic sources, and to increase your ability to produce sustained, accurate language in both speech and writing.
  The objectives of the language element of the module are to enable you to:

(i)   recognise a wide range of constructions, particularly verbal constructions, and to use them accurately in oral and written contexts;
      The elements of the course designed particularly to achieve this are grammatical exercises (including those available in the Computer Assisted Language Learning classes), translation work from English into the language, usually highlighting points of grammar arising from the weekly video presentations, and essay writing in the language.
(ii) appreciate the differences between familiar, normally spoken, language and a more formal, often written, register;
      The elements of the course designed particularly to achieve this are the weekly video presentations and translation work from the language into English.
(iii) converse naturally in the language, speak for several minutes on a topic of broad contemporary interest, participate in the discussion of such a topic and write a short essay in the language (about 200 words) on an aspect of life likely to be relevant to someone studying at university.
      The elements of the course designed particularly to achieve this are the oral classes, which also include the practice of essay writing in the language.

More generally, both the language and literature elements aim to encourage you to develop habits of independent study, individual resourcefulness and time management and to enhance your analytic and communicative skills – all of which will prove valuable to you in any sphere of employment.

(Adapted from: http://www.arts.gla.ac.uk/)

FIGURE 6.1 *Typical aims and objectives*

We have already discussed in our introductory chapter how this conception has come to permeate institutional discussions of the role of modern languages. They became simply a means to doing something else – languages *for* business, or engineering, or medicine, or law. We are asked to provide a liberal supply of chisels, hammers, planes, nails and spirit levels – but we have nothing to say about the building of the ship, no role in determining the ethics of creating nuclear submarines or the desirability of luxury cruise liners.

In this comfortable and reassuring world of 'language for purposes' a situation produces a 'correct' response, and an impersonal one. Because learning outcomes are by definition general and normative, individuality, creativity, *difference* can have no place there. The assessment template could never work if this were not the case. 'The student shall develop the ability to speak, read, write and understand the language'. That may be why the fifth skill, and the most important, does not characteristically appear – thinking. It may also be why ontological dimensions – dimensions of being – are masked out of the discourse on outcomes. Perhaps because it is not a skill in the same sense that the others are, critical reflection does not make the list; yet it is the only skill that can make sense of the others, whose expression demands language.

But we would go further still, and require not just the insertion of *critical reflection*, but the active **critical being**
encouragement of Barnett's critical being (Barnett, 1997). Languaging – actively being intercultural, allowing the energy, the rising panic, the excitement, the purposive dilation of pupils, indeed the sheer love of this way of being to enter our performative, individualistic classroom contexts – would be to overturn the false but stubbornly held belief that we can measure performance.

Although he then goes on to explore ways of assessing the disposition, Byram (1997: 50) refers to the wide-eyed and receptive curiosity that can be read off the facial expression of a schoolchild on their first language exchange as a key attitude and objective for the development of intercultural competence. Putting these facial expressions and spontaneous questions into our classrooms has to be one of our aims. We want to teach eyes that sparkle and question, which make visible the embodied, skilled practice of languaging, not the sad eyes of passive-aggressive disappointment or fear.

Languaging Aims and Outcomes

This course aims to skill you in the practice of languaging. By engaging with another language and the life of the people who live it and use it as one of their powers of expression you become part of a network of relations – through interaction and exchange of your experiences of life, your imagination, your ideas, the books you have read, the food you have eaten, the people you have met, the things you can do, your likes and your dislikes.

In this course you can expect to be challenged. University is the place where we encounter ideas, theories, ways of appropriating the world, ways of representing the world that are 'too difficult'. The process of life can only be lived reflectively, can only be acted out critically, if we engage with what is 'too difficult'. The unexamined life, as Socrates famously said, is not worth living. In the university you will have the chance to learn how to make the library your friend, how to learn from your lecturers and tutors as your critical guides. You will be scaffolded in your reading and thinking, with people and resources around you to help you become skilful in dealing with the 'too difficult'.

In a course on languages and intercultural studies of the 'too difficult' there will be moments when you struggle to articulate your ideas to those who speak another language. In the times when you are undertaking field work and projects you will discover moments of ease and flow alongside others of frustration. Being intercultural is not about being safe in your knowledges and ways of doing things, it is about working away as border crossers, making the links, filling in the gaps and then taking time to be quiet, to listen and to reflect.

We cannot possibly know with any degree of certainty whether the practice you have of crossing borders, reflecting and being critical of established structures of knowledge and understanding, of yourself and of those who live and speak differently to you will get you a good job. We cannot know whether the reflection and *experience of cultural and linguistic difference and distance will make you materially wealthy.*

The questions that will accompany you throughout are these:

- *What difference does it make that I speak this language in this time and place?*
- *What difference does it make that this book, person, film, meal, building is expressed in ways strange to me but which are becoming my own?*
- *How might I find a way of understanding and living with difference?*
- *How have I been transformed by this language inside me, by those with whom I use it to relate?*

REFLECTIVE SPEAKING, CRITICAL LISTENING

All this may seem banal, obvious. Yet it would seem entirely legitimate to ask what is spoken, what is heard, what is understood in the written or aural text. Answering that question requires an extensive and complex response. We make assumptions about our students. That they arrive with knowledge and concerns – yet we do not mobilise them in the context of language learning; when they are used in a 'conversation practice' context, we isolate the means from the ends, the form from the content. And it cannot be otherwise, once we have artificially separated what is thought from how it is expressed. This does not in any way invalidate the use of 'formal' texts, of other genres. Poetry and literature in general will enrich and add to that 'structure of feeling' which we understand culture to mean throughout this volume.

The question, of course, is whether liter- | text and cultural meanings |
ature should be privileged in the business of language learning. We deal with this issue at length in another chapter. But it should be said here that the value of a text in this process is not adduced from its aesthetic achievement understood narrowly. The text is valuable as a bearer, transmitter and reviser of cultural meanings; these are many and varied. Successful language learning will leave the learner with a repertoire of symbolic values and social registers and of the appropriacy of their usage in context. We certainly should not be cornered into becoming the spokespersons for a kind of canon of adequacy in linguistic expression. The only criteria that can function are specific to the task: can

the learner mobilise sufficient expressive resources to convey the depth, richness and complexity of a given text (defined in the broadest sense, as we explore later) from her personal stock, or the stock of others, or through the mining of other comparable texts and contexts? It may be that each form of communication has rules, measures and conventions of its own; our task is to provide the widest possible glossary of conventions and means of judging their aptness or otherwise.

Then there is the talking. Consider the topics of discussion deployed by native language assistants (and let us be very clear that this is in no way criticism of NLAs who are often unsupported and undirected, treated in many senses as the sherpas to our sahibs). Plucked from the air, these might include topics of contemporary concern – war, abortion, human rights, religion, the meaning of the blues. This could be an enormously fruitful exercise, were the class to be seen as a place of exchange in which the NLA in some way represents the 'structure of feeling' of a generation meeting its fellows in our institutions. Then the conversation would be the collaborative and mutually enlightening process it may be in other contexts, an equal exchange of symbolic goods. Instead, the NLA is more usually placed in the position of a linguistic arbiter, assessing and correcting the form of expression and in doing so interrupting and fragmenting the meanings embedded in the flow of self-expression.

Let us imagine a different situation, in which the conversation class was an exchange and comparison of stories, of living tales told by people whose encounter is based on a mutual recognition of autonomy. Of course, this certainly happens already in many cases, quietly and unacknowledged in the manuals. What would arise in the conversation would then provide a direction for the learning that followed; it would enter and leave a continuous flow of communication. It might, indeed almost certainly would, involve the introduction of other supports of expression, materials, actions, role-playing exercises, evidence and testimony, body language, tunes and songs half-remembered, the visual references (photographs, paintings, faces in the street) that enrich and complete our own understandings. These then would become the 'texts' of the language learning process. And they are not merely 'realia' – a rather vague notion that suggests condiments and decoration, flavouring ingredients to create a sense of place or, more probably, of 'otherness' (like 'background').

Why should advertisements, songs, magazine articles, recipes, medical advice, radio programmes, theatrical performances not act as texts in this sense? After all, they are 'meaningful' language acts, communicative inter-

exchanging stories

ventions in the world, yet each of them carries a significant aura (in Benjamin's sense of the 'here-and-now'-ness (Benjamin, 1973)) and a cultural resonance which is equivalent but not identical from one culture to another.

And why should this collection of multiple texts, and this 'here-and-now-ness' always be assumed to be contained in language textbooks, the 'realia' of one or more authors, with their own particular perspectives on the life of the language? It is the experience, in the classroom, of seeing those 'saying-doing-being-valuing-believing combinations' (Gee, 1989: 6) lived and acted out in a myriad of different, often spontaneous ways, by the teacher as well as by those who have their own experiences to relate as learners, that helps create the context for languaging and meaning-making.

Discovering and locating those meanings is in every sense a language-learning exercise; identifying points of difference and similarity, making sense of one in terms of the other, is the most meaningful of cultural encounters – and the most expressive.

Teacher: *OK. Can you open your books at page 33. We're starting a new grammar section today and looking at declension of nouns, nouns and articles and also at compound nouns and their formation in German.*

Student puts garden gnome on the table. Teacher cannot help noticing and laughs.

Teacher: *So…why have we a garden gnome in class today?*

Student: *He wants to learn German.*

Teacher: *Well, let's give him a text book too.*

Gnome sits in front of an open text book.

Teacher: *So, who can give me the German for Garden Gnome?*

Student: *G – nom- e?*

Teacher: *Well that works for gnome but not quite…*

Another student: *'Garten…err…Gartenzwerg?'*

Teacher: *And here we have our first example for the day of a compound noun!*

Laughter

Teacher: *So is it der, die or das – based on what you've learned so far?*

Student: *Der.*

Teacher: Why?

Student: Well it's a guess, but both Garten and Zwerg are masculine.

Teacher: And with compounds the gender always refers to the last part of the compound. Do you think our Gartenzwerg should have a name? What about Markus – seeing as he isn't here today?

Another student pulls out an A4 poster from his writing pad with a picture of a gnome in the local park. Underneath it says: 'Could you give a Gnome a good time?'

Teacher: Well – our Gartenzwerg is certainly having a good time here.

The rest of the class follows with students working in pairs or threes on structural grammar exercises. They test each other, read out the sentences and work out the different logics. Every now and then I stop them when I want to correct pronunciation. I ask them to repeat words after me, but all together – they feel safe that way. I exaggerate the Ü sounds – these are difficult for anglophones. I tell them to purse their lips, to exaggerate, to concentrate on the feel of their tongue on the roof of their mouths and to try again. They all get the giggles, of course. They are used to this kind of phonetic and physical reflexivity in my classes by now but it never ceases to be a source of amusement. If I don't like what I hear I get them to repeat it again and again. It is rather like a pantomime. And they are, of course, acting – trying on phonetic identities – feeling their physicality, becoming skilled practitioners.

There is absolutely no reason why this cannot fruitfully occur in a higher education environment, but there is an administrative or material prerequisite for it to happen. It has to do with context. The successful conversation takes place unexpectedly, follows unpredictable paths, is a social context. The ones that really work happen in the park, or in a café, or over a beer; in other words, the meaningful language exchange is a function of something other than itself – it is a way of knowing and being known, of approaching another, of resolving tasks collaboratively with others. That is hard to reproduce in the classroom with its fixed arrangement of furniture, in a time slot defined by tradition and the ease of tracing squares on paper.

But why should it be an hour, why at a fixed time, why in a group of 6 or 26, and why necessarily in a classroom? Is it to do with a notion of 'seriousness' – that communication only has academic validity when it is formalised or structured? That seems contradictory, considering the way in which languaging actually takes place.

AND IS THERE TEACHING STILL TO BE DONE?

It will be clear by now that our emphasis is on the capacity of the learner to impel her own learning, that motivation is the impulse that drives the learner and the process of skilling, rather than an externally imposed system-building activity. We do not wish to claim that systems are not valuable. Indeed they bring freedom and rewards of their own if understood and applied for their profundity and creative potential, rather than for their capacity to motivate through fear or for the satisfaction of completing a task skilfully.

> Is learning the result of a problem-solving drive, a fascination with grammar as system? In the majority of cases no, though I recall a friend and ex-student, one of the best linguists I have ever encountered, who moved smoothly and easily from learning a range of languages (including Chinese) to repairing car engines to computers. Having cracked the complex structure, he seemed to move restlessly and continuously to the next. He, I firmly believe, is the exception rather than the rule.

For the most part system-building is an automatised process which does not adapt to language-learning. The reasons? Precisely because languaging, as the skilled practice of meaning-making, is an exchange and a creative one. Of course system-building can be a creative process too, but the join-the-dots approach belongs to the spoon-feeding school of learning and teaching. Thus the primary motivation is the desire to communicate (Chambers, 1999), to negotiate a shared space and to develop that communication. That notion of development seems crucial – otherwise the 'survival method' of language learning, which lays out a range of limited and specific procedures for limited and specific needs, would be sufficient.

We have to assume language learning is far more than task-based, that it is
culture-driven in the sense of achieving understanding in a double and simultaneous sense – understanding the Other *and* making oneself

communication not survival

understood *to* the Other. Knowing the linguistic code may be a necessity but cannot be a sufficient condition for that understanding to occur.

The issue here is what is the relationship between linguistic and cultural (attitudinal) outcomes, what is the influence of the learner's perception of the other language culture on the language learning itself? Our position is that they are intimately interrelated, and that the language classroom is a site where that connection is explored, developed and elaborated. Indeed, we understand language rather as anthropologists do. Without actually learning the language of the culture they are studying anthropologists know that they will not be able to do fieldwork, that they will be reliant on highly subjective and problematic translators and interpreters, that they will never get under the skin and into the thick of the culture and beyond.

In modern languages we have only very recently begun to understand our enterprise as anthropological.

Successful learning requires negotiation by the learner of what she already knows in the face and in the light of the new – so does communication. (Benson and Voller, 1997: xii)

That negotiation is a constant in the language- **negotiating tasks** learning process, but it is also its starting point. We have discussed the limiting and repressive consequences of a classroom arranged around a concept of authority. It is also our conviction that the subversion of that physical arrangement is almost certainly a first and indispensable moment in the learning process. But the very next step – and this at any level of advancement in the language process – is to determine what is to be done. This might suggest a task-based approach – and indeed that may well often be the approach best suited to this negotiation. But the tasks are culture and communication-driven. In the reality of a classroom in which the majority of students are non-native speakers of the other language, the issue may often be – what is it I want to say about myself? That does not necessarily imply an endless retelling of our individual stories – though that is a fundamental part of the learning, because the 'I' who speaks is the same in either language; it may also be an exploration of 'saying' and 'listening' as performance, as experience, as mobility. In other words, it may also involve functioning in that environment – but functioning as a fully complex person in that other milieu.

The role of the teacher is important here – we distinguish what we are advocating from a notion of autonomy that in fact abandons the student to a series of self-assessed exercises of a mechanical kind, before the page or the screen. The dialogic process on which this whole discussion rests requires an other, not an antagonist but a responsive voice. And while the approach must be learner-centred and anti-authoritarian, it cannot in any sense deny the wealth of experience and knowledge that the teacher may bring to the dialogue as an exchange.

> *I would argue that a teacher has the responsibility to plan deliberately for a possible transfer (and not merely 'facilitate'). (Barnett, 1994: 142)*

What is important here is that there is a double process: the issue of what is said and how it is said. In the traditional language classroom it is often the second, the form, that determines the first, the content. And in many cases, the content is also a given. The upshot is to demotivate the student, withdrawing her autonomy. At root, where the learner is without choice, she is also without motive. The autonomy of the learner, then, is in the first instance an acknowledgment of the learner's capacity – and indeed right – to bring to the community the subject matter. The motivation to learn to speak, listen, read, write in any language, one's own or another, is the desire to express a content, to intervene in an exchange. As Benson puts it 'A language cannot be described adequately by reference to its forms and structures unless these are related to the meanings conveyed in specific interactions' (Benson and Voller, 1997: 21).

Important consequences flow; knowledge – of a language or in a language – are not veins waiting to be revealed by the judicious and persistent use of a pedagogic pickaxe. It is constructed in the learning, the product of a critical engagement with the world. In this sense, learner autonomy is neither a simplistic libertarianism, in which the student is left to flounder in chaos, nor a one-to-one relationship with a computer screen or a tape recorder in a science-like language laboratory.

What then is the role of the language teacher the language teacher in the classroom? It is not enough simply to throw in buzzwords like 'facilitation' or 'empowerment'. In the first instance, to empower is not simply to add to the stock of personal confidence and knowledge, but to relocate individual learning in a community – that of the classroom, of the learning group (because all is exchange) but also, by analogy, with the community of the language learned. Thus to a notion of empowerment must be added a dimension of collective cultural work (Giroux, 1992).

The irony is how much language work, while conducted in a situation where significant numbers of people are present, is actually conducted at an individual level. To move from desk to desk, privately correcting errors and whispering advice, negates the centrality of dialogue and exchange. Forging a community is critical to successful language teaching; movement – physical and communicative – is the core of the exercise. Hence – forgive the repetition – the emphasis on flexible furnishings.

forging a community

We are insisting here, not on key skills, but on enthusiastic and embodied skilling. Languaging is a manifestation of the skilled practice of communicating with conviction, enthusiasm and indeed knowledge, it is an attitude where no learners are adversely afraid of or impressed by another's knowledge – while disengaging that knowledge from power. The learner must feel his or her own power over the learning process increasing in the course of things – that is the important sense of autonomy. But that is not a justification for the disappearance of the tutor; on the contrary, her role should be to reinforce and animate that sense of autonomy, offering the means for complex expression, socialising each moment of understanding through the class, suggesting possibilities, offering instruments of 'how' in response to the 'what'.

In between this class and our last one I've sent the students away to read a piece by Gramsci, to get their heads around hegemony, and to have a go at seeing how these ideas apply to the case studies on 'popular German culture' that they have been examining so far. Although I have prepared a plan and have written out my aims and outcomes, and followed up on all the correct documentation, this class will only 'work' if the students come to it ready to engage and exchange with each other and with me. I begin by asking them, not if they have read the passage, but how they found it. I know by now that they are readers, capable of having a go at tough stuff.

They have been getting together in small groups to discuss what they read and recently I've been asking them to tape their discussions for me to follow up on later. What is clear is that these conversations lack focus. The students open up in the groups at differing speeds, some confident, some gentler with their exploring, but gradually all begin to explore and to ask each other questions.

'What did you understand by page 43, paragraph 2?', 'I didn't think that was what he meant?', 'How does this relate to hegemony?', 'What is hegemony anyway?', 'Why can't these people write in ways we can understand?'

The different groups come back with their settled thoughts and their questions, if not with any clear conviction, and we open the dialogue out again. This always feels like learning. It always feels hard to control, as though my job is to listen, to test, to question, to open out new directions, to compare and to constantly affirm and support.

In these measurable times these unfolding conversations and moments of awkwardness are hard to quantify. And yet, when asked which part of the course was the one where they felt they we really getting somewhere they always point to these conversations. They refer affectionately, by this stage, to 'the question of the week'. They have a whole discourse, co-created, for representing the experience of the course.

The learner thus owns what is said and what is thought; the classroom ceases to be a place where a power struggle is conducted, to become a place of exchange, of dialogue, of mutuality.

TEXTS AND UNTEXTS

We will return later to the question of texts – particularly literary texts – and reading as a component of 'being intercultural'. In the language classroom, however, and particularly in higher education, 'texts' are often the material substance of the act of translation and the measures of achievement. In that sense, we do need to address not so much *which* texts are or should be employed as *whether* texts are strong or broad enough to bear the responsibility. It might be assumed, for example, that the kinds of exchange that we have discussed are entirely verbal exchanges – communications at the level of speech.

There are two ways of responding to that assumption: first, by saying that communicative acts are complex and themselves involve, well if not texts then at least multiple discourses; second, that they are not necessarily verbal exchanges in any event – or to put it another way, that complex speech acts can and should occur around texts of a wide variety of genres. After all, there are no speech acts which do not find an equivalent in corresponding or accompanying discourses. These are embodied in material objects, printed words or parallel modes of communication – like gesture, register, the absorption of the surrounding ambience, the use and reference of objects, body language, as well as the many other varieties of 'formal text'. We might be speaking here of radio or television programmes, photographs (with or without captions), advertisements, newspapers and magazines, song lyrics and so on.

In that sense there are two interconnected regions of practice which correspond to those different experiences of *languaging*. Let's call them, for want of other terms, the interpreting milieu and the manipulation of texts.

manipulating of texts

By interpreting we refer not to the professional vocational training process, but rather to the liaison interpreting exercise as a mode of language learning. This is not the place to explore its procedures in detail, but it is worth looking broadly at its methodologies and purposes. Essentially, what is invoked is an instant translation of verbal communications from another language, and at a later stage into that language too. The ideal group for the purpose is a mixed group (in terms of native language) at a fairly advanced level of linguistic awareness. But its practices may be relevant to a much earlier stage of language learning.

In an advanced class, an essential part of the class involves preparation by the student group, familiarising themselves with the discussions and debates around a contemporary issue previously agreed. In that sense, the lexis associated with specific areas of knowledge and experience is accumulated as a kind of growing repository that is common to the group and to which all can refer. But the initial stages of preparation are less concerned with specific lexical issues than with issues of register – complex meaning where utterances are reinforced, or interpreted by parallel discourses like tone, gesture, body language and context. Recognition of that knot of interwoven meanings is a cultural practice; it is not less or more so because of the complexity of the utterance.

The exercise can begin within the native language of the learners. There is a general principle to be learned about language as cultural exchange which is not specific to source or target language, but to language itself. This is not necessarily to argue a 'universal grammar', but to address the way in which language is both reflection and construction of reality. Learners are perfectly able to perceive that at the earliest stages of language learning. Thus face-to-face repetition of words and phrases will reactively involve considerations of context (cultural and material – the classroom, the society beyond, gender, class, age and profession and so on) which are signalled in ways often not articulated but learned (to continue with Chomsky) as a 'deep structure'. Register, the complex transmission of meaning and attitude, gives content to form. Do we transmit simply the 'Yes I should think so!' or do we reproduce the nuances added by other discourses of gesture, tone, facial movement, body language and so on. In so far as that represents a recognition of deep structure, it is also an introduction to grammar. The same procedures apply in reproducing meanings in the target language, however simple; and the same vocabulary of cultural signs needs to be adduced to respond to register as well as form.

It is important of course that such interlingual expression be authentic, possess that multiplicity of dimensions. The 'texts' that a language class may use should provide that authenticity and that connection. Authenticity is of course a problematic concept and has been the subject of much cultural abuse. Essentially we are suggesting texts that have complexity embedded within them and texts which have not been fabricated for the sole purpose of use in the classroom context. They can be of almost any kind – written, oral, visual, material, musical – in so far as they enrich and fill out the semantic context of the original utterance. In that respect, the task of the teacher is to introduce relevant and illuminating materials in as creative a way as possible – to have a stock available rather than necessarily a limiting text. But it is not solely the task of the teacher to unearth the most meaningful materials in the stock – the search (or research) for those materials should be a key part of the learning process. The grammar – the route taken – of such a series of encounters can be signalled but is not a different kind of knowledge by its nature inaccessible to the investigative learner. In that sense the business of learning should be 'rule seeking rather than rule remembering' (Krashen, in Byram, 2000: 146).

It is in this sense that the time and space of   *a manner of speaking*
the learning environment is a place of discovery, and it is as much self-discovery as discovering the Other. For the capacity to acquire a language is the product of a desire to understand. At some point, of course, formal issues intervene – questions of structure and form. But the grammar of a language is not, as so many of us have learned to see it, merely a toolbox – a set of inert rules; grammar is linguistic conduct, a manner of speaking and being, shaped by culture, history and the social. Drawing general procedures from linguistic

behaviours is an entirely different business from learning them as givens in isolation from use. Thus when we ask students to rehearse forms of expression it should include, wherever possible, an attempt to place them in their framework. 'Students must be willing and able to adopt various aspects of *behaviour* [our emphasis], including verbal behaviour, which characterize members of other linguistic, cultural groupings' (Chambers, 1999: 19).

The reality, of course, is that we are located in a room somewhere quite distant from that context. The question, then, is to what extent we are able – as teachers – to recreate something of that other milieu. We have virtual access to it, that is true. There is a pedagogical problem here, however, to which we shall return: its usefulness will depend on how far real interactivity is possible there. But even without that there are other levels of engagement. Newspapers, television, radio are now almost instantly accessible via the Internet; we can read what they are reading in Madrid, Berlin, Paris or wherever at the same time as they are reading them over croissants or café con leche or Frühstuck. And if that is a common experience to the group of learners then it is entirely possible to enact the responses and commentaries that the material awakens in the learners' group. How would a lead story be received elsewhere? How would it differ from our own responses?

I am standing in front of my class struggling with them with the juxtapositions of direct and indirect object and subject pronouns. We are using a textbook – a good one in my own opinion – but they are not engaging with the aridity of this particular grammar exercise. They have probably sensed that I am not excited by it either! So I pick up Mark's pencil, Karen's pen and my own book – to their amusement and surprise – and we begin to make these objects our own, weaving our own stories around them. I give Karen Mark's pencil and the class tell me what I've done. I take it back again, I change between registers of formality that match my facial expressions. They mimic this practice. The students repeat the formula but they do so creatively – and in the course of the fun languaging occurs, eyes lighten up and we make our own stories. I overhear the students talking excitedly about this class to their friends – 'and then we did this with the pencil...' Somehow something gets lost in the telling – their interlocutor doesn't quite 'get it' – the story and experience of picking up pens and pencils was ours. And I smile.

Answering cultural questions and creating stories from limited resources is a much more complex activity than it might appear to be. It involves self-awareness as much as understanding others; it involves, to repeat, exchange; it involves preparation and then translation as an active exercise. It requires the preparedness to participate. And it can find expression in any of the multiple ways in which we express ourselves in other areas life – speech, gesture, song, role-play. And it is in this context that what some might describe as 'formal language learning' can take place. For in a higher education environment in which modern languages play the core role that we envisage, all activities can be attended or followed by critical reflection upon them.

Here the original issue of authority enters the fray yet   authority
again. Monopoly of access to information and its sources
may be a reassuring source of power, but it is a betrayal of learning. As teachers we have a duty to lead the learners to those sources and make them accessible so that learners can genuinely use them without magisterial intervention. And that requires the conviction that learners can discover the structures of language themselves, with guidance and encouragement. That is the real significance of autonomous learning (Mann, 2001).

> I have a problem. I've been told – by someone in authority – that I have to stop using the textbook that I know to work well and change to a new one, for the sake of change and in line with what I perceive to be pernicious ideologies of learning. Having made my argument along the lines 'if it ain't broke why fix it', I capitulate – after all, surviving in the university today is about knowing which battles to fight. This one just wasn't worth it. The textbook selected for me to use is, in my view, essentialist and even borders on the racist. The exercises it uses for language learning are prescriptive not dialogic. The book is American. This is not in itself a problem, but it does mean that all the examples – which in a rather problematic text are of course manifold – require me to have an intimate knowledge of the world's dominant power, which I do not possess.
>
> Critical reflection is my only hope. I do not buy the argument, outlined to me, that students need to be made to feel comfortable

with essentialist concepts and representations of Germany. I stand by my view that learning and the university is about 'the too difficult' – if this is taught in scaffolded ways. When I teach from this book, with my students, it is to deconstruct its assumptions, to reconstruct its texts, to critically question the assumptions, to laugh near it and to find ways of using the potential creativity that the tensions it supplies may engender.

BECOMING....

The purpose of this chapter has been to set the broader discussion of languaging in time and place in a recognisable learning context, to address the where and the how at an early stage. For those who hoped for a manual, a methodology, it will have been a disappointment. But that is not, we hope, because it has failed in its purposes. On the contrary, the objective has been to reopen the classroom, to erase the harsh lines that separate the classroom from the world, to make it permeable to the experience and knowledge of all those engaged in the learning process. For all that knowledge and understanding, formal and informal, synchronic or diachronic, practical or intellectual, has a place in the language learning process. It is after all, as we have repeatedly emphasised, a process of *exchange*. We aspire to a practice of languaging that is serious and yet full of laughter, that is critical and ironic, that is disciplined in its playfulness. In looking at the framework of learning, we have explored the circumstances and practices that can make such an exchange possible – or inhibit it where they are absent. Once the shape of that environment is agreed and formed, the business of being intercultural can begin in earnest.

Key references

Byram, M. (1997) *Teaching and Assessing Intercultural Communicative Competence.* Clevedon: Multilingual Matters.

Carter, R., McRae, J., (eds) (1996) *Language, Literature and the Learner: Creative Classroom Practice.* London and New York: Longman.

Gee, J. (1989) 'Literacy, discourse, and linguistics', *Journal of Education*, 171(1): 5–17.

Giroux, H. (1992) *Border Crossings: Cultural Workers and the Politics of Education.* London: Routledge.

Ingold, T. (2000) *The Perception of the Environment: Essays in Livelihood, Dwelling and Skill.* London and New York: Routledge.

Kramsch, C. (1993) *Context and Culture in Language Teaching.* Oxford: Oxford University Press.

Websites
http://www.lang.ltsn.ac.uk/resources/guidecontents.aspx
http://www.ltsn.ac.uk/genericcentre/index.asp

Encyclopedia

Byram, M. (2000) *Routledge Encyclopedia of Language Teaching and Learning.* London and New York: Routledge.

Being there

POINTS OF DEPARTURE

Alison: My 'year abroad' wrought powerful changes in my life. In the summer of 1988 I had nothing to do but anticipate. I remember always wanting to have a year abroad. I remember the stories of my teachers at school and of watching them at ease in both French and German as they lived and laughed in the languages I was struggling to make grow inside of me. I remember those hesitant steps on school exchanges as I stumbled around unfamiliar words and newly fashioned friendships. I remember just knowing, with a strange kind of pride, that I too would live abroad for a year.

The college discourse was full of such knowing. Friends on three-year courses marked 'us linguists' out as different; the residence abroad being a prior exoticism in our relationships at home. Tutors processed forms and sent us off at the end of the year telling us to enjoy ourselves and to come back eager for finals. I was not the only one anticipating the transformations that would follow a period of residence abroad.

But apart from this prior ontological knowing, there was little preparation. I was perhaps lucky in that I had already travelled and talked my way through travelling encounters. I was predisposed to enjoyment and convinced – though hardly experientially – of the 'good' that would come of a year in a small Swabian town.

Mike: I probably enjoyed a different sort of privilege, and a different sort of loss. My abroad was in London, where I grew up in a curious sort of no man's land between two universes. On the one side, my *mother's family, Jews exiled from Vienna after the Anschluss, spoke an animated if slightly adapted German – Viennese style. On the other, my father's circle of Civil War exiles from Franco's Spain, lived in permanent anticipation of returning – and failed to see the point of embedding themselves in an English-language world. I suppose you could say that my space was a place between – not hybrid, because these two pre-existing worlds never really merged, nor produced a new culture out of their meeting. My father's political circle lived in an unresolved past; my mother's family inhabited a kind of permanent transience; her parents had moved on from eastern Europe, she in turn became British. I spoke neither German nor Spanish – only the English of the place where I lived – though I learned both later with ease. My ear, after all, resonated with their sounds. I felt, by turns, pride in my cosmopolitanism, and occasionally lost in my lack of place.*

Where are we now? We have rehearsed and played with different kinds of being and insisted that languaging is a kind of being. Languages no longer reside solely abroad. The whole point of our method is to demonstrate that as our ways of being in the world change under the flux of material circumstances, so languages will take residence in our ways of being in new, exciting forms. What we have to say in this book, and specifically in this chapter, inescapably implies a new curriculum both before and after residence abroad. The work of forming and shaping such a curriculum is collective, cultural and political.

All that has gone before in our discussions of languaging has been the preparation for an 'art of travel' and a way of being 'abroad'. Residence abroad, like language itself, does not need to be curricularised and exercised into separate courses. It also, importantly, needs to be lived as part of languaging. However, in the languages classroom 'abroad' is largely, though not entirely, an imagined place. It is also constructed through different ideological and educational discourses, but it bears an anticipation in the body of the learner and teacher of exchange and transformation through an encounter with 'the real'.

> living and languaging

If our lives are dominated by a search for happiness, then perhaps few activities reveal as much about the dynamics of this quest – in all its ardour and paradoxes – than our travels. They express, however inarticulately, an understanding of what life might be about, outside the constraints of work and the struggle for survival. Yet rarely are they considered to present philosophical problems – that is, issues requiring thought beyond the practical. We are inundated with advice on where to travel to; we hear little of why or how we should go – though the art of travel seems naturally to sustain a number of questions neither so simple nor so trivial and whose study might in modest ways contribute to an understanding of what the Greek philosophers beautifully termed eudaimonia *or human flourishing. (de Botton, 2002: 9)*

For the most part modern language degrees in the UK require residence abroad as part of their programmes. This is not the case in other countries, where there is not so much a requirement as a strong recommendation that this will be of clear benefit. It is a common-sense assumption of modern language *learning* that the best way of ensuring the development of the language is by going to the country and speaking it for a sustained period of time.

The stress here on *learning* is deliberate, for the same assumption does not hold for *teaching*. The common-sense assumption of modern languages teaching is that the immense emphasis on structure in the years prior to residence abroad is no longer required in periods of residence abroad. In relation to residence abroad, the lack of curriculum development has been seen as a positive virtue; indeed, it is usually assumed that the process of learning that occurs during that time requires little other than nebulous pastoral support.

'Being there' can mean two very different things. Implicit in the current arrangements is the supposition that languages will be learned by osmosis – simply as a result of being physically present in a place for a length of time and by being detached from 'home'. But throughout this book we have used the term 'being' as an active, agentic, conscious and creative category. 'Being', for us, requires understanding, engagement, enthusiasm, exchange, a willingness to risk openness to the other and to try out new steps.

Students, like anyone else, can, of course, 'be there' without 'being there', by hunting in packs and creating subcultures where only English is spoken. We are all familiar with the advice commonly given precisely not to spend time with one's compatriots in order to gain the most, linguistically and interculturally, from a period of residence abroad.

In this vein, some see the year abroad as a time when students should cut the umbilical cord and learn to stand on their own two feet; students will only really develop their language skills and learn about the local culture if they are immersed in it and have little or no contact with tutors back home. A parallel suggestion is that too much prior knowledge about the culture can detract from the experience. Finally, it is argued, it is not an academic's job to deal with pastoral issues or to provide information to parents or guardians, especially when the students are over 18.

There is some virtue in these views. They express respect for the students' need for freedom, space and immersion in language.

However, in terms of 'being intercultural' and 'being there' the only way to genuinely engage comes through the impulse to live in and through the language, an impulse that is social and comes from the creative desire to exchange, make meaning, connect. And this requires energy, time and a commitment to making sense of a life lived in a new 'provisional home' (Henderson, 1995), away from the distractions of other homes. It requires what Clifford terms 'dwelling-in-travel' (Clifford, 1997). It requires the agency of active engagement and exchange.

> *Real life has no authors save the persons who are already living it, and these persons, if they would build, must already dwell. Thus every act of building is but a moment in a continuous act of dwelling. This process [...] is one through which persons and their environments are reciprocally constituted, each in relation to the other. (Ingold, 1996: 116)*

It could seem as though time abroad is an interruption in this process of the continuous constitution of the self and at first sight the building of a 'provisional home' abroad does seem to confirm this. Curricularising residence abroad may appear to maintain the business of constituting the self through educational structures. However, the continuous act of dwelling abroad requires students to be freed up to be self-constituting, languaging, reflective actors and agents. This does not require an interruption to either languaging or being intercultural, merely an intensification of experience over reflection, and a different vantage point in the world of social relations.

However, what has been evident from research on the impact of residence abroad on students is that travel does not necessarily broaden the mind. Coleman's (2001) large-scale research on the subject has drawn some disturbing conclusions which many modern language professionals, in our experience, might wish to deny:

travel does not necessarily broaden the mind

A pilot study of 124 students of German undertaken in 1993 found that, compared to the British, the Germans are thought to be serious, unemotional, logical, efficient, hard-working, competent, not lazy or shy in the slightest, arrogant, confident, impatient, intolerant, ill-tempered, loud, and relatively unfriendly and ungenerous.

Returning students find the Germans more competent, more hard working, rather more efficient, less emotional etc. (Coleman, 1999: 152)

The mismatch between the sense of flourishing, excitement and sophistication that greets staff when their languaging students return from a stint abroad and research findings that suggest unreflective attitudes to experience, gives pause for thought. After all, one of the much-vaunted ideological reasons for studying modern languages today, alongside employability, is a common-sense belief that languages break down cultural barriers. Research that suggests the exact opposite is unlikely to be welcomed.

CUTTING THE CORDS

In a large-scale survey in 1998 (Coleman, 2001), teachers were asked whether preparation for residence abroad, such as linguistic, intercultural, academic and study skills etc., was included in degree programmes. For some three-quarters of the respondents courses on the politics of France or on contemporary Spain and classes with native language assistants fulfilled the role, and they answered affirmatively.

Now, most academics filling out statistical questionnaires in a performative environment are likely to answer 'yes', however wearily, to almost any question. And yet …

If I were asked these questions of my own courses I would give the same response, fully aware of the contingent nature of the climate in which I am labouring. Yes I do teach courses on contemporary Germany, yes the NLAs do talk about living in Germany and they even go so far as to help students fill out 'Scheine' and 'Überweisungsformulare'. No, of course I don't hold briefings for parents. The students are over 18 and are therefore legally responsible for themselves. And anyway, I've more than enough to do as things stand.

In discussions of a more critical nature with colleagues who share a creative passion for languages and their lives, my answers to such questions, contextualised more dialogically, will be different. No, what we give to students does not equip them in any way for the transformations that living encounters with others will effect in their lives. No, none of the courses I teach give experiential, creative or critical preparation to students to enable them to understand themselves and their encounters. No, I do not think the students are able to reflect on the constructedness of their images of other cultures and languages, and I do not think they realise that difference is always present and prior as a result of the images and education they have received thus far.

So, if the courses available fail to provide the kind of 'creative and experiential' foundations for life in the 'provisional home', what might such courses look like if they were available? How might we be equipped for anticipation, arrival, meetings and deepening encounters, working alongside and within different systems of culture, language and thought? What might the result be of such heightened awareness of language and life as opposed to specific knowledge of the federal structure of the *Bundestag*, the significance of 1968 or the role of contemporary French women writers?

Of course we are not suggesting here that the institutions of political life or key historical experiences are not important in a modern languages curriculum. But they go only part of the way. Disengaged from their place in the complex of social life and language, they represent only more elaborated 'background', more data removed from the lived experience. It is important that the time and space of residence abroad for the purpose of cultural learning and of languaging be both structured and reflexive, both flexible and free and informed. The map with which we travel provides the framework; the contours and nuances of the terrain become apparent only when we feel them beneath our feet.

What matters most, as Alain de Botton suggests, is not so much the *where* of travel, but the *why* and *how*. *Where*, after all, is easily explained; the student traveller will be sent to places where their languages are nationally recognised. Most modern languages students will find themselves in European countries – Spain, France, Germany etc. – or occasionally in their ex-colonies in Latin America, South East Asia, West Africa or the

Caribbean. The reality, however, is that the other is no longer conveniently and neatly located in specific geographical frames. Indeed, in an *age of liquid modernity* (Bauman, 2000) we may travel far only to find ourselves face to face with ... ourselves, and by contrast we may find stranger and less familiar worlds a block or two from home.

The experience of residence abroad can be a more intense and concentrated experience than language learning at home, though for the British colonials it was a more intense and concentrated experience of Britishness than of otherness. But ultimately it is a question of degree. It is perfectly possible to act as an intercultural being without going abroad.

There is more to cultural immersion than simply travelling, since the urban centres of a globalised world will almost invariably contain a familiar landscape of neon brand names and invocations of metropolitan utopias – 'Come to Marlboro Country' or Aya Napa. On the other hand, Spanish is the normal medium of the majority of the population living within a few miles of Hollywood, yet it is rarely heard except as the idiom of domestics in the representations of Los Angeles.

There is a fundamentally important point here. Intercultural being is not just about how you feel and perform vis-à-vis different countries. It is more profoundly about how one lives with and responds to difference and diversity. You cannot be truly intercultural and racist. Being intercultural is about much more than policies of tolerance. It is about living out the network of diverse human relationships – not just abroad, but down the road as well.

Academic rehearsal of the institutional history and culture, that is to say of teaching the *Bundestag* or French women writers, if it prepares the student traveller at all, anticipates only a formal connection, an encounter with the monuments of a society. It does not prepare for ways of living and being intercultural. It prepares for a museum visit, in specific ways, but not those that work to understand what actually is occurring when you chose to exhibit culture in museums. Beyond this, there may be an unspoken assumption that the components of daily life in the non-institutional sphere will be familiar or at least manageable with the tools of ordinary living at home. These are, paradoxically, precisely the tools and knowledges which are characteristically excluded from the classroom, as we saw in our previous chapter.

In Britain, the Residence Abroad Project (one of a number of similar projects) has evolved a 'taxonomy of the objectives of residence abroad' under the following five headings – Academic, Cultural, Linguistic, Personal and Professional (http://lara.fdtl.ac.uk/lara/). In our view, these distinct categories compound rather than resolve the problem of 'preparation'. Essentially, they are performance targets rather than cultural competences. Under 'Cultural Purposes', for example, 'insight into ways of life and institutions' are deemed capable of 'overlapping with academic objectives' – yet the section on 'Academic Objectives' simply sets out curricular requirements. The 'Intercultural Objectives' put forward begin commendably with 'Awareness of the relativity of cultures, including one's own', yet offer a final 'work-related' justification. Quite separate from these are the 'Linguistic Objectives', which simply rehearse the need to acquire linguistic instruments. 'Personal Objectives' make the usual nod in the direction of independence and self-reliance. Most telling perhaps, are the 'Professional Objectives', a now familiar list embracing 'transferable skills', 'objective-setting', 'time management' and all the other quasi-managerial attributes which betray the project's framing values.

The problem with this kind of technicist, performative and operational approach to the *why* of residence abroad is that it may make for easy measurement, but it does not make for fluent living:

> To reduce human action to a constellation of terms such as 'performance', 'competence', 'doing' and 'skill' is not just to resort to a hopelessly crude language with which to describe serious human endeavours. In the end, it is to obliterate the humanness in human action. It is to deprive human being of human being. (Barnett, 1994: 178)

If neither taxonomies of performance targets and objectives, nor laissez-faire non-approaches to residence abroad are sustainable ways of living in linguistic, cultural and intercultural fluency, how might our project here be reconciled, both in theory and in practice? How might we enable our students to develop fluent arts of dwelling-in-travel? How do we reconcile risk and danger, safety and scaffolded learning in such a way that creative and critical fluency can occur?

How to be fluent

Speaking a language actually equates to living in the language; the speech has to be to some purpose that is not contrived and contingent upon the classroom. It is perfectly possible for students to acquire a high degree of competence in written language, grammar and syntax. But for the skills of listening comprehension and the development of an ease or fluency with the spoken language – in other words, with the embodiment of language – there is no substitute for immersion, for the daily round and routine of speech acts. Languaging is living.

> *There is just nothing in the world to compare to this feeling. I'm in the middle of a conversation with a stranger I've met on a train. We are discussing the journeys we've both made. I'm not having to grasp for words, struggle for constructions, slip in hopeful anglicisms – it's just all there and complete. I feel alive, bright, happy and entirely trusting. I know that I'm fully present to my companion. And then the inevitable happens. I'm asked where I'm from. I'm feeling playful. 'Guess', I say, in German. And we begin an interesting tour of southern Germany. I'm not German I venture – helpfully – hugging myself with utter delight and pride. Austria – comes the reply. I'm not a native speaker, I allow. 'Dutch, Danish, Scandinavian...' 'English!' 'No way!' 'But your parents are German?' 'No – I've learnt it the hard way.' But you must have grown up here? No – I've been here since the autumn – I'm studying German. 'But you are completely fluent,' – ' Sie sprechen aber fliessend Deutsch.'*

To be 'fluent' in a language is a profound, living thing; it is far more than a technical skill. Yet it is also attainable, in a way that 'native-speakerdom' clearly is not. Second (third..., fourth...) languagers can never, of course, *be* native speakers, but they *can become* fluent (Kramsch, 1993).

> **Fluent:** *flowing easily; not settled, liable to change; graceful, easy; copious, coming easily, ready; expressing oneself quickly and easily. (Oxford English Dictionary)*

It is well known that for students a primary objective is to attain fluency in their chosen language – and that the period of residence abroad is the prime opportunity for them to seek fluency. But it is a matter of some importance, in the light of debates and discussions we have already referred to, that the preparation for the experience should include a discussion as to what fluency means.

Gaining a convincing local accent and a greater speed of delivery may seem to be the purpose; in fact these are technical achievements which are not the central experience. For the year abroad is much more an opportunity to develop skills and understandings that involve not merely immersion in the language but much more importantly, living and dwelling (Ingold, 1996). It is not just how a thing is said that changes in another cultural context, it is what is said, where and to whom; it is about what matters in that world, what needs to be clarified or concealed, what values prevail and what actions make sense there. When all aspects of life are lived in and through the language then the actions of everyday life and language together with new discursive domains attain an ease, a grace, they flow readily – that is, they may reach fluency.

To the language learner, however, fluency does not necessarily come easily; it is the product of work. It cannot be, as it is for the native speaker, a reflection of the naturalness of being within a language, and it is purposeless to disengage ease of expression (accent, speed of utterance and the rest) from being at ease within the cultural universe of that language, as if the first could be acquired as a technical skill without the development of the second – which is a cultural capacity.

As debates about theatrical performance have so often reiterated (Schechner, 1985), *ease* of perform- **fluent practice** ance does not come *easily*; it is the product of reflection, thought, identification and – most crucially – of *practice*. But it is critical that we clarify our use of the term 'practice'. We do not mean by it a mindless repetition of structures (or even a sophisticated repetition!) which presumes that perfection is achieved by mechanical reiteration. On the contrary, we understand 'practice' to embrace all those areas of reflection, cultural understanding, values – in short, of living in another language.

Overcoming awkwardness, halting pauses, breaks is not a simple matter of endlessly revisiting sound patterns, but of coming to recognise why and in what circumstances a thing is said, where and by whom. Fluency is the bedding of rehearsals – *practices* – into the body and material life. It is an accumulation of stories, connection, memory, material, history, routine and ritual, work and reflection. And that is learned, developed in the context of languaging as opposed to mere language acquisition. It cannot simply be absorbed through the ether; this cultural appropriation or assimilation is a conscious process, an act of will and desire.

In the real institutional context in which we work, of course, this throws up difficult, if largely material, issues. It is almost certainly convenient for teachers under pressure as well as accountants with a sharpened knife to encourage the 'thrown-into-the-world' approach. There are time and resource implications in this insistence on a preparatory process for being abroad – and one that addresses the philosophical contradictions of multiculturalism in a resolutely monocultural polity, of critical self-development in an instrumental and vocationalised educational milieu where everything is to benchmarked, weighed and measured. Diversity and difference, after all, make a poor national standard.

If fluency is the bedding of practices into the material self, then this will require encounters with the material world. Bedding down requires more than a passing, fleeting cognitive acquaintance with people or places. It takes us therefore beyond travel into a place where new lives can be built on the basis of exchange. This is what we understand to be at the heart of what Byram terms sojourning (Byram, 1997).

BEYOND TRAVEL

With many others speaking your language the Planet is not such a Lonely place. Not only do the guide books deliver the travellers to the same places the world over but the language of the guide books creates a sensation of linguistic homogeneity. The independent traveller armed with the divining rod of the guide books finds by charmed coincidence that many of the other travellers in the guest house/hostel/café speak his/her language. This is hardly surprising if the same guide in the same language has brought the travellers there in the first instance. (Cronin, 2000: 86)

Cronin is obviously suggesting that this controlled homogeneity of travel guided by *Lonely Planet* is limited – that there are other ways of travelling for which interpreters (physical or printed) cannot exist that are likely to prove more meaningful and creative. Languaging presumes a creative, unpredictable encounter – and in some sense, so should the period of residence abroad.

In our view, Byram's distinction between the tourist and the sojourner is a useful one in the discussion about developing intercultural communicative competence (ICC):

Although tourism has had major economic consequences, it is the sojourner who produces effects on a society which challenge its unquestioned and unconscious beliefs, behaviours and meanings, and whose own beliefs, behaviours and meanings are in turn challenged and expected to change. The tourist hopes for quite the opposite effect, first that what they have travelled to see will not change, for otherwise the journey would lose its purpose, and second that their own way of living will be enriched but not fundamentally changed by the experience of seeing others. (Byram, 1997: 1)

The two are not so easily or absolutely separate as this suggests, of course. Those sojourning abroad will at times adopt the role of tourist and move in and out of domains and discourses that are more fluid and complex than Byram suggests here. Nonetheless, the definition allows us to distinguish the different attitudes and responses that might inform travel and some of the shaping influences; class, for example is an important one. Byram, for instance, is clear that in the West, at least, sojourning has been either the activity of a social elite or 'of much larger groups of people of low social status, especially migrant labourers' (Byram, 1997: 1). We should recognise that the routes our students follow are largely those of the middle-class sojourner; they will be very unlikely to take the (usually clandestine) roads of the asylum seeker or the economic migrant. For a start, they are legal travellers whose journeys will be undertaken with the relevant documentation and in a degree of comfort, or usually so.

I'm quite childish, I always get excited when I see 'Willkommen in Deutschland' ('Welcome to Germany') on the road signs or in the airport, but I always feel a bit paranoid. Even when I know that I've got my passport, and that it's valid, I feel paranoid. And I always think they're going to find something on me, like drugs. Even though I don't take drugs and I don't have them on me, I always think that there's going to be something. When somebody asks for my passport and I've given it to them, I always feel a bit sort of like 'phew'. I feel quite.... sort of.... relieved

(Student interview, quoted in Wilkinson, 2002: 22)

May 1989: *We've just arrived at the Czechoslovak border. I'm here with a bus load of German pupils on a school trip to Prague. We've been waiting for a while. The driver has twelve cans of Coca Cola by the door which he hands over to the border guards. Our passports are collected and we sit quietly, somewhat apprehensively, waiting. Guards have guns. I'm the only one with a British passport. I'm the one called off the bus, questioned, searched, asked for additional papers.*

October 1999: And once again I'm telling this story, and others from my languaging experiences of being there, border crossing and living through the ferment of change that came in 1989 and 1990. My students are only seventeen and are learning about contemporary Germany culture not as experience but already as distant memory of news items, excited parents and teachers, as history. Raymond Williams' structure of feeling, Turner's liminality, all these concepts are made to come alive in my stories, their memories, video footage and the tales of those I invite to talk to this class.

The social justice issues that pertain to the question of the actual languages that inhabit school and university curricula also apply to countries deemed suitable for residence abroad. Just as we are not working hard to teach citizens to learn to live together through Urdu, Arabic, Turkish, Chinese, Gaelic, neither are we suggesting India, Africa, Iraq or Afghanistan as suitably experiential places for a learning sojourn. In addition, following on from anti-terrorism legislation, we see the diversity of our own campuses curtailed as we 'tighten up' our admissions procedures for those from countries we have listed as suspect. There are clearly some truths about the globalised, globalising world that we do not wish – in Byram's words – to see 'challenge our unquestioned and unconscious beliefs, behaviours and meanings'. Sojourning for the purposes of language learning should be safe. Heterogeneity is all very well in regulated doses.

Distance from home, therefore, is no longer a guarantee of otherness; nor is the fact that those encountered elsewhere exist under different legal systems or with different official languages. The fact is that even these are increasingly under pressure to globalise – though resistances may sometimes come from surprising quarters, – as for example the United States's refusal to accept the International Court of Justice. Yet there is difference in cultural patterns and in the structures of ordinary life. The key is to go beyond virtual travel – which can involve physical movement but not cultural translocation – into that experience of *being in, dwelling in*, another place, another culture.

It is clearly a key consideration that 'sojourning' abroad, for the academic institution in an age of litigation, should be safe. This is an entirely logical concern, given that our students are overwhelmingly young and for many of them this will be a first experience of independent travel. In a world of globalisation and resistance, of terrorism and counter-terrorism, of racism and xenophobia, of sexism and homophobia, the international milieu may often seem to be a deeply insecure place, full of unpredicatable risks and dangers. Sensible warnings and preparations are essential. These should not, however, be simply components of the institutional discipline, chapters in a manual of pre-digested information, or – even worse – presumptions embedded in the list of areas recommended by departments. It is as critical that the learner makes their assessment of risk and desirability – of *where* – on the basis of information informed by their own experience and judgement. For there is a crucial difference, a key line of division, between the physically dangerous and the culturally unfamiliar – where questions of *how* and *why* become paramount.

'Making safe' is a procedure which has very different implications in these two distinct cases. In the first, what is 'out there' is seen as threatening and the choice of place will necessarily arise from considerations of safety and the known. The more domesticated and familiar, the better. In the second, what is required is a deeper understanding rooted in a narrative of cultural distance in which overcoming is the core impulse. Without it, what appear to be simply instructions become instead an unspoken, inhibiting narrative of self and other as enemies.

Preparation and support: Problem solving

Alphabetical Index (starting after the Introduction)

Introduction: Accompanying partners: AIDS: Attack or assault: Children: Differences from the home: environment and student expectations: Documentation: Drugs: Food hygiene: Good information about country, region, town: Good information about the placement itself: Harassment at work: Health and security issues: experience of returners and L2landers

Illness: Insurance Illness: Precautionary measures: Information about the new setting: the basis: Keeping staff informed (in home and host countries): Learning about cultural difference: Link person abroad: role and location Link person: consultations Link person: Courtesy Medical help abroad: Mental illness or depression Parents: briefing Parents: homesickness Parents: up-to-date addresses and contact numbers: Partners and special friends: Partners at home: Partners abroad: Personal safety: Phone/Fax: Preparation for independence: Problems: Protection against theft: Reflecting on the experience: Seeking help abroad (see also link person abroad): Sensible groundrules for safety: Sensible precautions: Socialising and integration: Staff visits: Theft: Insurance: Victims of Theft: Video conference: Virtual visit and contacts: E-mail

Source: http://www.lang.ltsn.ac.uk/languagesbox.aspx (2003).

FIGURE 7.1 *Residence Abroad: hyperlinks for students, staff and parents.*

To take an example, the Residence Abroad section of the LTSN Subject Centre for languages, linguistics and area studies contains the hyperlinks for students, staff and parents shown in Figure 7.1.

We are indeed 'inundated with advice', as de Botton states (2002). Thus portrayed residence abroad is located within the discourse of safety, not the discourse of experience, learning and teaching or sojourning, let alone that of human flourishing. Before students even leave their home university this site suggests all manner of potential horrors and precautions. In cultures of blame and of risk assessment, such a development is hardly surprising and is perhaps even to be welcomed as a small, sensible dimension to experiential learning. The problem, of course, is that such a taxonomy of problems and potential pain can also begin to determine the kinds of narratives that then accompany student experiences. Students are already predisposed to expecting homesickness, difficulty, danger, even death.

This is a fundamental dimension to all experience of travel, as the anthropologist Nelson Graburn pointed out in his work on departures (Graburn, 1978: 22):

> In spite of the supposedly happy nature of the occasion, personal observation and medical reports show that people are more accident-prone when going away; are excited and nervous, even to the point of feeling sick … a symbolic death… is implied in phrases such as 'Parting is such Sweet Sorrow', or even 'To part is to die a little'. Given media accounts of plane, train and automobile accidents, literally as tourists we are not sure that we will return. Few have failed to think at least momentarily of plane crashes and car accidents or, for older people, dying on vacation. Because we are departing ordinary life and may never return, we take out additional insurance, put our affairs in order, often make a new will, and leave behind 'final' instructions concerning the watering, the pets, and the finances. We say goodbye as we depart and some even cry a little, as at a funeral, for we are dying symbolically.

Where to go and how to do so merge in the safety advice – a certain disposition for action is already created here that uses the tools of safety and security, not of risk and danger. Again, both the 'health and safety' lobby and the 'sink or swim' lobby have valid points here. We cannot suggest to students that they take on whatever risks that may come through travel to and residence in specific countries unless they are carefully given the tools, support and experiences that will prepare them for such encounters.

We have suggested a response based on an idea of 'critical being' – and it is important to reiterate that we understand that as 'being in the world', as theory and practice. In the same sense, the knowledge of cultural otherness is bedded in the body and lived experience of the learner. Learning after all is not about the absorption of pre-existing truths but about testing and exploring ideas in and against reality, and then reflecting upon the process. In many academic subjects – medicine, engineering, geography, anthropology and education for example – this dynamic relationship between theory and application is structured into the curriculum. Students regularly experience recursive learning, leaving the classroom to apply their learning to practical ends, returning to the classroom to reflect and ground their experience back into the theory through fieldtrips, placements, clinics and so on. In modern languages residence abroad has long been understood as an applied dimension standing *outwith* the curriculum and, until relatively recently, has not been subject to the kinds of rigorous preparation and recursive reflection that are part of the applied aspects of other disciplines. Such preparation has now long been a feature of courses in anthropology and in geography, for instance, where a different set of social justice issues pertain.

LANGUAGING AS ETHNOGRAPHY

Of course, if modern languages have as their principal purpose the reception and assimilation of a canon of texts representing timeless and universal values, the filter of experience is entirely unnecessary. If the text is the sole landscape through which the learner is expected to travel, then all encounters are predictable and resolved by the application of general, abstract rules. If, however, the learning of modern languages is at every stage an encounter and an engagement with the living world of that language, then different approaches are needed.

One of the most exciting and radical developments in modern languages in the UK in recent years is comprehensively described in Roberts et al's *Language Learners as Ethnographers* (Roberts et al., 2001). This happy research is the outcome of the highly successful *Ealing Ethnography Project* that ran at Thames Valley University during the 1990s. Members of the modern languages section became ethnographers, worked alongside anthropologist colleagues and developed a programme around tenets drawn from anthropology, ethnography, cultural studies, linguistic anthropology, ethnography of communication etc., in order to demonstrate that language learners can become ethnographers, particularly during periods of residence abroad.

There is neither the space, nor indeed the need, to repeat the detail of the Ealing Project here. Numerous examples are given in *Language Learners as Ethnographers* (Roberts et al., 2001) and on the Learning and Residence Abroad website of developing curricula for residence abroad, student ethnography projects, home ethnographies, ethnographic writing and dense description. The stories of the staff-training element interweave with those of student voices and a sense of excitement and passion for new ways of being language-and-culture-learners – what we are terming languagers, not just linguists – is communicated strongly through the book. Its authors make a strong case for the kinds of integrated under-standings of and multidisciplinary approaches to language and culture that we are advocating here.

> *Ethnography can be broadly described as the study of a group's social and cultural practices from an insider's perspective. It is both a method involving the detailed observation and description of particular forms of behaviour and a written (sometimes audio-visual account) based on social and cultural theories [...]*
>
> *The attraction of ethnographic principles and practice for language learning lies in this combination of the experiential and intellectual which are so often presented as dichotomous in language programmes. (Roberts et al., 2001: 3)*

So what ethnography provides is a *network of bridges* between areas of the modern languages curriculum that have otherwise been stand-alone: language and background; language and literature; speech and writing; application and theory; residence abroad and study at home; literature and culture; experience and reflection. Just as languages have long been understood and used by anthropologists as key ethnographic tools so ethnography becomes a key tool in the process of languaging. At the same time, language is itself the object of reflection and exploration

Ethnography provides more than just a tool. Once the leaner picks up the 'tool' her being is extended and changed and she will create connections and conversations, in and through the medium of language and as both linguistic and ethnographic translator. In *Living the Ethnographic Life* Dan Rose (1990) maintains that ethnography is about real-life connections and bridges made between people in relationships. It is not about cognitive schema-connecting, but about people meeting in human encounter and in ways which may change the way they see the world.

I'm reflecting, in the final session of the year, with my honours option class. They are all dressed up and have come to class excited and nervous, ready to act out what they have learned. They have been using language and ethnography through the course. It's been their first encounter with ethnographic method and at times its been very bumpy for them. They have constantly tried to make their data quantitative and scientific. This is hardly surprising in such a 'scientific' age. Some of their German 'informants' have come along to watch what they have produced. It's lovely seeing students adopting debating roles and dressing up to be Mary Douglas, Kay Milton, Pierre Bourdieu and Karl Marx. The course has been all about 'rubbish' and what Germans do with it. Some of them are carrying black dustbin liners – they have literally brought their rubbish to class.

They have changed a lot since the course began. Back in October we had a session where we brainstormed all the ways in which Germany is 'green'. They were full of knowledge and excited to know so much from their own experience. This course was going to work with this knowledge, and often against the grain of this knowledge, through encounter with critical arguments and through exposure to ethnography.

The surprise for them all was the encounter with themselves. They were set the simple task of finding Germans in Glasgow and talking to them about environmentalism. We had some really tough classes when they were bringing their findings back for discussion. 'How dare they think the things they do about how we live?', 'why are they so negative about us?' These were, as always, the precarious points of learning, where the relationships and encounters had only developed reaction, not understanding. But as the action of reading, talking and time did its work I was privileged to see the fruits of their learning and to see them become languagers. 'The moral order informs the social order', 'dirt is matter out of place', 'some of this behaviour is caused by grid-group patterns of social behaviour', ' there is a problem in this idea because it is deterministic', they wrote.

When they were writing their essays I was exhausted. They were constantly beating down my door, borrowing my books, trying out ideas. They were intensely involved in the process of understanding the very complex array of data they had collected. Their bodies were excited bodies, wanting more, wanting to share what they were discovering. This was the hard work of being intercultural – of finding their understandings of the world turned upside down and becoming people who could articulate an understanding of this transformation, through their knowledge. In order to understand the learning process myself I'd asked them to tape record some of their group discussions of theory and data and I'd been amazed at the sheer conceptual mess. At times, it seemed, there was nothing to build with, but bit by bit, by having time and space to talk, to think, to read and to wait, they distilled their thinking and became intercultural beings.

Roberts et al. point out that the same conditions as we have described earlier pertaining to non-preparation for the year abroad also pertained in the field of anthropology until the 1960s:

Up until the 1960s, anthropology students went out into the field with little more advice than to take a notebook and pencil with them. Precisely how ethnographic study was to be conducted and then written remained a mysterious process. The methods of participant observation, interviewing and analysis are now the subject of numerous methods books and it is increasingly evident that doing ethnography is an enormously skilful task, involving the whole social person. (Roberts et al., 2001, 38)

Their point – and ours – is not to present anthropological and ethnographic dimensions to language learning as 'the answer' – but rather to argue for their incorporation into the formal and informal structures of modern language teaching in higher education as a way of reimagining and enlivening the subject.

Hannah Arendt addresses these issues with a characteristically pithy term. She emphasises that this critical sojourning cannot be conducted from a detached point of view; instead, she sees this manner of learning as 'training the imagination to go visiting'. The point here, of course, is twofold – first that the development of critical understanding requires movement in the world – and secondly that that mode of travel should be attended by the imagination, the exploration of possibilities for the traveller as well as the world travelled. It may be argued that this is too political, too subjective a procedure – our point is that no learning of language can be conducted in isolation from living through it.

OTHER LIVES, OTHER WORLDS

In the past scholarship in modern languages, as we have seen, has been concerned with ways of becoming a 'cultured' person, with knowledge of 'great European literature' and languages. Research has striven for depth, digging deeply into literary aesthetics and linguistic constructions for detail. Oeuvre, authors and ages were mined constantly for their gems, and, we hope, as we discuss in the next chapter, this attention to texts may continue. However, this form of work may be termed 'epistemological heaviness'. It is work which requires a density of knowledge and was long assessed in final examination papers by attention to an outward display of factual knowledge – such as dates, overview of works, discussion of reception, etc. For a 'cultured' age, as we have discussed earlier, such an ideology of knowledge is understandable. However, in an age when fluent communication requires much more than knowledge management, when the 'epistemological heaviness' of the modern era now finds itself parodied in popular culture in the form of *Trivial Pursuits, Who Wants to be a Millionaire?* and the pub quiz, there is a need, we are arguing, for an ontological rebalancing. Communication gets stuck in heavy 'cultured' knowledge. Communication requires lightness.

We do not wish to say here that we are, in a simplistic sense, 'against' detailed, careful and rigorous research, teaching and learning. These are vital to the real work of developing languagers and intercultural beings with a thirst for understanding, through knowledge assessed critically and carefully. We do wish to avoid the trap of students simply learning facts about cultures or authors. We are against the kinds of fixed, heavy knowledges, such as those found in the work of Hofstede or Hall (Hall and Hall, 1990; Hofstede, 1984) which suggest that 'Germans will behave like this because they live in low context cultures' or that 'The Chinese will have this communication style because they live in collectivist societies.'

These ways of teaching and learning about cultures weigh heavily and build barriers to communication by creating the 'problem of culture'. We are also not wed to the ideology of 'liquid modernity'. Under ideologies of flexibility, communication, lightness of travel, heavier, time-bound aspects of life – such as community, relationships, etc. – things which are inherently messy and which often require life-long engagement – become equally problematic. For us, languaging, epistemologically, has both heavy and light qualities precisely because it is about the way knowledge is worn to become a part of the self, of intercultural being, dwelling-in-travel.

Scaffolded learning, an openness to using theory and practice from anthropology, ethnography, cultural geography etc., a preparation for risk, can make possible the development of a different habitus in language learners – that of languaging (Walker, 2002). We return again, to underscore this point to Bourdieu and to his notion of agency as the embodied and bodily living out of knowledges gained through experience in the world as a learned disposition for action. In other words, through all manner of human and material encounters our learners engage with the world in myriad ways. To work with these encounters, with the feel of engagement, to enable learners and teachers to dig continuously into the places where they live out difference and connection, puzzlement and understanding, is to develop the languaging *habitus*, is, in Bourdieu's terms again, to understand epistemology as ontology – knowing becomes being.

Languaging in the context of residence abroad is about living, or being in what Habermas terms a *Lebenswelt*. The *Lebenswelt* is produced out of the dialectic between system and the struggle to become or create a 'life-world' that is characterised as dialogical, reflective, shared. It is in the life-world that 'social and economic structures interpenetrate with action and consciousness' (Pusey, 1987: 58). Barnett draws on Habermas to capture 'a view of human being located neither in operations and technique, nor in intellectual paradigms and disciplinary competence but in the total world experience of human beings' (Barnett, 1994: 178).

The kinds of competences – or perhaps more accurately arts of dwelling-in-travel – that Barnett's synthesis suggests can be developed through expanded understandings of the crucial role of living away from the familiar, either here or abroad. Teaching can be rethought as a practice that has mobility and fluidity at its core, that encourages students to notice, describe, analyse and reflect on their own sense of identity and difference, that shows the systems and structures that are at work in any form of communicative action. It can provide an environment for the sharing and exploration of transformative experiences when they do not just speak another language fluently, but dance and sing in it, as ethnographers, anthropologists, as readers and writers of text. In that shared narrative, the 'banking' knowledges incorporated in the authoritative teacher can give way to the creative knowledges born of a reshaping of the world and the self.

All of this is not just a utopia, but is achievable. It is demonstrated by the Ealing Project – and the proliferations of such modes of teaching that have followed in its wake. Such a rethinking of residence abroad and an attention to the central questions of where, why and how to travel and dwell do not threaten the traditional practices of modern languages.

Rather, with the emphasis on methods and on writing in anthropology, the concern with questions of cultural representations, they create spaces in curricula that may open fresh ontological perspectives onto studies of 1968, French women writers or the *Bundestag*.

> *Human concerns, aesthetic sensitivities, collective will-formation, action-based understanding, value choices; these are indicative of the much wider range or resources of understanding which we might wish to marshal in the life-world. (Barnett, 1994: 180)*

We have addressed in this chapter how these arts may be developed and recognised in the journey to the other world. That journey, however, does not end with the return – or should not if modern languages is to be more than mere survival in foreign places. On the contrary, that engagement with the life-world of other cultures should inform and continue into a transformed culture, a place of continuing and extending narrative, a place as much owned and shaped by the learning as the street encounters of the time abroad. In that sense, texts are spaces for anthropological encounters as rich, as important and as unexpected as those that should have occurred in the phase of travel, sojourning and visiting ourselves and others.

Key references

Barnett, R. (1994) *The Limits of Competence: Knowledge, Higher Education and Society.* Buckingham: Open University Press.

Clifford, J. (1997) *Routes: Travel and Translation in the Late Twentieth Century.* Cambridge, MA: Harvard University Press.

Coleman, J. (2001) 'What is residence abroad for? Intercultural competence and the linguisitic, cultural academic, personal and professional objectives of student residence abroad', in R. Di Napoli, L. Polezzi and A. King (eds), *Fuzzy Boundaries? Reflections on Modern Languages and the Humanities.* London: CILT, pp. 121–40.

Kramsch, C. (1993) *Context and Culture in Language Teaching.* Oxford: Oxford University Press.

Roberts, C., Byram, M., Barro, A., Jordan, S. and Street, B. (2001) *Language Learners as Ethnographers.* Clevedon: Multilingual Matters.

Websites

http://www.lang.ltsn.ac.uk/resources/guidecontents.aspx
http://lara.fdtl.ac.uk/lara/intercultural1.html
http://www.hum.port.ac.uk/slas/rapport/
http://www.lancs.ac.uk/users/interculture/

Encyclopedia

Byram, M. (2000) *Routledge Encyclopedia of Language Teaching and Learning.* London and New York: Routledge.

8

Resonant reading

Imagination has a history. There are changing and conflicting interpretations of what it is and of its value. Imagination also has a structure, at once grammatical and historical, in the tenses of the past, present and future. (Williams, 1983: 259)

There were ten people in the first-year Hispanic Studies tutorial; we were meeting to discuss an early novel by García Márquez.

I asked whether anyone had any questions about the book, and one student asked what exam questions they might expect. Rather than answering directly, I asked them what issues they might want to address if they had been setting essay topics. Jane suggested 'something on style'.

I wondered what they understood by 'style' and suggested that we might go round the room and get each person to mention a book they had read and how they would describe its style. Natasha talked about Hardy's Mayor of Casterbridge, Emily brought up Angela Carter and her magical realism, Michelle talked about Toni Morrison's Beloved, Suzie described Grassic Gibbon's Sunset Song (which she wasn't all that impressed by), Matthew asked whether the James Bond novels had a style at all or were simply formulaic. Everyone had a book to suggest.

Any other suggestions for essays? Something about Macondo (the fictional setting for most of García Márquez's novels) perhaps? How did they read this fictional world, or understand its relationship to the material reality? We went round the room again – Narnia, Animal Farm, science fiction were offered as examples. The discussion drifted towards the differences between allegory and metaphor.

This was a randomly chosen first-year tutorial group on a Tuesday afternoon.

And they say that students don't read any more.

HOLY WRIT

In the heavy handbook of bibliographies, course descriptions, examination regulations and instructions which are the student's Baedeker through a year of work, the word 'Text' – starkly emboldened – sits at the head of pages. Where literature or the literary model has provided the framework for explorations of language-in-action, the 'Text', thus underlined, is authoritative and sacrosanct. It is more than the piece of continuous writing to examine and be examined on; it is the holy writ of quality, the exemplar of aesthetic achievement, the embodiment of the great work. The term 'canon' has particularly deep resonances. It represents not simply the weight of literary achievement; it seems to have an existence somewhere *outside* time which gives its components a universal voice and an exemplary role. The text exists, unassailable, in its own right. Shakespeare, Dante, Calderón, Racine – were these not always, from time immemorial, the recognised emblems of national expression? The truth, of course, is otherwise; each age has acknowledged, or refused to acknowledge, *its* Dante, *its* Shakespeare.

These are not the only sacred texts. In a postmodernist variant, philosophers or critics may come to occupy the sanctified chairs; in a feminist canon, Virginia Woolf may replace Shakespeare or Sarraute replace Racine. Universality is an oddly contingent category. But the point, of course, is not the content of each list of sacred texts, but the very notion of a consecrated canon. It may be argued that the concept has been intellectually challenged in recent years (Eagleton, 2000). Yet much of the practice of teaching texts in modern languages still rests firmly on that foundation.

The authority of these works and their pride of place in the curriculum may appear to students to be beyond question. But if we ask them what they think the canon is *for*, or what it actually represents, they become perplexed. The answer may be that they *have been chosen*, and that must be because they say universal things in universal ways; thus their intellectual authority is established not in the act of reading, but in some earlier process. These texts are somehow 'best', but 'best for what'? It is significant that there is no subject of the act of choosing; the voice here is passive. But how often are the philosophical underpinnings of these lists ever made explicit or addressed? In Spanish departments around the globe, for instance, *La Celestina* has alternated with *Don Quixote* in an incontestable round for as long as anyone can remember.

Until very recently neither the reasons for their inclusion nor for the exclusion of unnamed others have been open for debate. This is more than an evasion for reasons of institutional convenience (though it is also that – a denial of the right to ask why or for what). It embeds the criteria of selection in an unassailable aesthetic fortress the key to whose massive doors is available only to those who have the secret, the password, the earned right of access. And, with a blindingly circular logic, that right is earned by the assimilation and transmission of the canon.

In some literature departments, aspects of popular culture are introduced and acknowledged. Yet they carry their mark of origin with them always, and are addressed either as a factor in the high/low culture binary, or they are as it were 'rescued', recovered from their unjust fate and reconstructed as great works in their own right. Carlos Monsivais, the Mexican cultural critic, calls one of his extraordinary books on popular culture *Entrada libre* or 'Free Admission', precisely because, for him, popular culture is defined by its democratic access, its availability to those not possessed of formal criteria of judgement or validation. The irony of this relatively recent inclusion of works or texts from popular or mass culture is that their inclusion does not, curiously enough, challenge the ideology of the authoritative text – but on the contrary, expands and adjusts the canon in order to legitimate it.

I'm sitting in the exam hall with my first-year German literature examination paper in front of me. I've loved the course this year, loved the literature, loved the chance to read and think, though I've never really had a sense of how to do this or what 'reading' actually means. I've worked really hard for these exams. I always do – methodically going over notes, re-reading passages, learning quotations, reading crits. I have no idea whether this is the way I should work or not. I have a list of themes to work from and am prepared to answer on a range of texts. I'm hoping for something on Goethe. The question that makes my heart beat with excitement and challenge and stimulation is this: 'First-year undergraduate students are not yet of sufficient maturity to read Goethe's poetry. Discuss.' I brought anger and passion to my sustained argument in response. This question touched me deeply, made me determined. I answered of course in the affirmative. I now know that a good critic can answer any question from any position and today I probably could make a good case the other way. But for me my life had been enriched and worlds had been opened, my imagination had gone travelling, so how could I possibly agree with such an outrageous suggestion. So what that essay did, scribbled furiously in the three hours I had for the paper, was demonstrate as best I could, that Goethe's poetry had a place on the first-year syllabus.

There may be from to time works conceived in the realm of popular culture which prove to possess deep hidden veins of aesthetic value; buried beneath the surface of Eugene Sue or operetta or comics or horror films may lie coded messages whose import is as universal as Joyce or Proust or Rabelais. These are then subjected to the intervention of the heavy toolbox of aesthetic criticism and relocated within the canon, harmless marauders from another world that are soon domesticated, tamed by literary criticism.

What does the toolbox contain? In its first compartment are the general criteria, the 'standards' of judgement against which any given work may be measured; these general categories might include 'taste', 'sensibility' and 'artistry'. In the drawer beneath are the individual instruments with which to deconstruct these classifications – 'language', 'symbolism', 'plot', 'character'. Together they provide a template derived from an unnamed series of prior works which have, apparently, thrown up the necessary categories. In reality they provide a ranking method, and a recommended mode of reading – what Williams describes as a 'theory of consumption', a guide to reading (Williams, 1977).

A third compartment in the toolbox may well contain a number of recommended approaches to questions of literary production – these include 'biography', 'genre' and the methodologies of micro-description. But what all kits have in common is their purpose – the production of a canon, a hierarchy of excellence against which to judge any new aspirant to the hallowed ground. And so much of the work of judgment is little more than an assessment of suitability. The erection of new canons – many discourse theories, for example, or classifications of works in popular culture – does not offer an alternative *method*, only an alternative content.

In these circumstances, the journey through literature becomes a kind of paper chase, a search for those clues whose accumulation may eventually yield the whole password. The students are detectives, seeking out a hidden logic, a pattern whose beauty and elegance will eventually be revealed after some time spent flailing around in a world of chaos. And the whole process of exploration is conducted under the keen eye of a teacher whose authority is affirmed by their obvious possession of the final answer; they are initiates, the learners mere aspirants. Probably the best we can expect is an enigmatic nod or a wink as we are 'hot' or 'cold' in our closeness to a revealed (or revealable) truth.

> Jorge Luis Borges, the great Argentine writer of 'fictions', plays cruel games with such expectations – though he was a believer in one of many great traditions. In Death and the Compass, his extraordinarily well-read detective patiently sifts the clues left by a murderer who is clearly a theologian of profound understanding. Eventually the detective is able to reproduce the complex thought patterns of the pursued criminal and to anticipate his next thought. Yet he is wrong the first time, having discerned a possible, but not the only, pattern. He succeeds at the second attempt – when he finds himself in the exact spot for a murder at the exact time of its commission. The victim, of course, is himself. Yet it is not that he has finally reached the truth, only a truth arbitrarily closed by his own death.

This perception of the literary quest, subject to ironic, playful destruction by Borges, is also present in Calvino's *If on a winter's night a traveller* and in the multiple charts to unknown islands that Umberto Eco has uncovered. The text, then, is a given; it is authoritative and unique. Its links with other texts are based on genre or period, broad framing categories which are by definition inflexible and formal. *Teaching* such a text is no more than revelation.

The problem, once again, is in the relationship between the self-transformation involved in learning and the openness of the object of that learning, its permeability. If the Text is not available for languaging, for embedding in the whole social world of the reader, it is just there for discovery and revelation, the object is closed and the process (to the extent that there is one) entirely one of passive assimilation. Reading is just the acquisition of facts, not a creative process of appropriation.

By way of contrast, we might disinter the outmoded idea of 'literary appreciation', with its implicit acknowledgement that the teaching of literature, at its best, is a shared experience of reading. It can be languaging as a reliving of the pleasure of discovering excitement and passion and personal revelation. With barely a farewell, such notions have been consigned to a realm of amateurishness, of reading as an activity of displacement or a mere social grace, while the far more serious business of deconstruction or practical criticism takes over. As Eagleton (2000) has commented in relation to the learning of Shakespeare, the literary and the critical canons become straitjackets, impeding access beyond the masterworks. Indeed, acquisition of knowledge about the key texts is specifically distinguished from developing a more inclusive critical apparatus. There is no link made between the learning of Shakespeare and an exploration of wider human concerns; it is as if the insights encapsulated in the endless array of books of quotations from the Bard had acquired the status of holy books. They are the sacred texts which are the fetish items of 'learning' defined, in a wholly circular way, as the accumulation of knowledge of these texts.

If our criteria for the process of learning are exchange and engagement – in a word, **exchange and engagement** being – then it manifestly cannot happen where understanding is in a sense only the acquisition of the wisdom of others, together with the regulations and criteria embodying that understanding. In this context any discussion of value, meaning or significance will serve only to reinforce those externalities and *distance* the learner from the text while simultaneously promising access and revelation. Perhaps it is time to restore concepts like 'pleasure' and 'appreciation' to an honoured place in the curriculum – even if that seems at first to negate the idea of studying texts as opposed to living them.

Our starting point is this. Can the text offer an opportunity for the learner to move from a *study* of literature, whose purpose is a knowledge *about* literature as defined and ringfenced, to the *use* of literature in the process of developing critical self-awareness – a step in a process of intercultural being (Carter and McRae, 1996)? In this process-centred experience, value becomes value *for*, meaning becomes meaning *for* and so on. Can the encounter with the text add value to life, rather than additional skills to an employment portfolio?

'What do you think the father is like, in this play?' I ask my first-year class.

When I ask this question I know that it will be met with silence, hesitation, something approaching fear and several 'don't knows'. But it is still a good question. There is something of a tussle going on, in this question, between me and them. They want me to give them the answer. I am determined to show them they have answers themselves. Sometimes it is just so much easier to give in, to pour forth a monologue on role, characterisation, interaction, language. I try a different tack. 'OK, if you had a line of men outside this door to audition for the role, what do you think the father would look like physically?

'He's small, kind of fat, wears built-up shoes, medallion man'...'What else?' I push...'keep going...' ...'What about his face...does he have a beard?' ...'No'...'OK, so how do you know...' 'He's shaving in the opening scene...' ...'OK'...'So what does his skin look like ...' 'A bit red, stubbly' ...'Go back to that scene where he's shaving, what's happening?' ...'He cuts himself...' ...'Why?'...'he's too stingy to put on the light...' ...'So what does his face look like...' '...shaving cuts, plaster...' And so it goes on and we build up a vivid picture of a man that none of them like.

ONLY CONNECT

The text that is defined as *literature* lives within a narrow and defined role, constrained by *unlocking the puzzle* genre, enclosed by period, chained, unchained then rechained to movements or schools. Further, it has been singled out, canonised and isolated even from its most obvious fellows. In these terms it is made distinct from all other texts, descriptively and by dint of a kind of graded aesthetic judgement. The results of reading in this way are *teaching* outcomes – the student will unlock the puzzle whose secrets are already known to the teacher. The method of interpretation is given and reaffirmed, and the method as well as the inescapable conclusions of its application are passed on to a new generation. Discovery, such as it is, can lead only along pre-established routes (though sometimes with permitted diversions and lay-bys) towards a 'correct', previously concealed and above all *examinable* conclusion. The achievement is in the ending, the culmination of the search in the revelation.

The consequence in the modern languages classroom is the confirmation of the line of authority, the dependence of the learner upon the teacher. Truth, meaning, pleasure, emotion all lie with the twin authority figures, the author and the teacher. This is what Freire (1998) calls 'banking education' – the accumulation of existing cultural capital in a credit account. Interest is accrued as accumulation progresses. From the perspective of the teacher it is secure, safe, unchallenging. It is the very definition of the 'linear, serialist' method.

And it is the polar opposite of that creative meaning-making experience that makes of us all open travellers in a world of cultures. This process has been described, a little forbiddingly, as 'a connectionist rather than a linear and serialist form of meaning-making practice' (Carter and McRae, 1996: xiii). It is a process at once creative, risky and almost entirely unpredictable. It cannot be otherwise. Our argument is that being intercultural implies the engagement of the imagination. It represents journeys into imaginary worlds and translated worlds and in the company of the imagination of others, past and present. It is a journey whose consequences and impacts will both continue and parallel the real-life journeys of actually 'being there' and languaging discussed in the previous chapter. And it is one that is no less exciting, subject to sudden leaps and changes or full of unexpected encounters. Literature, far from being marginalised as a 'useless ornament', should be central to learning to be intercultural.

It's the last class of the course, the class before their assignments are due. The title I have set them is difficult; it is open-ended, and it is not immediately clear which lecture or text or set of ideas it relates to, out of all those they've been offered through the course. There are no right answers, I tell them. There may be the need to quibble with some facts, but at the end of the day the best answers are the best arguments – and, 'no, I will not tell you what I think'.

Throughout the course I have been raising questions, delighting in the chance to be unpredictable, to tell stories and to unsettle. I have let the students know that I am genuinely enjoying the chance to teach them. A colleague stopped me in the street, just after the course began, to tell me how refreshing the students have found this, how they had talked with her about what I had said to them and what I had done in their language class. I love it when these stories return. I love the way they are embellished. When the stories fail to return to me I know I am tired:

It is through the fictions and stories we tell ourselves and others that we live the life, hide from it, harmonise it, canalise *it, have a relationship with it, shape it, accept it, are broken by it, redeem it, or flow with the life. (Okri, 1997: Aphorism 29)*

There is a perpetual creativity involved in storytelling. Stories make people more creative, negatively or positively. (Okri 1997: Aphorism 61)

I put the students into small groups, the title on the board, and just get them to write down all the things that they believe are problems. After about fifteen minutes, during which the room hums with debate, I pull all the problems together into a list on the board, affirming each, teasing out more, pushing them for precision – we are all really working hard, with focus, concentration and laughter.

'So, what do you think?' I throw the question back at them. More of an exchange. 'Yes, that's one way of looking at it. What feels right to you?' More struggle for meaning, for a place to stand. And then, in the silence, a gently exasperated voice that is open and accepting, not hostile or resigned; 'Oh please, just give us a spoon.' And we all laugh.

These students had 'got it'. They had the answer at this moment and in this way. This is what learning looked liked here.

Once the laughter had died down, I said: 'Let me tell you something about my life. When I have your essays I will take them home and mark them. The phone will be ringing, I will have a million other things to do, I will want to go out to meet friends, see a film, enjoy a walk, dig the allotment. My partner will want to cook with me, clean with me, shop with me. Your job, with your essays, is to write for me in ways that hold me, that stop me getting up half-way through reading to put on the kettle. Your job is to make your argument so compelling as to grip me, entice me, delight me, or even, repel me, but to keep me reading. If all I read are forty bored versions of my own position, written in poor prose, badly presented, then I will not sense your authority and I will not be held by your voice. Find something you believe to be true and exciting in answer to these questions and then give it to me straight between the eyes.'

And what were their essays like in the end? They were rich, diverse, vibrant, engaged. They held my attention.

In his *Beyond All Reason: Living with Ideology in the University*, Ronald Barnett writes of institutional energy and of ways of working with, through and around the pernicious ideologies that have come to dominate life in the university:

> *Ideologies are quietened by new counter-energies being released on campus. As with 'recovery', 'release', too, has a dual structure. It speaks of virtuous energies having previously been thwarted and of creative efforts that may weaken pernicious ideologies. The acts of releasing virtuous energies have, therefore, an end and a beginning all at once: they end barriers to institutional and personal growth and they begin the spreading of institutional energy. (Barnett, 2003: 176–7)*

Laughing – Barnett speaks of 'smiles' – is one of the releases for creative energy in these classrooms. A recovery of ways of being forgotten by the students since childhood, a boundary crosser, enjoyable contempt for less wholesome ways of learning, a place where movement and light become lively and playful.

The 'connectionist' method, as we may call it, begins from what is recognisably a 'text', a work of literature, in the formal sense; yet here it is a point of departure for a series of reflections that lead back into memory and experience, and produce a cultural practice. A good reader, after all, is not only capable of analysing and interpreting but also of relating literature to life. It might be argued, and often is, that only great literature, inspired and original, is able to awaken this exercise of connection; hence its pride of place among texts. It may be the case that some texts are more complex, more profound, more daring in their exploration of the unknown, more 'defamiliarising' than others. In a learning context, however, those 'objective' criteria are not what determines the value of a text. The question to be asked is 'What will my students get from the text? How will they change as a result?' (Carter and McRae, 1996).

POETRY UNDER PINE TREES

> *Ein kleines Haus, unter Bäumen am See*
> *vom Dach steigt Rauch.*
> *Fehlte er, wie trostlos dann wären*
> *Haus, Bäume und See*

A small house, under trees, by a lake
smoke rising from the roof
If it were lacking, how desolate
the house, trees and lake.

Alison (having read poem out loud): 'So your task for next week is to learn this poem by heart. I suggest you write it out on a card and recite it to yourselves at the bus stop, or waiting to go in to lectures, or at night. I'll be testing you on reciting it in the tutorial.'

The following week: The students all, hesitantly, recite the poem. I write it up on a white board. 'I'm going to do something a bit different this week and I need you to take a few risks with me. This won't be like your normal classes but I hope you will be able to see the point of it. Right. I'd like you to close your eyes and listen while I read the poem to you. You all know this by heart now, but I'd like you to try and picture the scene for me. I'll read the poem a couple of times' ... 'OK you can open your eyes now. Could you all picture the poem?'

Students: 'Yes'.
A: 'What was the mood you felt?'
Students: 'Slightly melancholy.'
A: 'I wonder why that was?'
Student: 'It was words like fehlen and trostlos.'
A: 'I'm terrible at drawing, as you will see in moment, but what I'd like to do is have a go at drawing the scene you imagined when I read the poem. So, what do you want me to draw?'
Student: 'A house.'
A: 'Like that?'
Student: 'No, I thought it was more like a croft and single storey.'
A: 'So, like this?'
Students: 'Yes.'
A Student: 'Hmmm, I'm not sure.'
A: 'OK let's go with the majority and come back to this in moment. What else?'
Student: 'Trees.' (I draw pine trees)
Student: 'No, not that kind.'
Student: 'Yes — I thought of pine trees.'

A: 'OK how about mixed woodland as a compromise.'

(Students laugh)

A: ' Mountains.'

Students: 'Yes...No ...' (Laughter)

Student: 'The sea.'

A: 'Ahhh – now is it...?'

Another student: 'It's a lake.'

A: 'How do you know?'

Student: 'Its 'am See' – so it has to be a lake because 'Die See' is feminine and means the sea.'

A: 'Good, so we have a lake, a croft, trees, possibly mountains – like this.' (I draw mountains that look like the Alps)

Students: 'No – they are more rounded.'

A: 'OK – like this?'

Students: 'Yes.'

A: 'What else?'

Students: 'Smoke.'

A: 'Straight up or blown by the wind?'

Student: 'It's a calm day, so straight up.'

A: 'Great. People?'

Students: 'Hmmm.'

A: 'Let's look at the poem again. Why does it have that title?'

Students: 'Because it's about smoke.'

A: 'Is it good smoke or does it spell danger?'

Student: 'It shows someone lives there.'

A: 'So...people!'

Student: 'But it could spell danger. I mean Brecht was in exile, wasn't he? It could be the roof burning or something.'

A: 'But what about the line 'fehlte er'? If it was a fire then it wouldn't be a bad thing if it wasn't there, would it?' (Students laugh) 'Now, the interesting part for me here is to ask you why you described this scene the way you did and why the house, the mountains and the trees had to be the way you described them – and why some of you disagreed?'

Student: 'I used to go on holiday to the hills and they were rounded not pointy and the cottage was like that.'

Student: 'But I'm from Spain and the hills and houses and trees look different.'

Student: 'And there are lots of pine trees in Germany and not as many trees here in Scotland. We don't really have forest, we have lone Scots pines.'

A: 'So what does this tell you about how you interpret poetry?'

Student: 'Well, I suppose we see it through our own experience and lives.'

A: 'Yes, you have certain expectations, what we might call cultural constructions, that are automatic ways of understanding the language you hear. Signs with signifiers, in linguistic terms. Which one of you has the RIGHT answer?'

Students: 'You?' (Laughter)

A: 'All of us.'

This was the first time any of the students in this class had read poetry in German. In fact, when asked when they had last read a poem they all said it was in primary school. Could they remember those poems? They all said they could and had vivid memories of writing shape poems or drawing pictures of Tam O'Shanter.

The 'connectionist' method is horizontal, structured in general but not in particular, fluid and mobile. It is not, however, a matter of simple mental association; this after all is a search for communicable meaning, and the communication of it is the core of the process. In so far as this is a collective process, what is pursued is shared meaning that can later be articulated or, to persist with our use of the term, languaged. At the risk of repeating ourselves, this is a learning experience whose shape and direction is determined by the search for meaning and coherence at the point of understanding. It is not a teaching procedure whose limited purpose is to convey an already existing interpretation.

The text – whatever text it is – has value as a *learning* stimulus to the extent that it

> text as a learning stimulus

can mobilise languaging and a critical awareness of self. This is more than simply an awakening of memory or an act of recognition; learning is, as we have emphasised at every stage, an act of critical appropriation of the world and ourselves. Where the classroom is merely an arbitrary collection of individuals, the best we can aspire to is that the individual learner will recognise the views and purposes of the instructor. In a community of learners, however, the recognition of self is a result of the acknowledgement of others – it is the fruit of exchange.

What then is the role of a teacher in this common exploration of the constellation of meanings that settle on and around a text? It would be quite wrong to imagine that there is no role, other than a kind of care-taking. It is true that there are times when the best decision on the part of a teacher might be to absent him or herself. At other times, however, their presence is indispensable. It is easy enough to employ terms like 'enabling', 'empowerment', 'guidance' and so on, but we are all aware that they can embrace a multitude of sins and indeed simply mollify the anti-authoritarians with a mask of collaboration which will fall at the first provocation to reveal an authoritarian in casual dress.

Neither of us has ever encoun-   **bringing knowledge and experience**
tered a student who resented our
experience or particular knowledge; their presumption, on the contrary, was that we were there precisely to bring that accumulated body of knowledge and experience into the learning space. The point was to share it openly, to make it fully and unconditionally available to them. They and we have plenty of examples of a drip-feed method in which knowledge was given on a need-to-know basis without providing the tools to reach those conclusions independently. The question is, what is the opposite method?

> *Discourses are not mastered by overt instruction (even less so than languages, and hardly anyone ever fluently acquired a second language sitting in a classroom), but by enculturation ('apprenticeship') into social practices through scaffolded and supported interaction with people who have already mastered the Discourse. (Gee, 1989: 7)*

Selection of material and provision of texts gives some real power, but it also enables the provider to address certain key questions. That choice is a legitimate teaching decision. If in Spain centralism and nationalism are touchstones of peninsular history, then they can be an important catalyst for a process of cultural understanding; if the role of intellectuals is key to French culture, where it may not be so in an anglophone society, then that paradox may serve as a particularly appropriate point of cultural encounter. The legacy of empire may explain the dominant ideology in late nineteenth-century Spain, but not in the Spain of 1945; in France, by contrast, this is a central cultural issue in the postwar arrangements. We cannot assume that prior knowledge on the part of learners; we can assume, however, that with the necessary analytical instruments understanding will be accessible to learners, and that in the discovery they will develop a means of understanding and response which will then be more generally applicable.

This, then, is the second consequence for the teacher: the responsibility to provide tools of cultural understanding. This may include theoretical instruments, but not only these; the toolbox must include the means for interrogating the reality, the language of explanation, the means of cultural research. There has always been, and remains in the discourse of higher education, an insistence that 'research' may only be undertaken at a postgraduate stage. The joy and pride of undergraduates who find that they are able to research the world, to meaningfully explore another culture, is palpable. The central conclusion that arises here is that the learning process is collaborative and communal; the teacher offers her toolbox, the student brings to the table her accumulated stock of meaning and practices. Experience and analysis provide meaning in the community of learners. Collective inquiry replaces learning and teaching.

The text, therefore, may be literary or not, it may be aural, visual …

Give the students as much scope as they possibly can to choose what they want, because I find that in this course we had a choice…Mike took us in, he said, 'right, tell me what you want to do' and you know, we threw about some ideas but we finally came to soap operas and it was something I never thought we'd be able to do. So I don't think it necessarily has to be academic. If it's fun, you know…and there was an academic side to it, because there was a lot of research…I think giving the students the opportunity to decide about what they want to do for themselves and obviously the support, and we did have him for support if we needed it, then that's important.

(Excerpt from a student discussion about history projects in Hispanic Studies)

If we understand Gee's concept of 'discourse' more widely than simply to mean direct verbal communication, but instead all the practices and expression of cultural being, his definition of 'scaffolded and supported interaction' may provide a guideline for the connectionist exploration of texts in a modern languages context. It will also allow us to establish what criteria we might use to select and prioritise texts. Until now, the inbuilt and usually unquestioned assumption is that the text is chosen on the basis of its inherent qualities, whether those be aesthetic or narrowly defined cultural criteria. In either case, the presumption – to repeat an earlier point – is that the landscape we travel is the text itself, and that on the way we will uncover signposts cleverly hidden by previous travellers which may indicate which way we should now go to reach whatever objective it is that shall be revealed to us in due course. Once framed in that way, the text itself becomes the object of study – and the only debate is a rather recondite one as to which among a small selection of printed texts contain the greatest number of universals.

COMMUNAL EXPLORATION

Our presumption is a very different one, whose starting point is exchange and inquiry rather than learning and teaching. Our question is what text will best provide an opportunity or a stimulus to that exploration of self and other, that exercise in making meanings that we call languaging. The community that gathers around the text – the seminar group or workshop – furthermore finds its unity in the shared experience of exploration and the accumulation of common knowledges; its collective purpose is *not* to reach, in unison, a single interpretation under the authoritative guidance of the tutor. In some sense, the most successful text class will be cacophonous, at least at some points; it will be a place of many voices, understandings and interpretations. The later stages of this encounter should be an exchange – a process we have repeatedly set at the heart of our understanding of teaching and learning modern languages – in which the individual learner is enriched and the community is rendered more complex and profound by the exchange and (non-competitive) comparison of the processes of critical thought that have produced a response. Once again, the role of teacher is changed and changed utterly; there can be no central authority in a federation of approaches. Yet the teaching role is key – firstly, as we have argued, in selection and later in facilitating exchange.

But it has to be said that the text as focus need not be, and often will not be, literary. Indeed, given the closed and pre-emptive nature of literature teaching, it may be that the texts of the literary canon(s) are less suitable than others whose imaginative complexity may be less great but whose capacity to provoke critical responses may be greater.

> *The most one can hope for is to help, as circumspectly as possible, to encourage, or simply to* allow, *the conditions and climate within which culture can come into its own… It may be useful to think of this 'own' by thinking of culture, not as a content or a series or cluster of contents, but most especially as a constantly developing cluster of structures…What we are confronted with in culture is not an expanding, yet finite, set of 'things', of 'events', of 'actions', of 'products' or 'processes' – but with things, events, actions, products and processes which, through their inter-relationships* produce meaning. *(Brink, 1983: 223–4)*

We return to the matter of selection and choice. Do we choose 'good texts' over 'bad'? Yes, but the criterion for determining their value in this respect is whether a given text may produce stories of passion and involvement or of sadness and rejection, whether they may induce understanding or the failure to understand. The text is a terrain on which an intercultural process – of comparison, evocation, perplexity and illumination – may take place. And those possibilities are drawn out by placing and locating the exercise of imagination in time and place, 'opening' the text and not closing it down or locking it into a fixed posture. In other areas, like film, learners are beginning to do things with their material; until now, too often, the text has been sacrosanct and inviolable. This teaches only recognition, reverence perhaps; it does not invoke reading as a journey through myriad resonances and reminders through which the learner may make their own.

As teachers being intercultural allows us the opportunity to make different selections of texts based on different criteria – those of intercultural being and languaging as creative, collective communication. In so doing we need to be critical of what has gone before, testing and sifting out texts together with our students against the aims of intercultural being, not the ideals of previous canons, yet fully aware of the canonical potential of such cultural work of selection. In other words, as teachers of texts we have the task of exploring imaginary intercultural worlds and guiding our students through their delights, possibilities, resonances and pitfalls at the same time as allowing them to take our imaginations travelling into their worlds.

And when we are travelling in imaginary worlds in other languages there is one further border to cross and recross, until the frontier disappears and all share the disposition to live in translated worlds.

Key references

Bourdieu, P. (2000) *Pascalian Meditations*. Cambridge: Polity.

Brink, A. (1983) *Mapmakers: Writing in a State of Siege*. London: Faber & Faber.

Carter, R. and McRae, J. (eds) (1996) *Language, Literature, and the Learner: Creative Classroom Practice*. London: Longman.

Eagleton, T. (2000) *The Idea of Culture*. Oxford: Blackwell.

Gee, J. (1989) 'Literacy, discourse, and linguistics', *Journal of Education*, 171(1): 5–17.

Okri, B. (1997) *A Way of Being Free*. London: Phoenix House.

Williams, R. (1977) *Marxism and Literature*. Oxford: Oxford University Press.

Websites

http://www.lang.ltsn.ac.uk/resources/guidecontents.aspx

Encyclopedia

Byram, M. (2000) *Routledge Encyclopedia of Language Teaching and Learning*. London and New York: Routledge.

Living in translated worlds

Tradittore, traduttore. *In the kind of translation that interests me most, you learn a lot about peoples, cultures, and histories different from your own, enough to begin to know what you're missing. (Clifford, 1997b: 39)*

MINEFIELDS AT THE BORDER

Translation is not just 'expressing the sense of a word, sentence, speech, book, poem etc. in or to another language' (Oxford English Dictionary). Translation, we argue in this chapter, is a powerful agent of cultural change. Translators effect transformations. Translators are border crossers. Working with words through the activity of translation does things to the lives we lead. It is consequently not possible to teach translation and to help form translators in ways which are objective, neutral and devoid of being. The creative, human activity of translation is at the heart of languaging and being intercultural.

> *Translation is considered as a mode of engagement with literature, a kind of literary activism [...] Translators contribute to cultural debates and create new lines of communication. Translators are necessarily involved in a politics of transmission, in perpetuating or contesting the values which sustain our literary culture. (Simon, 1996: viii)*

Anthropologists, pedagogues and translators are all border crossers and are all languaging in important ways. Expanding the powerful work with words that translators have effected in the field of aesthetics and seeing it as a part of an anthropological curricularising of modern languages opens up new possibilities (Clifford and Marcus, 1986). When translation as metaphor meets translation as practice and the one is allowed to revive the other, the potential is cultural and political because it is poetic. Translation, we shall argue here, is about much more than texts. It is about imagining new worlds and new possibilities through languaging. It is at once exchange and encounter, collective and creative.

I'm feeling nervously confident. It is 9 a.m. on a Friday morning. I'm sitting waiting for the professor to start my first ever prose-translation class at university. I'm nervous because this is new. I'm confident because translation, at least at school, is something I know I can do and do well. My mind wanders for a moment and I'm back in Germany, standing up in front of 300 young people translating for them from German into English, making sure that they all know how to live together for the three-week youth camp I'm part of. I see my words bring laughter, understanding, recognition and respectful action. I see the worries and questions and fears flow through me and turn and find safety and security, a smile of encouragement, a nod of approval, a twitch or a glint and another stream of words for me to make mean. Translation is a wonderful feeling, it is a way of being with others in the world. It feels like magic, like a current of energy flowing through my body to connect people together. I see translation, my act of translation, actually making a difference to how these people come together and are together in this place at this time. Why, after this, should I be nervous?

The professor arrives and hands out a text by Coleridge which we are to translate, unseen, into German. It is impossible. The words don't follow. I have no tools to assist me. My dictionary, already loved and worn at the edges, has to stay on my shelf. I know I've just messed up a grammar point, it won't change the meaning but the sentence is now wrong by the objective measures of accuracy. I leave the room, having handed in my text, worried, frustrated, alienated, angry and wondering what my own lived experience of translation has to do with this.

A week later I am only nervous. The professor has decided to give back each text with an individual public commentary on the grade he has awarded and the ability of the student thus demonstrated. He gets to my name. 'I assume you went to a state school. It shows you know. You can't do this. You must go for remedial work on your grammar along with some others.'

I never did learn how to translate in a way that would satisfy the cravings of the powerful awarders of grades. I was taught by excellent, loving linguists and inspiring teachers, as well as by those who got their kicks in the way I describe above. Another professor charmed me constantly with a generous sensitivity to the power of language and a reading of literary passages that could show me their power, if not give it to me.

Even today, when I come to a class to teach translation these memories are more powerful than those that preceded them. I have empathy for my students when they feel frustrated by the experience. Translation, I now say, isn't actually something I can do, I'm not 'very good at it', 'someone else should do it'. I envy my colleagues their seemingly effortless ability and enjoyment when they come to translate literary texts. I usually feel a complete fraud in the classroom. Who am I to teach translation?

The point of this story is not therapy following the traumas of past language classes in higher education, though that may not be a bad thing for many of the scarred language learners who walk the world. We are constantly amazed at the powerful negativity of those who grimace at the thought of having to translate or utter words in another language. They tell us, as the knee-jerk response to our statement of profession, that they failed 'O' level French, that their teacher was a tyrant, that they never got anywhere with languages, that they can't translate for toffee (not that toffee is in and of itself easily translatable).

What interests us about this story for our purposes is what happened in and through **liberating and enriching** this particular experience of translation. Having experienced acts of translation as an everyday, necessary, border-crossing activity we found that our lived understanding of translation did not match the one we were subjected to in this class. We have found translation to be liberating, exciting and enriching. We have found it, most significantly of all, to be possible. Here it was dry, pointless and obfuscating, intended to discipline and punish. What the professor understood by 'translation' assumed there is a bull's-eye to hit. Actually, the activity needed a completely different term altogether: the ironically accurate term of *unseen*. What was tested was our ability to hit a moving target. Far from being a process of mutual transformation and exchange, unseen translation exercises test precisely the opposite; there is no change or transformation and if there is it is 'an error'.

Even at the level of this one word 'translation' we can already see the extent of the different intralingual difficulties that come when we try and put our experiences of life into language. In this situation there was the same kind of dissonance (Cronin, 2000) as British English speakers may experience when they speak with American English speakers. The professor may just as well have been from another planet, where they spoke the same language, but failed to communicate. There was a gulf of life and stories, between the expectations and the ultimate experience.

Translation as an intractable activity was the *exercise or exchange* preserve of experts and not for the uninitiated (Schäffer 2001), an unfair, predictive exercise in decoding and deciphering. Translation as a lively, living experience had been 'translated' into a different world. Translation was no longer exhilarating, no longer fundamentally an exchange at a number of different levels, powerfully centred on intercultural being. This switch was never explained, intellectually. The explanation of the process of translation, the powerful human effects of shifting from being intercultural to excising the self from the translation process were not the subject of critical thought or of academic reflection.

It is our aim here to bring the human activity of translation to the fore, to reflect on the ways in which claiming and centring translation in a world of dehumanised textuality without critical reflection makes languaging and intercultural being highly contested states, rendering them invisible, or at best marginal. Far from being a languaging, mediational activity translation becomes a highly codified quest for equivalences. For us, 'Translation becomes the act of reclaiming, of recentering of the identity, a reterritorializing activity' (Brisset, in Venuti, 1999: 346).

The benchmark statements for the UK for the area of languages and related studies have this to say of translation:

Many language programmes seek to enable students to mediate between languages by means of translation and interpreting across a wide range of media. These activities require knowledge of how language systems relate to one another and of the techniques which permit mediation between languages. Where language mediation is a significant part of the curriculum explicit knowledge of the practice of translation will be a key feature.

Translation and mediation skills may be assessed by unseen papers but also by other means, such as prepared translation with commentary, and post-editing/correction of a draft translation. (QAA, 2002b: 5.4.1)

It is worth noticing that, in this scheme for learning outcomes in higher education for those studying language, very little mention is made of translation, except in the context of summative assessment. Does the reluctance to mention translation indicate at least a tacit acknowledgement that translation isn't actually working as a pedagogical tool for the communication age? The old ideology is still clearly present at the level of assessment. It is not human beings who meet and exchange with each other in translation, but systems of language. There is a curious silence throughout this policy document that does perhaps point to a shift.

The frustrated sense of the pointlessness of some translation activities has produced student feedback such as 'when am I going to need that word?', 'How on earth can I be expected to unpick that piece of prose', 'I didn't understand a word of the text', 'I can only remember all the gaps I had to leave or all the guesses I had to make',' Why can't we engage with something more up to date or relevant?'

We have sat through staff–student meetings and feedback sessions and focus groups where an anger and sense of alienation have prevailed and we have marvelled as colleagues have found ways of justifying this kind of activity to the students, painstakingly pointing out to them the need for a sophisticated reading of prose, for the ability to manipulate sentences, for the necessity of careful reading of text and learning of vocabulary. All of which is, of course, perfectly cogent. We have seen the ways in which languages and especially Latin and Greek were taught in the past being perpetuated unchanging into the future.

Again and again we have seen our own teachers read out fair versions of **translation and assessment** translation but refuse to distribute copies. The sound reasons for not doing so reflect the broken nature of this as a teaching technique and as a form of assessment. If there are no final, finished, accurate translations then how on earth can translation – in this form – be a suitable medium for assessment? We act and mark as if there is such a thing as a final, finished account, and yet we know that in the humanities, in the slippery world of texts and language and representation, there is no such thing. Again and again, through our assessment practices and through our positivistic pedagogy in this area of unseen translation, we have to wrestle the life of language back into easily manageable, quantifiable form.

So does this mean that translation should not be part of the work of teaching languages in higher education? No it does not. If anything, the ambiguities and complexities that make it such a lousy tool for assessment make it a wonderful place to language. The benchmark statements, for all their problems, offer some real hope here in describing translation as a mediation activity. Although mediation is not actually defined here, it too may be linked to the notion of *languaging* outlined previously.

> **Mediate:** *form connecting link between; be the medium for bringing about (result) or conveying (gift etc.). (Oxford English Dictionary)*

Having to teach translation of texts under systems of assessment and pedagogy such as those outlined above provides many challenges. The need we have both felt to develop ways of enabling students to experience translation as mediation and themselves as forming and forging links between goes to the very heart of revisioning languages more widely and in intercultural terms. In these ways we will be able to help our student languagers learn to reflect on the fact that 'we all live in translated worlds' (Simon, 1996: 135) rather than experiencing translation as a distant, separate, impossible, intractable, unseen, error-ridden and pointlessly deracinated activity.

SEEKING TRANSLATION

Where might we go for a vision of translation if we do not find what we seek in modern languages? The concept and metaphor of translation is frequently found in anthropology, for example (Asad, 1986; Clifford, 1997; Geertz, 1973; Ingold, 1993). Here it presupposes experience, reflection, the ability to language, to stand at the crossroads between different cultures and not just to act as link, bridge, mediating point – as is the case in translation between pre-existing texts – but to create the bridge from the resources of language as culture. James Clifford describes translation for anthropologists as an activity that is not centred and rooted but is part of the dynamics of 'being between':

> *Thinking historically is a process of locating oneself in space and time. And location [...] is an itinerary rather than a bounded site – a series of encounters and translations. [...] all broadly meaningful concepts, terms such as 'travel', are translations, built from imperfect equivalences. (Clifford, 1997: 11)*

Here we see anthropology move into the territory of the humanities at the same time as we, following others (Peck, 1992, 1989; Roberts et al.,

2001; Seyhan, 1997), are suggesting that a way of materialising and enlivening the study of other languages and cultures may lie in explorations of anthropology, cultural studies and other related human sciences, as much as it lies in literature and thought. It lies not just in forging links between texts, but in being intercultural though material relations as well as textual ones.

Ingold sees translation as a sensory activity that develops out of the experience of direct perception (Ingold, 1993: 228). In terms of our project, Ingold's view of 'translation' helps us move beyond culture (see Chapter 4). In order to view translation as an itinerary, and translators as intercultural beings, then translators have to be envisaged as languagers, as forgers of mediational links born out of intimacy with language and close mutual involvement, rather than as creators and investigators of problems between us and them.

Clifford and Ingold, in particular, see beyond translation as mere equivalence and problem and show an awareness of some of the consequences of translation in cultural and critical terms, but continue to ignore the role of languages.

So what happens when we turn to the literature on learning and teaching modern languages? What kind of place is translation accorded? Books with the following titles would suggest a good place to start looking for help: *Inspiring Innovations in Language Teaching* (Hamilton, 1995), *Second Language Learning and Language Teaching* (Cook, 1996), *Strategy and Skill in Learning a Foreign Language* (McDonough, 1995), *Motivating Language Learners* (Chambers, 1999), *How to Teach Modern Languages and Survive!* (Pleuger, 2001).

The indexes of these books do not contain a single reference to the activity of translation. The writers include school teachers, university lecturers, specialists in linguistics, second language acquisition, teacher trainers, modern linguists. All *must* have been given text translations to do as part of their own degree-level language study. None refer to translation as a key activity, or even to translation as an activity in language learning or teaching at all. Lawrence Venuti has written extensively on what he calls 'the invisibility of the translator' (Venuti, 1995). This, it would appear, is nowhere more apposite than in the very place where it has been most taught and practised as an activity.

So where might we go to find help and resource? Given the intercultural arguments that lie at the heart of this book – arguments claiming that languaging is a border crossing activity, that translation and ethnography are about creative ways of social and material being – then we might expect the intercultural literature to be more promising. *Teaching and Assessing Intercultural Communicative Competence* (Byram, 1997), *Language Learning in Intercultural Perspective* (Byram and Fleming, 1998), *Developing Intercultural Competence in Practice* (Byram, Nichols and Stevens, 2001), *Intercultural, Communication* (Scollon and Scollon, 1995), *Inter-cultural Communication at Work* (Clyne, 1994), *Context and Culture in Language Teaching* (Kramsch, 1993).

And yet again, combing the indexes and reading through the books gives us no sense of translation as a key communication activity in inter-cultural situations. In these texts too translation remains an unspoken assumption.

Out of the 714 pages of the *Routledge Encyclopedia of Language Learning and Teaching,* edited by Michael Byram (Byram, 2000) and a truly excellent, forward-looking resource, we find less than three pages on translation, and five pages on translation theory. In her entry on teaching translation, Rogers sees translation in terms of mediation, and isolates the 'grammar-translation method', 'professional translation' and 'literal versus free translation'. While acknowledging the changes wrought by disillusionment with grammar-translation and the func-tional need for professional translators Rogers can offer little more hope than 'wider resources [websites, media, tourist brochures, legislation etc.] beginning to provide a rich source of innovative, communicatively based ideas for the use of translation in language teaching' (Byram, 2000: 637) in higher education.

Only when we get to Lindholm-Leary's essentially quantitative survey of dual language education programmes do we find a reference to what everyone knows to be true: 'For years, the task of translation has been taught to foreign language students' (Lindholm-Leary, 2001: 318).

Although we may struggle to find ref-erence to translation in the wider **mediation and interpretation** literature on learning and teaching modern languages, the reverse is true of the presence of translation in the modern languages curriculum as a form of assessment. Degree examinations still include passages for trans-lation at many UK universities. Translation is present in the form of Chomskian competencies or translation equivalence, i.e. in the form of scripting and literature, but it is absent, almost entirely absent, as a lived activity such as that described by Ingold or Clifford.

In Byram's work we find words such as 'mediation' and 'interpretation' and 'negotiation' but not 'translation'. For example:

Someone with intercultural communicative [emphasis in original] competence is able to interact with people from another country and culture in a foreign language. They are able to negotiate a mode of communication and interaction which is satisfactory to themselves and the other and they are able to act as mediator between people of different cultural origins. Their knowledge of another culture is linked to their language competence through their ability to use language appropriately. (Byram, 1997: 71)

Byram is right in using the phrase 'mediation' to implicitly critique the narrowness of the ways in which the business of translation has been rendered static and meaningless. The question raised by the absence or invisibility of translation from Byram's important work is whether intercultural communicative competence is about more than translation, is different from translation, is not translation, is only 'good' or 'effective' translation?

What we are saying is that translation, in our definition and understanding, is both what Byram terms 'mediation' and, in addition, it is what Ingold sees as an experience in the dissolving of borders. Both Byram and Ingold are wary of the fences, but both, in their understanding of translation, only get up to the border. Their thinking remains interdisciplinary in precisely the context where academic teaching and research has always been dynamically and, of necessity, transdisciplinary. Translation is a *trans* activity, transforming, transcending, transcultural, transdisciplinary, while at the same time succumbing, in a variety of fields, to the specific understandings and outworkings of disciplines. In modern languages it has become either 'professionalised' or remains a 'grammar-translation' discipline. In anthropology it works powerfully through the discipline as an experiential tool for nascent anthropologists. Theology lives and breathes translation, interlinear, the codex, Greek, Hebrew, Latin being fundamental for any serious student of the Bible. Every disciplinary field in higher education is powerfully touched, changed and challenged by languaging as translation. Only the relatively new disciplinary field of translation studies reflects on this.

FINDING TRANSLATION

Translation is not wholly invisible. There are some reasonably good, handy 'how to teach translation' books (Malmjaer, 1998; Sewel and Higgins,

1996). Work on translation theory has grown over the past two decades, ever since translation studies took a cultural turn and began to explore questions relating to the effects of translation, the ideological and political motivations that may be uncovered in translation activity and in translated texts. Bassnett (Bassnett and Lefevere, 1990, 1998; Bassnett-McGuire, 1980), Venuti (1995), Simon (1996) and Bhabha (1994), among others, have all made a significant contribution to the theorising of translation as a cultural activity.

Translations come to be seen as empirical artefacts showing the actual situation of cultural transfer, the relations of power, the flow of cultural capital. Translators come to be seen as 'literary activists' who 'contribute to cultural debates and create new lines of communication [...] necessarily involved in a politics of transmission, in perpetuating or contesting the values which sustain our literary culture' (Simon, 1996: viii):

> *It is in the domain of cultural capital that translation can most clearly be seen to construct cultures. It does so by negotiating the passage of texts between them, or rather, by devising strategies through which texts from one culture can penetrate the textual and conceptual grids of another culture, and function in that other culture. What we call the 'socialisation' process, of which formal education is a big, though not the only part, leaves us with textual and conceptual grids that regulate most of the writing and thinking in the culture in which we grow up. (Bassnett and Lefevere, 1998: 7)*

Translation theorists have also directed much attention to uncovering possible reasons for the invisibility of translators and translation activity, as we have mentioned earlier (Cronin, 2000; Venuti, 1995). In addition they have paid attention to the view of all translation as inevitably 'defective' because it is not 'originary', because it has been 'tampered with', 'modified' and thus is no longer what it was, because it never can hit the moving target. Translation has long been judged secondary to the 'real thing' of literary writing and any translation of the 'original' has been judged for its quality and not seen for its action.

> *Because they are necessarily 'defective', all translations are 'reputed females'. In this neat equation, John Florio (1603) summarises a heritage of double inferiority. Translators and women have historically been weaker figures in their respective hierarchies. (Simon, 1996: 1)*

In our own attempts to 'find' translation – to find the activity that has long been understood as the bedrock of language learning and teaching – Simon's insights are particularly illuminating. Not only were modern languages 'classics for women' and the mark of female accomplishment in the nineteenth century, as we have already discussed (see Chapters 3 and 4) but translation was largely a pedagogical tool as opposed to a professional skill. Latin and classics took their places in the professions of law and the church. Modern languages were taught alongside embroidery.

In *Vanity Fair* Becky Sharp is marked by her ability to speak French in interesting ways. Firstly, it marks her out for the woman's work as a governess; secondly Miss Pinkerton's lack of French highlights the status and social prestige, or capital, that speaking French carried with it. Becky revels in the fact that in this, it is she and not Miss Pinkerton who can claim the cultural capital. And thirdly the fact that it is subversive Becky Sharp who is given French shows the way that living languages have long been marked out as gendered activities, which, as largely the domain of women, render the forms they take defective and the activity of translation as subversive:

> I have been made to tend the little girls in the lower school room, and talk
> French to the Misses until I grew sick of my mother-tongue. But talking
> French to Miss Pinkerton was capital fun, wasn't it? She doesn't know a
> word of French, and was too proud to confess it. I believe it was that which
> made her part with me; so thank heaven for French. (Thackery, 1848: 47)

It is interesting to note that living languages have been gendered as *women's work* – the Mother Tongue, Speech (Cixous, 1992) – and that dead languages have been more male gendered. When to the 'double inferiority' of translation – as defective and therefore reputed female – is added the marginal and equally gendered activity of translation as a pedagogical tool, the absences we find in the literatures become much less surprising. Where translation is theorised it is done so in a more legitimate professional space – that of the new but nonetheless scholarly field of translation studies. Where translation takes place in the classroom as part of the marginal university activity of teaching it all but disappears from view.

What Venuti and others, as fully paid up translation studies scholars, succeed in rendering visible, is the work of literary translation. Languaging translation continues to remain invisible, though a constant of life. What we find occurring again and again in these discussions of the absences of translation as a serious field of study is the same kind of 'philologism' as Bourdieu terms it in *Pascalian Meditations* (Bourdieu, 2000) 'which tends to treat all languages like dead languages, fit only for deciphering'. Bourdieu is highly critical of this kind of apolitical work that blots out the material and social conditions of knowledge and of action. To quote him again: 'they tend to conceive every understanding, even practical understanding, as an *interpretation* [sic], a self-aware act of deciphering (the paradigm of which is translation)' (53)

The task we have before us then is, firstly, one of bringing the practical and material conditions of the action of translation to the fore, of making strange the practices of translation so as better to teach and to learn of translation as an instrument of action and of power. Secondly, we have to ensure critical reflection on the material and cultural production of language within our learning and teaching of languages. Thirdly, we have the task of understanding translation as *trans* – as a border crossing, border dissolving activity at the ontological heart of intercultural being. In short, our task is to help form people – languagers – who *are* in the language, not just thinking in the language.

The world student games are taking place in Sheffield, 1991. I've been working in France all year and in my spare time have run a youth group with the Guides de France. I've now brought them 'home' to Sheffield to camp for three weeks. They are between 11 and 14. They have minimal English, which they try out at every possible opportunity. As part of the overall programme we attend church one Sunday morning. We turn up – all 25 of us – unannounced. The hospitality extended to us is warm and generous. I suddenly see the people of my home town in an entirely new light. What was invisible becomes visible. They see me as French – it is the language I am living in here. They understand intuitively that part of the gift of hospitality is that of language. With no warning or preparation the service, the readings and the sermon become bilingual – a member of the congregation 'has French' and he uses it to make us feel at home, through translation. We are all astonished, humbled and at home.

Language learners as ethnographers

The other place where translation may be found is in the very recent work done to see language learners as ethnographers (Roberts et al., 2001). It is fascinating to find translation brought to the fore in this particular emergent field as it is a field that is removed from the kind of leisured, universalising philologisms that Bourdieu criticises and that is firmly bedded in the obvious relational and material conditions of practical language use. This is not to say that translation can only be theorised or understood as a practical tool. Far from it. What it does show is that in contexts and disciplines where there is a learned disposition for treating languages as living rather than dead – what Bourdieu terms a *habitus* – there emerge the hints of a theory of practice.

What Roberts et al. assume in *Language Learners as Ethnographers* is that language students 'are, *of course*, [our emphasis] familiar with the idea of translation' (Roberts et al., 2001: 91). What we would conclude from our review of the literature and our critical appraisal of translation as a pedagogical tool for language learning is that *students are not at all familiar with the idea of translation*. Unless they are studying translation theory, they will have engaged in the quest for equivalences and attempted to 'break the philological codes' but this 'idea of translation' is far removed from the anthropological understandings of translation we examined earlier.

As Roberts et al. (2001) acknowledge, 'the challenge for them [language learners as ethnographers] is not only to translate from one language to another but to present culture practices observed in one society in terms of their own and be reflexive and critical about the process at the same time' (91). Here we have the beginnings of a languaging view of translation, at last, that we would sustain and support.

a languaging view of translation

Translation is a learned disposition for action. It is a highly complex activity that requires both reflexivity and criticality towards the languages in play, the power in play, the cultures in contact. It is certainly not impossible or intractable. This is true whether it is undertaken in the leisured quiet of texts or in the immediacy and urgency of everyday life. The feel of translation depends not on translation itself, but on myriad material and social relations that make up every instance of translation. It is these that the work of Roberts et al. begins to show in action in the context of learning and teaching languages when they talk of cultural 'translation' (their punctuation) to show that they are not interested in the hunt for equivalences but in writing, mediating, interpreting and inscribing the practices that need to be in play to come to a translation.

> I've set a short task for my first-year class as I usually do at the beginning of the year. The activity is quite simple. They are numbered off (in German) into groups and then given the group task of creating a poster about a region of Germany, presenting it in a style suitable for tourists. They have two weeks to accomplish this task and have to use a certain variety of resources – the Internet, the language library, the university library, the Goethe Institute and, if possible, the Embassy. All staff, NLAs, graduate students and secretaries are invited along to the presentations that the students do of their work. The students pin their posters to the wall, present their material freely in German, answer questions and are proud of their design, their handiwork, their effort.
>
> Not all of the writing on the posters is in good German. Often the writing is particularly poor and it is clear that this is writing that hasn't been 'thought' in German but 'translated' from English sources into German. The students at this level just do not have the vocabulary or syntax or practice to enable them to take a piece of text from English and render it with the same syntactical and linguistic ease as a text in English. I question the students about their working method. And as I suspect those with a high number of grammatical errors but solid content wrote out their work in English first and then tried to translate.
>
> 'Don't translate,' I say to them, forcefully. 'Think in German'.
>
> An honours-level class with students back from a year in Germany. They have been back about four months and they have been set a piece of twentieth-century prose to hand in one week and then discuss the next.
>
> I've never quite been sure why we don't pool our resources in translation classes, all tackling the points of difficulty first and then going off to try and work on the text afterwards. In fact, despite the fact this is not the 'normal' way of proceeding with teaching I have used time in classes for this purpose and of course the results are much better and the questions thrown up more interesting.

I've marked the texts and one piece has clearly been done with the help of a native speaker. This is a grey area. As the work is assessed I have to speak to the student. I know – because I can recognise the difference between native-speaker German and fluent German – that help has been given. We sit down after class in my office and I ask how the student did the piece. She is a lovely student, typically diligent, typically motivated, typically terrified of failing. She cries. Says she had help. Wonders why that is wrong. Says she doesn't understand why she could be so good at German in Germany and yet get such middling marks. Says her parents are counting on her getting a 2.1.

'But it's you who is learning to think in German,' I say, 'not those who already can.'

Translation can bring tears. Since I changed my approach to teaching translation, since I told these stories and my own, since I made it clear that there are no right answers or moving targets, since I began to demonstrate the powerful effects of translation to the students, since I grew in my conviction that living languages have to be translated in critical, lively ways – the tears have dried up.

BEING IN TRANSLATION

[The] founding task of translation does not disappear by fetishizing the native language. Sometimes I read and hear that the subaltern can speak in their native languages. I wish I could be as self-assured as the intellectual, literary critic and historian, who assert this in English. No speech is speech if it is not heard. It is this act of hearing-to-respond that may be called the imperative to translate. (Spivak, 1999: 27)

We have argued, throughout this chapter, that translation should be at the heart of being intercultural and of languaging. In our efforts to discover what has happened to translation to make it an oppressive, pedagogical tool of subjection or a functionalist servant of employment prospects, we have unearthed common-sense understandings of translation as 'intractable', 'difficult', as reserved for 'experts', as 'a problem', and we see translators either rendered invisible or constructed as tricksters, fraudsters, manipulators, women.

Not only is translation in and of itself a powerful agent of change and challenge and conservation, but it is at one and the same time subject to the kinds of systemic, structural power that can conceal and prevent the asking of important, different questions:

> *Not asking certain questions is pregnant with more dangers than failing to answer the questions already on the official agenda; while asking the wrong kind of questions all too often helps avert eyes from the truly important issues. The price of silence is paid in the hard currency of human suffering.* (Bauman, 1998: 5)

Questions that have dominated translation have been questions such as: 'Is it a good translation?', 'What is the equivalent?', 'Is this sentence grammatically accurate?' Questions that have not been asked include: 'What are the material circumstances that lead us to translate?' 'What happens when texts are translated and received into other languages and human experiences, that are at once connected and often far removed from their originary ground?', 'What gets changed and challenged by translation?', 'What is the lived experience of those who translate?', 'What does it *feel* like to *be* translating?'

Asking these and other questions which undoubtedly follow enables us to put the understandings of anthropology, intercultural communicative competence and translation studies together into an enlivened and material way of understanding translation. Failing to ask these questions in the modern languages contexts has already led to the suffering of disciplines, to subjection and to tears.

Translation is at the heart of being intercultural. Translation, we have argued here, is about much more than texts. It is about language at the root of imagining new worlds. Translators both know and are grounded in languages. They are happy at home and they are itinerant beings. Translators do not just enable border crossing and mediation. They bring new worlds into being. By working along the seams of languages and different human experiences they are able to show what the world may look like from different vantage points. They are communicators, language lovers, movers through words and worlds. They are able both to transcend cultures, to move beyond cultures and also to respect the integrity of the people and places they have come from and are moving towards. At one and the same time they are being transcultural and being intercultural.

Key references

Bassnett, S. and Lefevere, A. (1998) *Constructing Cultures: Essays on Literary Translation.* Clevedon: Multilingual Matters.

Clifford, J. (1997) *Routes, Travel and Translation in the Late Twentieth Century.* Cambridge, MA: Harvard University Press.

Cronin, M. (2000) *Across the Lines: Travel, Language and Translation.* Cork: Cork University Press.

Roberts, C., Byram, M., Barro, A., Jordan, S. and Street, B. (2001) *Language Learners as Ethnographers.* Clevedon: Multilingual Matters.

Simon, S. (1996) *Gender in Translation: Cultural Identity and the Politics of Transmission.* London: Routledge.

Venuti, L. (1995) *The Translator's Invisibility: A History of Translation.* London and New York: Routledge.

Venuti, L. (1999) *The Translation Studies Reader.* London: Routledge.

Websites

http://www.lang.ltsn.ac.uk/resources/guidecontents.aspx
http://accurapid.com/journal/13educ.htm

Encyclopedia

Byram, M. (2000) *Routledge Encyclopedia of Language Teaching and Learning.* London and New York: Routledge.

Being intercultural

BEING LANGUAGERS

Languages are in crisis. This may be a good thing.

What does it now mean to be a student, as learner or teacher, of modern languages? The activities of studying have become a self-denying exercise. It is a very curious category. In economics, for instance, one studies structures and functions and relations that combine to make up an economic system; the same is true of sociology and history. Yet when we come to modern languages we drop the whole idea of interrelationship and we study that to the exclusion of all else. We isolate particular aspects from the totality. Modern languages, despite its name, actually refuses to look at totalities. It is forced to extract language from social encounters and literature from life.

Compelled by the functionalist arguments of serving literary study or of serving goals of employment, everything that relates to life and relation ends up being nothing more than a social accoutrement or a fabricated fetish. The heart of languages, which is intercultural being, is lost.

This is the crisis. Why is the functional argument so able to overwhelm us? Because we have offered no coherent argument in response. This book is an attempt to demonstrate that we have a powerful case to make. Unless we actually centre languages at the heart of life, at the heart of intercultural being, grounding a fresh curriculum in common experience, then the marginalisation will continue and our lives and curiosities for other worlds and other ways of being will continue to be eroded in the name, even more ironically, of the global market.

What, then, might modern languages look, **questions and answers** taste, feel and be like as part of a political project of engagement with questions of power and of being human? How can we teach and learn languages productively? How can we 'study' languages together, as teacher and student, when culture is slippery and imprecise and in constant process, when culture as a concept has become so overweening and imprecise as to make us assert that we would do well to move beyond the concept? What 'tools' may be useful in aiding an understanding of what we are working with when we are living lives that teach in and about languages? What sense can we begin to make from the fragments of our experience? How can we move beyond simple assumptions and adversarial positions that understand culture or language as being about 'us' as native speakers and 'them' as speakers of 'foreign' languages?

Our answers to these questions have been twofold. Firstly, languages are not skills to be added to an employability portfolio nor are they the technical means by which great works of canonical culture my be consumed for their cultural capital. No, *languaging* is a way of being, encompassing the whole social world.

Languaging is transformational. Languaging is in and of itself embodied knowledge. Languaging is *habitus*, it is about skilling people, not adding on detachable skills. Languaging demonstrates that 'ontology always trumps epistemology' (Barnett, 2003: 56). Through languaging people come to make sense of and to shape their worlds. Through languaging they become active agents in creating their human and material environments. Languaging is, as we have argued throughout, inextricably relational. It is a social way of being. To repeat: 'No speech is speech unless heard' (Spivak, 1999: 27).

As languagers we are people who move in and through words as actions, who develop and change constantly as the experience of languaging evolves and changes us. A languaging student and a languaging teacher are given a unique opportunity to enter the languaging of others, to open up the ways in which the complexity and experience of others may enrich life.

Secondly, we argue throughout this book that experiences such as translating, reading texts in other languages, sojourning abroad, singing in French, dancing in German, applying bandages in Urdu, eating meals in Gaelic, are all ways in which we are being intercultural. To isolate these phenomena, to see them as closed, reified, as bound by system or geography or history is neither practical nor ethical (Freadman, 2001: 293).

Opening these experiences out – in the manner of just the smoke rising from Brecht's poem, or of the particular beat of the dance of the tango, or the dominant use of caraway or dill in a regional cuisine – opens us all out. It opens us out as people who are always in the process of becoming intercultural beings, whose whole lives are a patchwork of cultural colours, who respect and understand and engage openly with the different ways of living life and understanding the world that we may encounter in others and in ourselves. Languagers are able to move in and through words, smells, sights and tastes, make meanings, find laughter and loveliness, and ask questions of cruelty and oppression. To be intercultural is to be beyond the captivities of culture.

We have argued for a *critical perspective* throughout this book in order to open up space for a fresh debate about modern languages. Languages are a social justice issue. And profoundly so. In an age of translation, technology and global English, we are taking a moment to consider some of the ways in which languages make us manifestly human. The repression and destruction of languages is an act of injustice, in the same way as the stockpiling of weapons of mass destruction or the scandal of trade injustice. Just as postcolonialism opened out debates and transformed subjects such as geography, sociology, English literature, anthropology, so these ethical and political questions engage us as modern languagers in a process of learning and relearning, of deconstruction and reconstruction. In the process of asking new questions of languages, of the difference made by the languages we live in and those we encounter, we learn something new, simultaneously about ourselves and about the people and places we visit.

Learning, unlearning and relearning can occur and be embodied in the reflections on everyday cultural practices and everyday objects that fill our classrooms. It can occur by instilling a spirit of inquiry into activities that mess with languages through ethnography or fieldwork, through the practical embodying of language-in-action. It is present in reflections, for instance, on languages, their history, their use, their ideological imperatives throughout the ages, their shaping into an educational project – of which this offering is, of course, also a part. Such critical, open teaching allows a structuring of experience which focuses on lived events, as well as concrete practices. The people, practices, spaces and processes that are brought by our students and which we also bring to the open exchanges in our classrooms can be surveyed, exemplified, examined critically and interpreted for the multiple and contested meanings they contain. Each encounter can be interrogated for the way it may bear the imprint of the past. Such work of examination is the duty of both teacher and learner, so that each person in each classroom experiences what it is to be both teacher and learner.

critical, open teaching

In living languages nothing stays still for long and trying to nail languages down to some kind of unity of nation or ethnicity is highly problematic. To try and understand languages in the contexts of nations and cultures is to limit them to often arbitrarily, politically and historically defined boundaries. This is just one of the ways in which we have tried, in modern languages, to make manageable what is actually utterly impossible. Encountering languages through unashamedly critical perspectives means encountering difference and familiarity in ways of doing things, in ways of seeing and understanding the world, in material objects. Languaging involves encounters with others, yes, but also, importantly, with ourselves, with our own expectations, false assumptions, likes and dislikes, and often deeply rooted unexamined opinions. To really engage with modern languages involves what Raymond Williams describes as 'a long and difficult remaking [...] a struggle at the roots of the mind [...] confronting [...] the hard practical substance of effective and continuing relationships' (Williams, 1977: 212).

This is because languages, ultimately, are about life – life as shared, unequal, irreducible 'while it is being lived', as always 'in part unknown, unrealized' (Williams, 1993: 334).

Languages are by nature gregarious, even promiscuous, interdisciplinary things. I can't imagine why we should keep them out of trouble by confining them in Arts Faculties. (Freadman, 2001: 282)

Language teaching is a dynamic, volatile, changing, messy business. The crisis in modern languages exposes this and much more. It exposes those who do not and cannot speak with love the languages that they teach, who have no relation to living in languages, to our concept of languaging. It also exposes those who, because of the acute nature of crisis in general and here specifically, have held on to modes of teaching which are moribund and which operate from a basis of mistrust of students and of the knowledges they already embody. It exposes those who have no love of the life of the language they teach, whose social relations in and through the language are halting, not fluent.

Knowing what it is like to experience life in a language means that you engage that life. To disengage from the language is to put it in a space which is labelled 'French, German, Spanish', but which has no history, because we never study its relations and the ways in which it is read and used. It is to be devoid of the kinds of fluencies for which we have argued in this book.

Many of those who work in this profession today have spent their lives working with and on texts that they attempt to make fit into preconceived categories by stripping them of languages, social relations, intercultural being. There are good, pragmatic reasons for this work but what we are left with at the core of our modern languages disciplines is something of a dried up husk, artificially denuded of life, intellectually devoid of theory and method, rather like Cinderella's ugly sisters who chop off their toes in order to try and make their feet fit the slipper:

> *In any event, where language departments or language programmes ended up was a very uncomfortable place indeed, and I can assert with some certainty that the project of teaching a whole national culture within a single department was doomed from the outset, either to outright failure, or to abject self parody. It is quite simply impossible to reproduce in miniature the integrated articulated unity of all the faculties for the purposes of representing the culture of any nameable language. (Freadman, 2001: 279–80)*

One of the lessons we learn from translation studies is the lesson of *renewal*. Texts taken from one language and transformed into another are taken precisely because they have something to offer, some life, or idea, or way of representing the world that can enrich beyond boundaries, which may infuse with new life. And so it is, in our argument, with modern languages. To bind what Freadman describes as the 'gregarious', 'promiscuous' quality of languages to study in the arts is to deny the fact that no single academic discipline has been untouched by languaging, ever. Equally, to bind modern languages in the functionalist belief that languages are *for* business, *for* tourism, *for* engineering is to deny the powerful, boundary-dissolving effects of languaging and of being intercultural.

As we have shown throughout, languages, in other contexts, ask different questions, open different ways of being, enable different ways of encountering people, 'allow the hard currency of human suffering' that Bauman speaks of (Bauman, 1998: 5) to be explored and addressed. This is not to say that important questions have not and are not asked in modern languages disciplines today. It is to say that these, as yet, remain insufficient to addressing the crisis. We have used a new language throughout this book in an attempt to move beyond functionalist discourse and to enable the asking of the kinds of questions that may lead us to conceive of a languaging curriculum.

PRACTICAL RESOURCES FOR UTOPIA

We are aware, in writing this book, that we are both, in our different ways, with our different histories and passions, coming to teaching confident, hopeful, taking pleasure in the task, believing in our students and ourselves. We are also aware that for many teaching evokes different feelings, different experiences. For the new lecturer or the graduate teaching assistant teaching may be just doing in the classroom as teacher what was done to oneself. Alternatively, it may be a zealous quest for different ways of doing things, it may be a teaching that grows out of opposition to ways of instructing that have been experienced. It may, and this is also our experience, be a daunting task, one which causes some sleepless nights, some anxious moments, soul searching and that struggle which Raymond Williams speaks of, 'in the roots of the mind', which accompanies the genuine hope for better ways of being. How can I *be* intercultural, *be* a languager? These are grand ideals and worthy hopes but in the unbelievable constraints – material, emotional even intellectual – of my life at this time, in this place, with the pressures to publish or perish, to charm or die, to oil the wheels of a screaming bureaucracy, how can I ever *be* these things to these students?

The ways of being intercultural, human, of languaging that we have narrated here, from our own lives and experiences of teaching and learning, may indeed seem utopian, impractical, unworkable. The glass, in modern languages at least, is indeed 'half empty'. The mood of the moment is of retreat. Is now really the time for blue skies thinking?

The structure and working method of this book, however, has the aim of modelling the brokenness and vulnerability and messiness of hopes-in-action through the stories that break into the text and the argument. Your contexts are ours too.

It's the first day back after Christmas. Over the vacation the temperature reached –20 degrees. The building I teach in is frozen solid. The pipes upstairs in the library have burst, water has been pouring down the stairs, part of the ceiling has fallen in. Water has seeped into some of the channels though which the electric cables run. The heating in my office isn't working…but, despite all of this, its still business as usual. Teaching is like theatre. The show must go on. So here I am, huddled inside coat and scarf and gloves, just like my students. I laugh. We should start by celebrating our showing up together, I think. But really, how do I deal with this? Ignore it in the hope it will go away? Continue the fallacy that bodies are not what matters in learning? My Austrian language assistant at university would have made us do aerobics in German at this point but I don't actually quite have the nerve. There is a loud noise of drilling above and bits of plaster drop from the ceiling onto the pages open in front of us. This time we all laugh. And somehow, we all begin to thaw. Sometimes teaching comes from the acknowledgement of the impossible, the ridiculous, and our common sense of just being in it together.

But it is not just our material circumstances that are daunting at times. Here we are, stuck in the middle of ways of doing things and ways of teaching things and ways of organising things which, in the light of the arguments of this book, may now seem untenable. But the only power we have is what we are to give away to our students as we teach. How, in the powerlessness of such teaching, such constraints, can we hope to be inter-cultural, to form languagers? And yet, it would be our argument and our practical story, that for all its potentially impractical utopianism, it is not as if the current set of circumstances represent a better alternative, an easy place to stay. In many ways what we are talking about here – with the hope for 'a constant struggle at the roots of the mind' – is permanent, velvet revolution.

The work we have done has always been small scale, sometimes it has been marginal, odd, on the edges of the mainstream of our departments and disciplines. This has been the work of the departmental lone ranger holding on to the belief in other ways of doing things. To work like this is indeed not to be pliant, docile, predictable, easy. It is about a commitment to seeking out the risky, arduous and vulnerable ways of being. It will cer-tainly entail mistakes and failures, false starts, innovative flops, rejection by those who prefer the well beaten tracks. This, as a disposition for teaching, for action, is also one of the dispositions which the university exists to promote. There can be no reflection on life, no break through, no sifting of thoughts, no testing of theory without such a disposition. By lan-guaging alongside our students, in this supercomplex world, we can continually learn how to be intercultural.

Bibliography

This bibliography offers some references which may be useful for further reading and indicates some of the work, key thinkers and fields of knowledge that have influenced the writing of this book.

Aaltonen, S. (2000) *Time-Sharing on Stage: Drama Translation in Theatre and Society*. Clevedon: Multilingual Matters.

Abu-Lughod, L. (1991) 'Writing against culture', in R.G. Fox (ed.), *Recapturing Anthropology: Working in the Present*. Santa Fé, NM: School of American Research Press.

Adorno, T. (1999) *Auf die Frage: Was ist Deutsch?* Frankfurt am Main: Suhrkamp.

Agar, M. (1994) *Language Shock: Understanding the Culture of Conversation*. New York: William Morrow.

Agar, M. (2000) *The Professional Stranger: An Informal Introduction to Ethnography*. London: Academic Press.

Altricher, H., Posch, P. and Somekh, B. (1993) *Teachers Investigate their Work*. London: Routledge.

Anderson, B. (1991) *Imagined Communities: Reflections on the Origin and Spread of Nationalism*. London and New York: Verso.

Apostolopoulos, Y., Leivadi, S., Yiannakis, A. (eds) (1996) *The Sociology of Tourism*. London and New York: Routledge.

Appadurai, A. (1986) *The Social Life of Things: Commodities in Cultural Perspective*. Cambridge: Cambridge University Press.

Appadurai, A. (1996) *Modernity at Large: Cultural Dimensions of Globalization*. Minneapolis, MN: University of Minnesota Press.

Arcand, J.-L. (2000) 'Development economics and language: the earnest search for a mirage?', *International Journal of the Sociology of Language*, 121: 119–57.

Archer, M. (2000) *Being Human: The Problem of Agency*. Cambridge: Cambridge University Press.

Aronowitz, S. (1992) *The Politics of Identity Class, Culture, Social Movements*. New York and London: Routledge.

Arteaga, A. (1994) *An Other Tongue: Nation and Ethnicity in the Linguistic Borderlands*. Durham, NC: Duke University Press.

Asad, T. (1986) 'The concept of cultural translation in British social anthropology', in J. Clifford and G. E. Marcus (eds), *Writing Culture: The Poetics and Politics of Ethnography*. Berkeley, Los Angeles and London: University of California Press, pp. 141–64.

Atweh, B., Kemmis, S. and Weeks, P. (1998) *Action Research in Practice: Partnerships for Social Justice in Education*. London: Routledge.

Austen, J. (1813) *Pride and Prejudice*. Harmondsworth: Penguin.

Austin, J. L. (1975) *How to do Things with Words*. Cambridge, MA: Harvard University Press.

Baboni, P. (2001) 'Cinderella might find Prince Charming, at last. New perspectives for languages teaching methodology as an autonomous science', in R. Di Napoli, L. Polezzi and A. King (eds), *Fuzzy Boundaries? Reflections on Modern Languages and the Humanities*. London: CILT, pp. 109–20.

Barba, E. (1994) 'Traditions and the founders of traditions', *New Theatre Quarterly*, X(38): 197–8.

Barba, E. and Savarese, N. (1991) *A Dictionary of Theatre Anthropology*. London: Routledge.

Barbour, S. (1996) 'Language and national identity in Europe; theoretical and practical problems', in C. Hoffman (ed.), *Language, Culture and Communication in Contemporary Europe*. Clevedon: Multilingual Matters, pp. 28–46.

Barnett, R. (1994a) *The Limits of Competence: Knowledge, Higher Education and Society*. Buckingham: Open University Press.

Barnett, R. (1994b) *Academic Community: Discourse or Discord*. London: Kingsley.

Barnett, R. (1997) *Higher Education: A Critical Business*. Buckingham: Open University Press.

Barnett, R. (2000) *Realizing the University in an Age of Supercomplexity*. Buckingham: Open University Press.

Barnett, R. (2001) 'Crises of the humanities: challenges and opportunities', in R. Di Napoli, L. Polezzi and A. King (eds), *Fuzzy Boundaries? Reflections on Modern Languages and the Humanities*. London: CILT, pp. 25–42.

Barnett, R. (2003) *Beyond all Reason: Living with Ideology in the University*. Buckingham: Open University Press.

Barth, F. (1969) *Ethnic Groups and Boundaries: The Social Organization of Culture Difference*. Oslo: Universitetsforlaget.

Barth, F. (1981) *Process and Form in Social Life: Selected Essays of Fredrik Barth, Vol. 1*. London: Routledge & Kegan Paul.

Barth, F. (1989) 'The analysis of culture in complex societies', *Ethnos*, 54: 120–42.

Barthes, R. (1973) *Mythologies*. London: Paladin.

Bartlett, T. (2001) 'Use the road: the appropriacy of appropriation', *Language and Intercultural Communication*, 1(1): 21–40.

Bassnett, S. (1997) *Studying British Cultures: An Introduction*. London and New York: Routledge.

Bassnett, S. (2001) 'The fuzzy boundaries of translation', in R. Di Napoli, L. Polezzi and A. King (eds), *Fuzzy Boundaries? Reflections on Modern Languages and the Humanities*. London: CILT, pp. 67–80.

Bassnett, S. and Lefevere, A. (1990) *Translation, History and Culture*. London and New York: Pinter.

Bassnett, S. and Lefevere, A. (1998) *Constructing Cultures: Essays on Literary Translation*. Clevedon: Multilingual Matters.

Bassnett-McGuire, S. (1980) *Translation Studies*. London and New York: Methuen.

Baudrillard, J. (1993) *Symbolic Exchange and Death,* trans. Iain Hamilton Grant. London: Sage.

Bauman, R. (1986) *Story, Performance and Event.* Cambridge: Cambridge University Press.

Bauman, R. and Sherzer, J. (1989) *Explorations in the Ethnography of Speaking*. Cambridge: Cambridge University Press.

Bauman, Z. (1996) 'From pilgrim to tourist – or a short history of identity', in S. Hall and P. du Gay (eds), *Questions of Cultural Identity*. London: Sage, pp. 18–36.

Bauman, Z. (1998) *Globalization: The Human Consequences*. Cambridge: Polity.

Bauman, Z. (2000) *Liquid Modernity*. Oxford: Polity.

Bauman, Z. (2002) *Society under Siege*. Cambridge: Polity.

Bausinger, H. (1990) *Folk Culture in a World of Technology*. Bloomington and Indianapolis, IN: Indiana University Press.

Bausinger, H. et al. (1991) *Reisekultur. Von der Pilgerfahrt zum moderneren Tourismus*. Munich: C. H. Beck.

Belsey, C. (1980) *Critical Practice*. London and New York: Routledge.

Bendix, R. (1997) *In Search of Authenticity: The Formation of Folklore Studies*. Madison, WI: University of Wisconsin Press.

Benjamin, A. and Osborne, P. E. (1994) *Walter Benjamin's Philosophy*. London and New York: Routledge.

Benjamin, W. (1973) *Illuminations*. London: Fontana.

Benson, P. and Voller, P. (1997) *Autonomy and Independence in Language Learning*. London: Longman.

Bentley, T. and Clayton, S. (1998) *Profiting from Diversity*. Aldershot: Gower.

Bertho Lavenir, C. (1999) *La Roue et le Stylo: Comment nous sommes devenus Touristes*. Paris: Editions Odile Jacob.

Bhabha, H. (1990) 'DissemiNation: time, narrative, and the margins of the modern nation', in *Nation and Narration*. London: Routledge, pp. 291–322.

Bhabha, H. (1994) *The Location of Culture*. London: Routledge.

Blake, N., Smith, R. and Standish, P. (1998) *The Universities We Need*. London: Kogan Page.

Bloch, B. (1996) 'The language–culture connection in international business.' *Foreign Language Annals* 29(1): 27–36.

Bloom, D. and Grenier, G. (1996) 'Language, employment, and earnings in the United States: Spanish–English differentials from 1970–1990', *International Journal of the Sociology of Language*, 121: 45–68.

Boissevain, J. (1996) *Coping with Tourists: European Reactions to Mass Tourism*. Providence, RI: Berghahn.

Borneman, J. and Fowler, N. (1997) 'Europeanization', *Annual Review of Anthropology*, 26: 487–514.

Bottomore, T. (1984) *The Frankfurt School.* London and New York: Routledge.

Bourdieu, P. (1977) *Outline of a Theory of Practice.* Cambridge: Cambridge University Press.

Bourdieu, P. (1984) *Distinction: A Social Critique of the Judgement of Taste*. London: Routledge.

Bourdieu, P. (1988) *Homo Academicus*. Cambridge: Polity.

Bourdieu, P. (1991) *Language and Symbolic Power*. Cambridge: Polity.

Bourdieu, P. (1993) *The Field of Cultural Production*. Cambridge: Polity.

Bourdieu, P. (2000) *Pascalian Meditations*. Cambridge: Polity.

Bourdieu, P. and Haacke, H. (1995) *Free Exchange*. Oxford: Polity.

Bourdieu, P. and Wacquant, L. (1992) *An Invitation to Reflexive Sociology*. Oxford: Polity.

Bourdieu, P. and Wacquant, L. (2001) 'NewLiberalSpeak: notes on the new planetary vulgate', *Radical Philosophy*, 105: 2–5.

Bourdieu, P. et al. (1999) *The Weight of the World: Social Suffering in a Contemporary Society.* Oxford: Polity.

Bradburd, D. (1998) *Being There: The Necessity of Fieldwork*. Washington, DC and London: Smithsonian Institution Press.

Brenner, P. (1989) 'Interkulturelle Hermeneutik: Probleme einer Theorie kulturellen Fremdverstehens', in P. Zimmerman (ed.), *Interkulturelle Germanistik: Dialog der Kulturen auf Deutsch. Frankfurt am Main*: Peter Lang, pp. 35–55.

Brink, A. (1983) *Mapmakers: Writing in a State of Siege*. London: Faber & Faber.

Brooker, P. (1999) *A Concise Glossary of Cultural Theory*. London: Arnold.

Brown, K. (2000) 'Creative thinking about a new modern languages pedagogy', in Green, S. (ed.), *New Perspectives on Teaching and Learning Modern Languages*. Clevedon: Multilingual Matters.

Brumfit, C. (2000) 'Modern languages within a policy for language in education', S. Green (ed.) in *New Perspectives on Teaching and Learning Modern Languages*. Clevedon: Multilingual Matters, pp. 94–104.

Brumfit, C. (2001) 'Humanities, language education and national responsibility', in R. Di Napoli, L. Polezzi and A. King (eds), *Fuzzy Boundaries? Reflections on Modern Languages and the Humanities*. London: CILT, pp. 81–94.

Brutt-Griffler, J. (2002) *World English: A Study of its Development*. Clevedon: Multilingual Matters.

Buber, M. (1954) *Die Schriften über das Dialogische Prinzip*. Munich: Verlag Lambert Schneider.

Buber, M. (1958) *I and Thou*. Edinburgh: T&T Clark.

Burns, P. M. (1999) *Tourism and Anthropology*. London and New York: Routledge.

Burns, R. (1995) *German Cultural Studies: An Introduction*. Oxford: Oxford University Press.

Burwood, S. (1999) 'Liberation philosophy', *Teaching in Higher Education*, 4(4): 447–60.

Byram, M. (1997) *Teaching and Assessing Intercultural Communicative Competence*. Clevedon: Multilingual Matters.

Byram, M. (2000) *Routledge Encyclopedia of Language Teaching and Learning*. London and New York: Routledge.

Byram, M. and Fleming, M. (1998) *Language Learning in Intercultural Perspective: Approaches through Drama and Ethnography*. Cambridge: Cambridge University Press.

Byram, M., Estarte-Sarries, V. and Taylor, S. (1991) *Cultural Studies and Language Learning: A Research Report*. Clevedon: Multilingual Matters.

Byram, M., Nichols, A. and Stevens, D. (2001) *Developing Intercultural Communication in Practice*. Clevedon: Multilingual Matters.

Byram, M., Zarate, G. and Neuner, G. (1997) *Sociocultural Competence in Language Learning and Teaching.* Strasbourg: Council of Europe Publishing.

Byrnes, H. (1998) 'Introduction: steps to an ecology of foreign language departments', in H. Byrnes (ed.), *Learning Foreign and Second languages: Perspectives in Research and Scholarship.* New York: Modern Language Association of America, pp. 1–22.

Byrnes, H. (ed.) (1998) *Learning Foreign and Second languages: Perspectives in Research and Scholarship.* New York: Modern Language Association of America.

Calhoun, C. (1996) 'A different poststructuralism', *Contemporary Sociology,* 25: 302–5.

Callinicos, A. (1989) *Against Postmodernism. A Marxist Critique.* Cambridge: Polity Press.

Carr, W. and Kemmis, S. (1986) *Becoming Critical: Education, Knowledge and Action Research.* Lewes: Falmer Press.

Carter, R. and McRae, J. (eds) (1996) *Language, Literature and the Learner: Creative Classroom Practice.* London and New York: Longman.

Chambers, G. (1999) *Motivating Language Learners.* Clevedon: Multilingual Matters.

Chambers, G. (2000) 'Motivation and the learners of modern languages', in S. Green (ed.), *New Perspectives on Teaching and Learning Modern Languages.* Clevedon: Multilingual Matters, pp. 46–76.

Chodorow, N. J. (1989) *Feminism and Psychoanalytic Theory.* New Haven, CT and London: Yale University Press.

Ciliberti, A. (2001) 'Language ideologies and the current state of language teaching in Italy', in R. Di Napoli, L. Polezzi and A. King (eds), *Fuzzy Boundaries? Reflections on Modern Languages and the Humanities.* London: CILT, pp. 95–108.

Cixous, H. (1992) 'From Sorties', in A. Easthope and K. McGowan (eds), *A Critical and Cultural Theory Reader.* Buckingham: Open University Press, pp. 137–46.

Clifford, J. (1986) 'On ethnographic allegory', in J. Clifford and G. E. Marcus, *Writing Culture: The Poetics and Politics of Ethnography.* Berkeley and Los Angeles: University of California Press, pp. 98–121.

Clifford, J. (1988) *The Predicament of Culture: Twentieth Century Ethnography, Literature and Art.* Cambridge, MA: Harvard University Press.

Clifford, J. (1992) 'Traveling cultures', in L. Grossberg, C. Nelson and P. Treichler (eds) *Cultural Studies.* New York: Routledge.

Clifford, J. (1993) 'On collecting art and culture', in S. During (ed.), *The Cultural Studies Reader.* London, Routledge, pp. 49–74.

Clifford, J. (1997) *Routes: Travel and Translation in the Late Twentieth Century*. Cambridge, MA: Harvard University Press.

Clifford, J. (2003) 'On ethnographic authority', *Representations*, 1(2): 118–46.

Clifford, J. and Marcus, G. E. (1986) *Writing Culture: The Poetics and Politics of Ethnography*. Berkeley and Los Angeles: University of California Press.

Clyne, M. (1994) *Inter-cultural Communication at Work: Cultural Values in Discourse*. Cambridge: Cambridge University Press.

Clyne, M. (1995) *The German Language in a Changing Europe*. Cambridge: Cambridge University Press.

Cohen, A. P. (1994) *Self Consciousness: An Alternative Anthropology of Identity*. London and New York: Routledge.

Cohen, A. P. (2000) *Signifying Identities: Anthropological Perspectives on Boundaries and Contested Values*. London and New York: Routledge.

Cohen, E. and Cooper, R. L. (1986) 'Language and tourism', *Annals of Tourism Research*, 13(4): 533–63.

Coleman, J. (1999) 'Stereotypes, objectives and the *Auslandsaufenthalt*', in R. Tenberg (ed.), *Intercultural Perspectives: Images of Germany in Education and the Media*. Munich: Ludicium, pp. 145–59.

Coleman, J. (2001) 'What is residence abroad for? Intercultural competence and the linguisitic, cultural academic, personal and professional objectives of student residence abroad', in R. Di Napoli, L. Polezzi and A. King (eds), *Fuzzy Boundaries? Reflections on Modern Languages and the Humanities*. London: CILT, pp. 121–40.

Colomer, J. (1996) 'To translate or to learn languages? An evaluation of social efficiency', *International Journal of the Sociology of Language*, 121: 181–97.

Conquergood, D. (1991) 'Rethinking ethnography: towards a critical cultural politics', *Communication Monographs*, 58: 179–94.

Conquergood, D. (1992) 'Ethnography, rhetoric, and performance', *Quarterly Journal of Speech*, 78: 80–123.

Cook, G. (1994) *Discourse and Literature: The Interplay of Form and Mind*. Oxford: Oxford University Press.

Cook, G. (2000) *Language Play, Language Learning*. Oxford: Oxford University Press.

Cook, G. (2001) 'Less work and more play: towards a ludicrous linguistics', in R. Di Napoli, L. Polezzi, and A. King (eds), *Fuzzy Boundaries? Reflections on Modern Languages and the Humanities*. London: CILT, 141–58.

Cook, V. (1996) *Second Language Learning and Language Teaching*. London and New York: Arnold.

Coulmas, F. (1992) *Die Wirtschaft mit der Sprachen*. Frankfurt am Main: Suhrkamp.

Coyle, D. (2000) 'Meeting the challenge: developing the 3Cs curriculum', in S. Green (ed.), *New Perspectives on Teaching and Learning Modern Languages*. Clevedon: Multilingual Matters, pp. 158–82.

Crawshaw, R., Callen, B. and Tusting, K. (2001) 'Attesting the self: narration and identity change', *Language and Intercultural Communication*, 1(2): 101–19.

Creme, P. (1999) 'A reflection on the education of the "critical person"', *Teaching in Higher Education*, 4(4): 461–71.

Cronin, M. (2000) *Across the Lines: Travel, Language and Translation*. Cork: Cork University Press.

Cronin, M. (2002) '"Thou shalt be one with the birds": translation, connexity and the new global order', *Language and Intercultural Communication*, 2(2): 86–95.

Crowley, T. (1996) 'Signs of belonging: languages, nations and cultures in the old and new Europe', in C. Hoffman (ed.), *Language, Culture and Communication in Contemporary Europe*. Clevedon: Multilingual Matters, pp. 47–60.

Cryle, P. (2002) 'Should we stop worrying about cultural awareness?', in S. Cormeraie, D. Killick and M. Parry (eds), *Revolutions in Consciousness: Local Identities, Global Concerns in Languages and Intercultural Communication*. Leeds: IALIC, pp. 23–34.

Cunningham, V. (1994) *In the Reading Gaol: Postmodernity, Texts and History*. Oxford: Blackwell.

Curzon-Hobson, A. (2002) 'Higher education in a world of radical unknowability: an extension of the challenge of Ronald Barnett', *Teaching in Higher Education*, 7(2): 179–93.

Dahlén, T. (1997) *Among the Interculturalists: An Emergent Profession and Its Packaging of Knowledge*. Stockholm: Stockholm Studies in Social Anthropology.

Dann, G. (1996) *The Language of Tourism: a Sociolinguistic Perspective*. Wallingford: CAB International.

de Botton, A. (2002) *The Art of Travel*. London: Hamish Hamilton.

de Certeau, M. (1984) *The Practice of Everyday Life*. Los Angeles and London: University of California Press.

de Certeau, M. (1986) *Heterologies: Discourse on the Other*. Manchester: Manchester University Press.

de Certeau, M. (1990) *L'Invention du quotidien: Arts de faire*. Paris: Gallimard.

de Certeau, M. (1997) *Culture au Pluriel*. Minneapolis, MN: University of Minnesota Press.

Delors, Jacques et al. (1996) *Learning: The Treasure Within*. UNESCO.

Denham, S., Kacandes, I. and Petropoulos, J. (1997) *A User's Guide to German Cultural Studies*. Ann Arbor, MI: University of Michigan Press.

Dorson, R. (2000) *Folklore and Folklife: An Introduction*. Chicago and London: University of Chicago Press.

Doughty, P. and Thornton, G. (1973) *Language Study, the Teacher and the Learner*. London: Edward Arnold.

Douglas, M. (1987) *How Institutions Think*. London: Routledge & Kegan Paul.

Douglas, M. (1996) *Natural Symbols: Explorations in Cosmology*, 2nd edn. London and New York: Routledge.

Douglas, M. and Isherwood, B. (1996) *The World of Goods: Towards an Anthropology of Consumption*, 2nd edn. London and New York: Routledge.

du Gay, P. (1996) *Consumption and Identity at Work*. London: Sage.

Dunbar, R. (1996) *Grooming, Gossip and the Evolution of Language*. London and Boston: Faber & Faber.

Dunbar, R., Knight, C. and Power, C. (1999) *The Evolution of Culture: An Interdisciplinary View*. Edinburgh: Edinburgh University Press.

Dundes, A. (1999) *International Folkloristics: Classic Contributions by the Founders of Folklore*. Lanham, MD: Rowman & Littlefield.

Duranti, A. (2001) *Linguistic Anthropology*. Oxford: Blackwell.

Eagleton, T. (1996) *Literary Theory: An Introduction*, 2nd edn. Oxford: Blackwell.

Eagleton, T. (2000) *The Idea of Culture*. Oxford: Blackwell.

Egan, K. (1997) *The Educated Mind: How Cognitive Tools Shape Our Understanding*. Chicago: Chicago University Press.

Ellen, R., James, W., Ingold, T., Littlewood, R. and Richards, P. (1996), '1990 debate: human worlds are culturally constructed', in T. Ingold (ed.), *Key Debates in Anthropology*. London and New York: Routledge, pp. 99–147.

Eriksen, T. H. (1995) *Small Places, Large Issues: An Introduction to Social and Cultural Anthropology*. London: Pluto Press.

Evans, L. and Abbott, I. (1998) *Teaching and Learning in Higher Education*. London: Cassell Education.

Evans, C. (1988) *Language People: The Experience of teaching and learning modern languages in British Universities*. Buckingham: Open University Press.

Even-Zohar, I. (1981) 'Translation theory today: a call for transfer theory', *Poetics Today*, 2(4): 1–7.

Faber, R. and Naumann, B. (1995) *Literatur der Grenze, Theorie der Grenze*. Würzburg: Königshausen & Neumann.

Fabian, J. (1983) *Time and the Other: How Anthropology Makes Its Object.* New York: Columbia University Press.

Fabian, J. (1998) *Moments of Freedom: Anthropology and Popular Culture.* Charlottesville, VA and London: University Press of Virginia.

Featherstone, M. (1990) *Global Culture.* London: Sage.

Fiske, J. (1989a) *Reading the Popular.* London: Routledge.

Fiske, J. (1989b) *Understanding Popular Culture.* London: Routledge.

Forgacs, D. (2001) 'Cultural studies: a non-discipline?', in R. Di Napoli, L. Polezzi and A. King (eds), *Fuzzy Boundaries? Reflections on Modern Languages and the Humanities.* London: CILT, pp. 57–66.

Foucault, M. (1980) *Power/Knowledge.* New York: Pantheon Books.

Foucault, M. (1991) *Discipline and Punish: The Birth of the Prison.* London: Penguin.

Freadman, A. (2001) 'The culture peddlers', *Postcolonial Studies,* 4(3): 275–95.

Freed, B. (1995) *Second Language Acquisition in a Study Abroad Context.* Amsterdam and Philadelphia: Johns Benjamins.

Freire, P. (1998) *Teachers as Cultural Workers.* Boulder, CO: Westview Press.

Friedman, J. (1994a) *Cultural Identity and Global Process.* London: Sage.

Friedman, J. (1994b) *Consumption and Identity.* Chur, Switzerland: Harwood Academic.

Gadamer, H.-G. (1989) *Truth and Method.* London: Sheed & Ward.

Gee, J. (1989) 'Literacy, discourse, and linguistics', *Journal of Education,* 171(1): 5–17.

Geertz, C. (1973) *The Interpretation of Cultures.* London: Fontana.

Geertz, C. (1993) *Local Knowledge.* London: Fontana.

Geertz, C. (2000) *Available Light: Anthropological Reflections on a Philosophical Topic.* Princeton, NJ: Princeton University Press.

Giddens, A. (1991) *Modernity and Self Identity: Self and Society in the Late Modern Age.* Cambridge: Polity.

Gilman, S. (1996) 'A near future at the Millennium', in J. Roche and T. Salumets (eds), *Germanics under Construction: Intercultural and Interdisciplinary Prospects.* Munich: Ludicium, pp. 9–13.

Giroux, H. (1988) *Teachers as Intellectuals.* New York: Bergin & Garvey.

Giroux, H. (1992) *Border Crossings: Cultural Workers and the Politics of Education.* London: Routledge.

Goffman, E. (1961) *Encounters: Two Studies in the Sociology of Interaction.* Indianapolis, IN: Bobbs-Merrill.

Goffman, E. (1968) *Stigma: Notes on the Management of Spoiled Identity.* London: Penguin.

Goffman, E. (1969) *The Presentation of Self in Everyday Life.* London: Allen Lane.

Gottowik, V. (1997) 'Begegnung mit einer Ethnographie des Eigenen: John J. Honigmann beschreibt die Steiermark und wir erkennen sie nicht', *Zeitschrift für Volkskunde*, 93(1): 17–30.

Graburn, N. (1978) 'Tourism: the sacred journey', in V. Smith (ed.) *Hosts and Guests: The Anthropology of Tourism*. Oxford: Blackwell, pp. 17–31.

Graburn, N. (ed.) (1983) The anthropology of tourism: special issue, *Annals of Tourism Research*, 10(1): 9–34.

Graves-Brown, P. M. (2000) *Matter, Materiality and Modern Culture*. London and New York: Routledge.

Green, S. (ed.) (2000) *New Perspectives on Teaching and Learning Modern Languages*. Clevedon: Multilingual Matters.

Greenblatt, S. and Gunn, G. (1992) *Redrawing the Boundaries: The Transformation of English and American Literary Studies*. New York: MLA.

Grenfell, M. (2000) 'Learning and teaching strategies', in S. Green (ed.) *New Perspectives on Teaching and Learning Modern Languages*. Clevedon: Multilingual Matters, pp. 1–23.

Greverus, I.-M. (1990) *Neues Zeitalter oder Verkehrte Welt: Anthropologie als Kritik*. Darmstadt: Wissenschaftliche Buchgesellschaft.

Griffiths, M. (1998) *Educational Research for Social Justice: Getting off the Fence*. Buckingham: Open University Press.

Grin, F. (1996a) 'Economic approaches to language and language planning: an introduction', *International Journal of the Sociology of Language*, 121: 1–16.

Grin, F. (1996b) 'The economics of language: survey, assessment, and prospects', *International Journal of the Sociology of Language*, 121: 17–44.

Grossberg, L. (1996) 'Identity and cultural studies: is that all there is?', in S. Hall and P. du Gay (eds), *Questions of Cultural Identity*. London: Sage, pp. 87–108.

Grossberg, L., Nelson, C. and Treichler, P. (eds) (1992) *Cultural Studies*. New York: Routledge.

Guilherme, M. M. (2000) *Critical Cultural Awareness: The Critical Dimension in Foreign Culture Education*. PhD thesis, University of Durham.

Guilherme, M. (2002) *Critical Citizens for an Intercultural World*. Clevedon: Multilingual Matters.

Gumperz, J. (1982) *Discourse Strategies*. Cambridge: Cambridge University Press.

Gumperz, J. J. (1982) *Language and Social Identity*. Cambridge: Cambridge: University Press.

Gumperz, J. and Hymes, D. (1964) 'The ethnography of communication', *American Anthropologists*, 66(6): 182.

Gumperz, J. and Hymes, D. (1972) *Directions in Socio-linguistics: The Ethnography of Communication.* New York: Blackwell.

Habermas, J. (1984) *The Theory of Communicative Action: Reason and the Rationalization of Society.* Boston: Beacon Press, Boston.

Hall, E. T. (1993) *An Anthropology of Everyday Life.* New York: Anchor Books.

Hall, E. T. and Hall, M. R. (1990) *Understanding Cultural Differences: Germans, French and Americans.* Yarmouth, ME: Intercultural Press.

Hall, S. (1996) 'Who needs "identity"?', in S. Hall and P. du Gay (eds), *Questions of Cultural Identity.* London: Sage, pp. 1–18.

Hall, S. and du Gay, P. (1996) *Questions of Cultural Identity.* London: Sage.

Hallam, E. and Street, B. (2000) *Cultural Encounters: Representing Otherness.* London: Routledge.

Hamilton, J. (1995) *Inspiring Innovations in Language Teaching.* Clevedon: Multilingual Matters.

Hammersely, M. and Atkinson, P. (1983) *Ethnography: Principles in Practice.* London: Tavistock.

Hannerz, U. (1990a) *Cultural Complexity: Studies in the Social Organization of Meaning.* New York: University of Columbia Press.

Hannerz, U. (1990b) 'Cosmopolitans and locals in world culture', in M. Featherstone (ed.), *Global Culture.* London: Sage.

Hannerz, U. (1996) *Transnational Connections.* London and New York: Routledge.

Harvey, D. (1990) *The Condition of Postmodernity: An Enquiry into the Origins of Cultural Change.* Oxford: Blackwell.

Harvey, D. (1996) *Justice, Nature and the Geography of Difference.* Oxford: Blackwell.

Haug, W. (1999) 'Literaturwissenschaft als Kulturwissenschaft?', *Deutsche Vierteljahrsschrift für Literaturwissenschaft und Geisteswissenschaft,* 73(1): 69–93.

Held, D. (1980) *Introduction to Critical Theory.* Cambridge: Polity.

Henderson, M. (1995) *Borders, Boundaries and Frames.* London: Routledge.

Hettlage, R. (1995) 'Der Fremde: Kulturvermittler, Kulturbringer, Herausforderer von Kultur', in A. Wierlacher and C. Albrecht (eds), *Fremdgange: eine anthologische Fremdheitslehre.* Bonn: Inter Nationes, pp. 91–3.

Hidalgo, M. (2001) 'Spanish language shift reversal on the US–Mexico border and the extended third space', *Language and Intercultural Communication,* 1(1): 57–75.

Hoffman, C. (1996) *Language, Culture and Communication in Contemporary Europe.* Clevedon: Multilingual Matters.

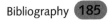

Hofstede, G. (1984) *Culture's Consequences: International Differences in Work-Related Values.* Newbury Park, CA: Sage.

Holstein, J. and Gubrium, J. (2000) *The Self We Live By.* Oxford: Oxford University Press.

hooks, b. (1994) *Teaching to Transgress: Education as the Practice of Freedom.* London and New York: Routledge.

Hurford, J. R. (1999) 'The evolution of language and languages', in R. Dunbar, C. Knight, and C. Power (eds), *The Evolution of Culture: An Interdisciplinary View.* Edinburgh: Edinburgh University Press, pp. 173–93.

Hymes, D. (1974) *Foundations in Sociolinguistics: An Ethnographic Approach.* Philadelphia: University of Pennsylvania Press.

Hymes, D. (1980) *Language in Education: Ethnolinguistic Essays.* Washington DC: Center for Applied Linguistics.

Ingold, T. (1986) *The Appropriation of Nature.* Iowa City: University of Iowa Press.

Ingold, T. (1993) 'The art of translation in a continuous world', in G. Pálsson (ed.) *Beyond Boundaries: Understanding, Translation and Anthropological Discourse.* Oxford: Berg, pp. 210–30.

Ingold, T. (ed.) (1994) *Companion Encyclopedia of Anthropology: Humanity, Culture, Social Life.* London and New York: Routledge.

Ingold, T. (ed.) (1996) *Key Debates in Anthropology.* London and New York: Routledge.

Ingold, T. (2000) *The Perception of the Environment: Essays in Livelihood, Dwelling and Skill.* London and New York: Routledge.

Irwin-DeVitis, L. and DeVitis, J. (1998) 'What is this work called teaching?', *Educational Theory.* 48(2): 267–78.

Jack, G. and Phipps, A. (2002) 'Mistaken consciousness: revolutionary exchanges on languages for intercultural communication', in S. Cormeraie, D. Killick and M. Parry (eds), *Revolutions in Consciousness: Local Identities, Global Concerns in Languages and Intercultural Communication.* Leeds: IALIC, pp. 43–54.

Jameson, F. (1984) 'Foreward', in *The Postmodern Condition: A Report on Knowledge.* Manchester: Manchester University Press. pp. vii–xxi.

Jameson, F. (1989) *The Political Unconscious: Narrative as a Socially Symbolic Act.* London: Routledge.

Jeggle, U. (ed.) (1984) *Feldforschung: Qualitative Methoden in der Kulturanalyse.* Tübingen: Tübingen Vereinigug für Volkskunde.

Jeggle, U. (1995) 'Fremdheit und Initiative', in A. Wierlacher and C. Albrecht (eds), *Fremdgänge: eine anthologische Fremdheitslehre.* Bonn: Inter Nationes, pp. 89–91.

Jenkins, R. (1996) *Social Identity*. London: Routledge.

Jenks, C. (1993) *Culture*. London: Routledge.

Jones, M. (1989) 'Identity, critique, affirmation: a response to Hinrich C. Seeba's paper', *The German Quarterly*, 62(2): 155–7.

Jordan, S. (2002) 'Ethnographic encounters: the processes of cultural translation', *Language and Intercultural Communication*, 2(2): 96–110.

Keesing, R. M. (1989) 'Exotic readings of cultural texts', *Cultural Anthropology*, 30(4): 459–79.

Keesing, R. M. (1994) 'Radical cultural difference: anthropology's myth?', in M. Pütz (ed.), *Language Contact and Language Conflict*. Amsterdam and Philadelphia: Johns Benjamins, pp. 3–24.

Kelly, M. (2000a) 'Mapping culture in language degrees', in N. McBride and K. Seago (eds), *Target Culture – Target Language?* London: CILT, pp. 81–92.

Kelly, M. (2000b) 'The stranger's gaze: the emergence of French cultural studies', in J. and L. J. Baetens (eds), Leuven: Leuven University Press, pp. 107–21.

Kelly, M. (2001) '"Serrez ma haire avec ma discipline": reconfiguring the structures and concepts', in R. Di Napoli, L. Polezzi and A. King (eds), *Fuzzy Boundaries? Reflections on Modern Languages and the Humanities*. London: CILT, pp. 43–56.

Kelly, M. and Jones, D. (2003) *A New Landscape for Languages*. London: Nuffield Foundation.

Kerdeman, D. (1998) 'Hermeneutics and education: understanding, control and agency', *Educational Theory*, 48(2): 241–66.

Kimbrough Oller, D. and Eilers, R. E. (2002) *Language and Literacy in Bilingual Children*. Clevedon: Multilingual Matters.

Kirshenblatt-Gimblett, B. (1998) *Destination Culture: Tourism, Museums, and Heritage*. Berkeley and London: University of California Press.

Kittel, H. and Frank, A. P. (eds) (1991) *Interculturality and the Historical Study of Literary Translations*. Berlin: Erich Schmidt Verlag.

Klein, J. T. (1998) *Notes Towards a Social Epistemology of Transdisciplinarity*. Paris: Centre International de Recherches et Études Transdisciplinaires.

Kopytoff, I. (1986) 'The cultural biography of things: commoditization as process', in A. Appadurai (ed.), *The Social Life of Things: Commodities in Cultural Perspective*. Cambridge: Cambridge University Press, pp. 64–94.

Kramer-Dahl, A. (1995) 'Reading and writing against the grain of academic discourse', *Discourse: Studies in the Cultural Politics of Education*, 16(1): 21–38.

Kramsch, C. (1993) *Context and Culture in Language Teaching*. Oxford: Oxford University Press.

Kramsch, C. (1998) 'Constructing second language acquisition research in foreign language departments', in H. Byrnes (ed.), *Learning Foreign and Second Languages: Perspectives in Research and Scholarship.* New York: Modern Languages Association of America, pp. 23–38.

Krashen, S. (1982) *Principles and Practice in Second Language Acquisition.* Oxford: Pergamon.

Kress, G. (2003) *Literacy in the New Media Age.* London: Routledge.

Kristeva, J. (1998) *Étrangers à nous-mêmes.* Paris: Librairie Arthème Fayard.

Kroeber, A. and Kluckhohn, C. (1952) 'Culture: a critical review of concepts and definitions', *Papers of the Peabody Museum of American Archaeology and Ethnology,* XLVII(1).

Kuper, A. (1996) *Anthropology and Anthroplogists: The Modern British School,* 3rd edn. London and New York: Routledge.

Larsen-Freeman, D. and Long, M. (1991) *An Introduction to Second Language Acquisition.* New York: Longman.

Lave, J. and Wenger, E. (1991) *Situated Learning: Legitimate Peripheral Participation.* Cambridge: Cambridge University Press.

Lave, J. and Wenger, E. (1999) 'Learning and pedagogy in communities of practice', in J. Leach and B. Moon (eds), *Learners and Pedagogy.* Milton Keynes: Open University Press, pp. 21–77.

Lave, J. and Roukens, J. (1996) 'The global information society and Europe's linguistic and cultural heritage', in C. Hoffman (ed.), *Language, Culture and Communication in Contemporary Europe.* Clevedon: Multilingual Matters, p. 27.

Lindholm-Leary, K. (2001) *Dual Language Education.* Clevedon: Multilingual Matters.

Lipiansky, E. M. (1993) 'Reflections on the notion of the intercultural', *Journal of Area Studies,* 2: 7–11.

Liska, J. and Cronkhite, G. (1995) *An Ecological Perspective on Human Communication Theory.* Orlando, FL: Harcourt Brace.

Little, D. (2000) 'Learner autonomy: why foreign languages should occupy a central role in the curriculum', in S. Green (ed.), *New Perspectives on Teaching and Learning Modern Languages.* Clevedon: Multilingual Matters, pp. 24–45.

Lodge, A. (2000) 'Higher education', in S. Green (ed.), *New Perspectives on Teaching and Learning Modern Languages.* Clevedon: Multilingual Matters, pp. 105–23.

Lutzeier, P. R. (1998) *German Studies Old and New Challenges.* Bern: Lang.

Lutzeler, P. (1989) 'German Studies in den USA', in A. Wierlacher (ed.), *Perspektiven interkultureller Germanistik.* Munich: Iudicium, pp. 679–91.

Lyotard, J.-F. (1984) *The Postmodern Condition: A Report on Knowledge.* Manchester: Manchester University Press.

Macdonald, S. (1993) *Inside European Identities: Ethnography in Western Europe.* Oxford: Berg.

Macdonald, S. (1997) *Reimagining Culture: Histories, Identities and the Gaelic Renaissance.* Oxford and New York: Berg.

Macdonald, S. and Fyfe, G. (eds) (1996) *Theorizing Museums: Representing Identity and Diversity in a Changing World.* Oxford: Blackwell.

MacIntyre, A. (1985) *After Virtue: A Study in Moral Theory.* London: Duckworth.

McDonough, S. H. (1995) *Strategy and Skill in Learning a Foreign Language.* London and New York: Edward Arnold.

McLaren, P. (1995) *Critical Pedagogy and Predatory Culture.* London: Routledge.

McWhorter, J. H. (2002) *The Power of Babel: A Natural History of Language.* London: Heinemann.

McWilliam, E. (1995) 'Seriously playful, playfully serious: the postmodern lecture and other oxymorons', *Taboo* 1(1): 31–43.

Malmjaer, K. (1998) *Translation and Language Teaching. Language Teaching and Translation.* Manchester: St Jerome Press.

Mann, S. (2001) 'Alternative perspectives on the student experience: alienation and engagement', *Studies in Higher Education,* 26(1): 7–19.

Marcus, G. E. (1997a) 'The uses of complicity in the changing mis-en-scène of anthropological fieldwork', *Representations,* 59: 85–108.

Marcus, G. (1997b) 'Afterword: ethnographic writing and anthropological careers', in J. Clifford and G. Marcus (eds), *Writing Culture: The Poetics and Politics of Ethnography.* Berkeley and Los Angeles: University of California Press, pp. 262–7.

Marcus, G. E. and Fischer, M. (1986) *Anthropology as Cultural Critique.* Chicago: University of Chicago Press.

Michel, A. (1996) 'Theory in German studies', in J. Roche and T. Salumets (eds), *Germanics under Construction: Intercultural and Interdisciplinary Prospects.* Munich: Iudicium, pp. 29–45.

Milich, K. and Peck, J. M. (1998) *Multiculturalism in Transit: A German-American Exchange.* New York: Berghahn.

Milner, A. (1993) *Cultural Materialism.* Carlton, Australia: Melbourne University Press.

Moore, M. (2002) *Stupid White Men ....and Other Sorry Excuses for the State of the Nation.* London and New York: Penguin.

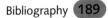

Morris, B. (1994) *Anthropology of the Self: The Individual in Cultural Perspective.* London: Pluto Press.

Nägele, R. (1997) *Echoes of Translation, Reading between Texts.* Baltimore, MD: Johns Hopkins University Press.

Needham, R. (1972) *Belief, Language, and Experience.* Oxford: Blackwell.

Nicol, D. (1997) *Research on Learning and Higher Education,* UCoSDA Briefing Paper Forty-Five.

Nixon, J., Beattie, M., Challis, M. and Walker, M. (1998) 'What does it mean to be an academic? A colloquium', *Teaching in Higher Education,* 3(3), 277–98.

Nixon, J., Marks, A., Rowland, S. and Walker, M. (2001) 'Towards a new academic professionalism', *British Journal of Sociology of Education,* 22(2): 227–44.

Nuffield Languages Inquiry (2000) *The Nuffield Languages Inquiry (2000): Languages: The Next Generation.* London: Nuffield Foundation.

Okri, B. (1997) *A Way of Being Free.* London: Phoenix House.

Pálsson, G. (ed.) (1993) *Beyond Boundaries.* Oxford: Berg.

Park, J. (1999) 'The politics of emotional literacy', *Renewal,* 7(1): 52–9.

Peck, J. M. (1985) 'Advanced literary study as cultural study: a redefinition of the discipline', *Profession,* 85: 49–54.

Peck, J. (1987) 'The institution of germanistik and the transmission of culture: time and place for an anthropological approach', *Monatshefte,* 79(3): 308–19.

Peck, J. (1989) 'There's no place like home: remapping the topography of German studies', *German Quarterly,* 62(2): 178–87.

Peck, J. M. (1992) 'Toward a cultural hermeneutics of the "foreign" language classroom: notes for a critical and political pedagogy', *ADFL Bulletin,* 23(3). 1–17.

Pennycook, A. (1994) *English as an International Language.* London: Longman.

Phipps, A. (1999a) 'Intercultural germanistics: a forum for reconstruction', in Nicholas Saul (ed.), *Schwellen-Thresholds-Seuils.* Würzburg: Königshausen & Neumann, pp. 289–303.

Phipps, A. (1999b) 'Provisional homes and creative practice: languages, cultural studies and anthropology', in D. Killick and M. Parry (eds), *Languages for Cross-Cultural Capability: Making Boundaries and Crossing Borders.* Leeds: Leeds Metropolitan University, pp. 19–29.

Phipps, A. (2001a) 'Busy foundries in modern languages and the humanities', in R. Di Napoli, L. Polezzi, and A. King (eds), *Fuzzy Boundaries? Reflections on Modern Languages and the Humanities.* London: CILT, pp. 185–93.

Phipps, A. (2001b) 'Measuring performance: some alternative indicators', in M. Walker (ed.), *Reconstructing Professionalism in University Teaching: Teachers and Learners in Action*. Buckingham: Open University Press.

Phipps, A. (2002) *Contemporary German Cultural Studies*. London: Arnold.

Pleuger, J. (2001) *How to Teach Modern Languages and Survive!* Clevedon: Multilingual Matters.

Pool, J. (1996) 'Optimal language regimes for the European Union', *International Journal of the Sociology of Language*, 121: 159–79.

Pusey, M. (1987) *Jürgen Habermas*. London and New York: Routledge.

Pütz, M. (ed.) (1994) *Language Contact and Language Conflict*. Amsterdam & Philadelphia: Johns Benjamins.

Read, A. (1993) *Theatre and Everyday Life: An Ethics of Performance*. London: Routledge.

Reid, I. (1992) *Narrative Exchanges*. London and New York: Routledge.

Richardson, R. (1990) *Daring to be a Teacher: Essays, Stories and Memoranda*. Stoke-on-Trent: Trentham.

Roberts, C. (1993) 'Cultural studies and student exchange: living the ethnographic life', *Language, Culture and Curriculum*, 6(1): 11–17.

Roberts, C. and Jordan, S. (2000) *Introduction to Ethnography*. Oxford: Oxford Brookes University.

Roberts, C., Byram, M., Barro, A., Jordan, S. and Street, B. (2001) *Language Learners as Ethnographers*. Clevedon: Multilingual Matters.

Roche, J. and Salumets, T. (1996) *Germanics under Construction: Intercultural and Interdisciplinary Prospects*. Munich: Iudicium.

Rosaldo, R. (1989) *Culture and Truth: The Remaking of Social Analysis*. London: Routledge.

Rose, D. (1990) *Living the Ethnographic Life*. London: Sage.

Said, E. (1995) *Orientalism*, 2nd edn. London: Penguin.

Said, E. (1998) *Identity, Authority and Freedom: The Potentate and the Traveller*. Cape Town: University of Cape Town.

Sandford, J. (1998) 'What does culture mean in German cultural studies', in P. Lutzeier (ed.), *German Studies: Old and New Challenges*. Bern, Lang, pp. 33–55.

Savory, T. (1968) *The Art of Translation*. London: Jonathan Cape.

Schäffer, C. (1996) 'Translation as cross-cultural communication', in C. Hoffman, (ed.), *Language, Culture and Communication in Contemporary Europe*. Clevedon: Multilingual Matters, pp. 152–64.

Schäffer, C. (2001) *Annotated Texts for Translation: English–German:* Clevedon: Multilingual Matters.

Schechner, R. (1985) *Between Theater and Anthropology*. Philadelphia: University of Pennsylvania Press.

Schiffer, M. B. and Miller, A. R. (1999) *The Material Life of Human Beings: Artifacts, Behavior and Communication.* London and New York: Routledge.

Schulman, L. S. (1999) 'Knowledge and teaching: foundations of the new reform', in J. Leach and B. Moon (eds), *Learners and Pedagogy.* Milton Keynes: Open University Press, pp. 61–77.

Scollon, R. and Scollon, S. W. (1995) *Intercultural Communication.* Oxford: Blackwell.

Scott, J. C. (1990) *Domination and the Arts of Resistance: Hidden Transcripts.* New Haven, CT: Yale University Press.

Seeba, H. (1989) 'Critique of identity formation: towards an intercultural model of german studies', *German Quarterly,* 62(2): 144–54.

Seyhan, A. (1997) 'Prospects for feminist literary theory in German studies: a response to Sara Lennox's paper', *German Quarterly,* 62(2): 171–7.

Shanahan, D. (1997) 'Articulating the relationship between language, literature and culture: toward a new agenda for foreign language teaching and research', *Modern Language Journal,* 81(2): 164–74.

Shell, M. (1993) *Money, Language, and Thought: Literary and Philosophical Economies from the Medieval to the Modern Era.* Baltimore, MD: Johns Hopkins University Press.

Sherzer, J. (1992) 'Ethnography of speaking', in R. Bauman (ed.), *Folklore, Cultural Performances and Popular Entertainments: A Communications Centred Handbook.* Oxford: Oxford University Press, pp. 76–80.

Simon, S. (1996) *Gender in Translation: Cultural Identity and the Politics of Transmission.* London: Routledge.

Spivak, G. (1999) 'Translation as culture', in I. Carrera Suarez, A. Garcia Ferandez and M. S. Suarez Lafuente (eds), *Translating Cultures.* Hebden Bridge: Dangaroo Press, pp. 17–30.

Stagl, J. (1980) 'Die Apodemik oder 'Reisekunst' als Methodik der Sozialforschung vom Humanismus bis zur Aufklärung', in M. J. Rassem and J. Stagl (eds), *Statistik und Staatbeschreibung in der Neuzeit.* Paderborn: F. Schöningh, pp. 131–202.

Staroster, W. and Roy, A. (2002) 'Gadamer, language and intercultural communication', *Language and Intercultural Communication,* 1(1): 6–20.

Stewart, M. and Talburt, S. (1996) 'The interplay of the personal and the pragmatic: language, culture and interpretation in the Spanish literature classroom', *Foreign Language Annals,* 29(1): 45–52.

Taussig, M. (1993) *Mimesis and Alterity: A Particular History of the Senses.* New York: Routledge.

Taylor, P. (1993) *The Texts of Paulo Freire*. Oxford: Oxford University Press.

Teraoka, A. (1989) 'Is culture to us what text is to anthropology? A response to Jeffrey M. Peck's paper', *German Quarterly*, 62(2): pp. 188–91.

Thackery, W. M. (1848) *Vanity Fair*. Harmondsworth: Penguin.

Thomas, N. (1991) *Entangled Objects: Exchange, Material Culture and Colonialism in the Pacific*. Cambridge, MA: Harvard University Press.

Thurlow, C. (2002) 'In the eye of the beholder: representations of "intercultural" communication among young "multicultural" teenagers', in S. Cormeraie, D. Killick, and M. Parry, (eds), *Revolutions in Consciousness: Local Identities, Global Concerns in Languages and Intercultural Communication*. Leeds: IALIC, pp. 197–208.

Tollefson, J. W. (ed.) (1995) *Power and Inequality in Language Education*. Cambridge: Cambridge University Press.

Trompenaars, F. (1993) *Riding the Waves of Culture*. London: Nicholas Brealey.

Turner, V. (1982) *From Ritual to Theatre: The Human Seriousness of Play*. New York: Performing Arts Journal Publications.

Turner, V. (1995) *The Ritual Process: Structure and Anti-Structure*. New York: De Gruyter.

Urry, J. (1990) *The Tourist Gaze: Leisure and Travel in Contemporary Societies*. London: Sage.

Valdés, G. (1995) 'The teaching of minority languages as academic subjects: pedagogical and theoretical challenges', *Modern Language Journal*, 79: 299–328.

van Lier, L. (1996) *Interaction in the Language Curriculum: Awareness, Autonomy and Authenticity*. London and New York: Longman.

van Wolde, E. (2000) 'The Earth Story as presented by the Tower of Babel narrative', in N. C. Habel and S. Wurst (eds), *The Earth Story in Genesis*, Sheffield: Sheffield Academic Press, pp. 147–57.

Vanpatten, B. (1997) 'How language teaching is constructed: introduction to the special issue', *Modern Language Journal*, 81(1): 1–5.

Venuti, L. (1995) *The Translator's Invisibility: A History of Translation*. London and New York: Routledge.

Venuti, L. (1999) *The Translation Studies Reader*. London: Routledge.

von Graevenitz, G. (1999) 'Literaturwissenschaft und Kulturwissenschaften: Eine Erwiderung', *Deutsche Vierteljahrsschrift für Literaturwissenschaft und Geisteswissenschaft*, 73(1): 95–115.

Vygotsky, L. S. (1978) *Mind in Society*. Cambridge, MA: Harvard University Press.

Walker, M. (1998) 'Academic identities: women on a South African Landscape', *British Journal of Sociology of Education*, 19(3): 335–54.

Walker, M. (2001) *Reconstructing Professionalism in University Teaching: Teachers and Learners in Action*. Buckingham: Open University Press.

Walker, M. (2002) 'Pedagogy and politics and purposes of higher education', *Arts and Humanities in Higher Education*, 1(1): 43–58.

Wenger, E. (1998) *Communities of Practice*. Cambridge: Cambridge University Press.

Widdowson, H. G. (1990) *Aspects of Language Teaching*. Oxford: Open University Press.

Wierlacher, A. (ed.) (1993) *Kulturthema Fremdheit: Leitbegriffe und Problemfelder kulturwissenschaftlicher Fremdheitsforschung*. Munich: Iudicium.

Wierlacher, A. and Albrecht, C. (1995) *Fremdgänge: eine anthologische Fremdheitslehre*. Bonn: Inter Nationes.

Wilkinson, J. (2002) 'Passports and the German border: who holds the key to the door', in A. Phipps (ed.), *Contemporary German Cultural Studies*. London and New York: Arnold, pp. 17–39.

Williams, R. (1977) *Marxism and Literature*. Oxford: Oxford University Press.

Williams, R. (1983) *Keywords: A Vocabulary of Culture ad Society*, 2nd edn. London: Fontana.

Williams, R. (1983) *Writing in Society.* London: Verso.

Williams, R. (1993) *Culture and Society*. London: Hogarth Press.

Williams, R. (1997) *Problems in Materialism and Culture*. London and New York: Verso.

Wilson, J. (1998) 'Seriousness and the foundations of education', *Educational Theory*, 48(2): 143–55.

Wilson, J. and Wilson, N. (1998) 'The subject-matter of educational research', *British Educational Research Journal*, 24(3): 355–63.

Wink, W. (1992) *Engaging the Powers: Discernment and Resistance in a World of Domination*. Minneapolis, MN: Fortress Press.

Young, R. (1996) *Intercultural Communication: Pragmatics, Genealogy, Deconstruction*. Clevedon: Multilingual Matters.

WEBSITES

The Interculture Project: http://www.lancs.ac.uk/users/interculture/
Learning and Residence Abroad: http://lara.fdtl.ac.uk/lara/
LTSN Languages, Linguistics, Area Studies (2003):
   http://www.lang.ltsn.ac.uk/index.aspx
Quality Assurance Agency (2002a) *Anthropology Benchmark Statements*:
   http://www.qaa.ac.uk/crntwork/benchmark/phase2/anthropology.pdf
Quality Assurance Agency (2002b) *Languages and Related Studies Benchmark Statements*:
   http://www.qaa.ac.uk/crntwork/benchmark/phase2/languages.pdf

Index

Added to a page number 'f' denotes a figure and 't' denotes a table.